A Higher Form of Killing

A Higher Form of Killing

THE SECRET STORY OF CHEMICAL AND BIOLOGICAL WARFARE

Robert Harris and Jeremy Paxman

HILL AND WANG, NEW YORK

A division of Farrar, Straus and Giroux

CONTENTS

ILLUSTRATIONS

between pages 114 and 115

ACKNOWLEDGEMENTS

This book grew out of a film we made for the BBC television programme *Panorama*, and we would like to thank Roger Bolton, *Panorama*'s editor, for the encouragement and advice he gave us at that time, and for the understanding that he, and others at the BBC, have shown since.

Thanks are due to so many people who helped in the actual research of this book that we cannot list all of them here. Considerations of space aside, many felt free to talk only with a promise of anonymity.

Among those who can be mentioned, however, we must record our gratitude to the staff of the Public Record Office, the Imperial War Museum, Churchill College, Cambridge, the US Army Public Affairs Department, and Edgewood Arsenal, all of whom assisted with documents and advice. The Church of Scientology also made available to us documents they had unearthed in their campaign against chemical warfare. Among other individuals who gave us their advice and information thanks are due to General Allan Younger, Professor John Erickson, General T. H. Foulkes, David Irving, Lord Stamp, Air Marshal Sir Christopher Hartley, Professor Henry Barcroft and Paul Harris.

Nicholas Sims, Lecturer in International Relations at the London School of Economics, and Adam Roberts, Reader in International Relations at Oxford University, were both kind enough to read and comment on portions of the typescript for the publishers.

Additional research in Washington was carried out by Scott Malone.

We would also like to thank Jeremy Lewis of Chatto & Windus, without whose initial enthusiasm this book would never have been written; and Elizabeth Burke, who steered our battered manuscript into production.

Although it is invidious to single out particular individuals from the many who have helped us, two in particular deserve our special thanks. One is Dr Rex Watson, the Director of Porton Down, who, within the confines of the Official Secrets Act and with no guarantee of a 'good press', gave us invaluable assistance. With his approval, we also enjoyed the help and advice of Porton's information officer, Alex Spence.

Our other great debt is to Julian Perry Robinson of the Science Policy Research Unit at Sussex University. He helped generously, both with time and advice, and read the book in its early stages, making many valuable suggestions. All students in this field owe Julian Perry Robinson a debt for the work he did in pulling together the information contained in the first two volumes of the six-part study of chemical and biological weapons published by the Stockholm International Peace Research Institute. Where we have drawn upon this, and upon the work of others who have investigated this subject in the past, acknowledgement is made in the notes at the end of the book.

If, despite the best efforts of all the above, we have made errors of fact or judgement, responsibility rests with the authors.

Robert Harris wrote chapters one to five of this book; Jeremy Paxman wrote chapters six to ten.

INTRODUCTION

One summer evening we were standing on the platform at one of London's major railway stations. A group of young soldiers pushed past, making for the only compartment with empty seats. They were laughing and joking and had obviously had a few beers, about to begin a period of leave in their home towns in the north of England. There being no other seats available, we joined them in their compartment.

They were, it transpired, on their way home after a period of what they cryptically referred to as 'NBC Training'. NBC, they explained, stood for Nuclear, Biological and Chemical. Their training involved them in wearing special protective suits, rubber gloves and gas masks for hours on end while they attempted to carry out all their normal tasks. As they broke open the case of beer they carried with them, they dismissed the final cataclysm of the nuclear battlefield with a cheery fatalism. Yet the prospect of biological and chemical war seemed to fill them with a particular dread. It was, one of them said, 'dirty'.

The image has stayed with us throughout the writing of this book. What is it about chemical and biological war, or as it is more popularly known, poison gas and germ warfare, that holds such a unique terror?

They are, first and foremost, indiscriminate weapons, somehow – as the young soldier put it – 'dirty'. They rely for their effectiveness on taking their victims unawares. By and large they are invisible, and do their damage from within the body. One may not see the bullet or bomb that kills you, but that external threat is somehow more easy to comprehend than the malignant tumour, the paralysis or the suffocation inflicted by an unseen weapon.

Poison gas and germ weapons turn civilization on its head. Diseases are not fought, but carefully cultivated; doctors use their knowledge of the functions of the human body to devise ever more effective means of halting those functions; agriculturalists deliberately induce fungi and develop crop destroyers. The chlorine that

Plato

poisoned our grandfathers at Ypres was available thanks to our grandmothers' desire for brightly-coloured dresses. Modern nerve gases were originally designed to help mankind by killing beetles and lice: now, in the hands of the military, they are, literally, insecticides for people. Chemical and biological warfare, as one writer has put it, is 'public health in reverse'.

Ever since the first gas attack during the First World War, man has attempted to come to terms with the impulse which led him to develop these weapons. And, largely, he has failed. Despite the efforts of the diplomats and the disarmers gas and germ warfare continues to exert a grim hold on the world's armies. Why this should be so, and why the attempts to rid the world of these weapons have failed, is one of the recurrent themes of this book.

Another is the secrecy which has always shrouded gas and germ warfare. Our experience has been that the story of their development is far more closely guarded than the history of nuclear weapons. Partly, perhaps, because of the moral dubiousness of their actions, governments have sought to conceal from their peoples the extent and the nature of their plans to wage war with chemicals and bacteria. It is only within the last few years that documents relating even to the use of gas during the First World War have become available. Almost all the papers detailing plans for the use of gas and germs during the Second World War will remain under lock and key until the turn of the century. Early in our researches we submitted a list of wartime files we would like to have declassified to the British Ministry of Defence. More than a year later, the Ministry and the Cabinet Office have yet to reach a decision: it seems likely that the material – now forty years old – will still be judged 'too sensitive' to be made public. It is perhaps because of the obsessive secrecy which cloaks the subject that no general history has yet been written.

We have attempted to break through the veil of secrecy, by obtaining previously classified information and by talking to many of the people who spent their lives working on what may with justice be called one of the most unknown areas of western military planning. In doing so, this book tries to explain why it is that a weapon developed seventy years ago should still induce terror in the soldiers of the 1980s.

In no future war will the military be able to
ignore poison gas.
It is a higher form of killing.

Professor Fritz Haber, pioneer of gas warfare, on
receiving the Nobel Prize for Chemistry in 1919.

ONE

'Frightfulness'

The 22nd of April 1915 had been a warm and sunny day, but towards the end of the afternoon a breeze sprang up. It came from the north, from behind the German lines, blew across No Man's Land, and gently fanned the faces of the Allied soldiers in position around the village of Langemarck, near Ypres.

They were new to the trenches – French reservists and Algerians from France's north African colony. To them the fresh wind must have seemed a good omen, for a few seconds later, as if on cue, the German guns which had been bombarding them all day suddenly stopped firing. An abrupt silence descended over the front.

A few hundred yards away, four divisions – of the 23rd and 26th German Army Corps – crouched in their trenches. They had waited there since dawn, unable to move for fear of giving away their presence. Now, just as it had begun to seem too late, the moment had come. The wind had changed. An attack.

At five o'clock, three red rockets streaked into the sky, signalling the start of a deafening artillery barrage. High explosive shells pounded into the deserted town of Ypres and the villages around it. At the same time the troops sheltering near Langemarck saw two greenish-yellow clouds rise from the enemy's lines, catch the wind, and billow forwards, gradually merging to form a single bank of blue-white mist: out of sight, in special emplacements protected by sandbags and concrete, German pioneers were opening the valves of 6,000 cylinders spread out along a four mile front. The cylinders contained liquid chlorine – the instant the pressure was released and it came into contact with the air it vaporized and hissed out to form a dense cloud. At thirty parts per million of air chlorine gas produces a rasping cough. At concentrations of one part per thousand it is fatal. The breeze stirred again, and one hundred and sixty tons of it, five feet high and hugging the ground, began to roll towards the Allied trenches.

Chemical warfare had begun.

The wave broke over the first line within a minute, enveloping tens of thousands of troops in an acrid green cloud so thick they could no longer see their neighbours in the trench. Seconds later they were clutching at the air and at their throats, fighting for breath.

Chlorine does not suffocate: it poisons, stripping the lining of the bronchial tubes and lungs. The inflammation produces a massive amount of fluid that blocks the windpipe, froths from the mouth and fills the lungs. In an attempt to escape the effects, some men tried to bury their mouths and nostrils in the earth; others panicked and ran. But any exertion or effort to outdistance the cloud only resulted in deeper breaths and more acute poisoning. As the tide of gas washed over the struggling men their faces turned blue from the strain of trying to breathe; some coughed so violently they ruptured their lungs. Each man, as the British casualty report was later to put it, was 'being drowned in his own exudation'.[1]

Advancing cautiously behind the chlorine cloud came the German infantry, all wearing crude respirators of moist gauze and cotton tied round their faces. They passed through an unprecedented scene of horror. The dead lay where they had fallen, arms outstretched trying to escape the gas. Interspersed with the corpses, the wounded and dying sprawled gasping and choking as their agonized lungs coughed up mouthful after mouthful of yellow fluid. Any metal object the chlorine had come into contact with was tarnished. Buttons, watches, coins: all had turned a dull green. Rifles were rusted and looked as if they had been left out in the mud for months. Most of the breech blocks on the sixty guns the Germans captured that day were unusable.

Any of the French still capable of movement fled. The British suddenly found the roads and bridges of their sector clogged with retreating soldiers, many of whom could only point at their throats in explanation. By six o'clock, even as far back as ten miles, the chlorine cloud was still making men cough and their eyes smart. By seven o'clock, the few French guns which had been left in action were ominously silent.

The first large-scale gas attack had taken the Allied commanders so completely by surprise that it was not until the early hours of the morning that they began to appreciate the scale of the disaster that had overtaken them. The Germans had torn a hole four miles wide in the Western Front, smashing in an afternoon defences which had held for months. The German commander, Falkenhayn, was as startled as his opponents by the overwhelming effect of chemical warfare. He had seen gas merely as an experimental aid to his attack and had insufficient reserves ready to exploit his advantage. But for that he might have been able to drive right through the Allied line to the Channel ports: the gas attack could have won the war for the Germans. Instead, as night fell over Ypres, the German soldiers dug in. Falkenhayn's 'experiment', the Germans reckoned, had cost the Allies 5,000 men dead and 10,000 wounded.

Thirty-six hours later, while the British and the French were still struggling to fill the breach in their defences, the Germans struck again. At 2.45 am, shortly before dawn on the 24 April, Captain Bertram of the Canadian 8th Battalion noticed some greenish-white smoke rising from the German front line about 600 yards away. Travelling at eight miles an hour, the cloud 'drifted along the ground towards our trenches, not rising to more than seven feet from the ground when it reached our front line'.[2] The bank of high-density chlorine rolled over the Canadians, whose only protection was handkerchiefs, socks and towels which they urinated on and then stuffed in their mouths. Over the next few hours they were subjected to successive waves of gas so thick they blotted out the sun. Once or twice through the clouds they caught glimpses of German troops apparently dressed as divers, wearing large hoods with a single glass eyepiece set in the front.

There was the same panic-stricken scramble for the rear. On a small stretch of ground leading from the advanced trenches to the supports Bertram counted twenty-four bodies of men killed trying to outrun the gas; he himself collapsed with vomiting and diarrhoea, unable to breathe, with a feeling 'of great heaviness in the bottom of the chest'.

The German gas and artillery attack killed 5,000 men. Sergeant Grindley of the Canadian 15th Battalion was one of hundreds carried off the battlefield into the primitive medical posts. The doctors had no idea how to treat gas casualties and two days later Grindley died, gasping for breath. The surgeon who treated him called it 'air hunger'. In blue pencil he scrawled a post-mortem report:

The Body showed definite discolouration of the face and neck and hands. On opening the chest the two lungs bulged forwards. On removing the lungs there exuded a considerable amount of frothy light yellow fluid, evidently highly albuminous, as slight beating was sufficient to solidify it like white of egg. The veins on the surface of the brain were found greatly congested, all the small vessels standing out prominently.[3]

Of those who survived the gas attack, 60 per cent had to be sent home; half were still fully disabled at the end of the war.

Neither for the first time nor the last, men like Grindley – 'lions led by donkeys' – suffered for the blunders of their commanders who for weeks beforehand had been warned of what the Germans were planning. Although the facts were suppressed at the time, we now know that on 13 April, over a week before the first attack, a French patrol had captured a German soldier actually carrying a respirator. The soldier, a twenty-four year-old private called August Jäger of Germany's 26th Army Corps, revealed the German plan to use gas and described the position of the cylinders (the existence of which had already been confirmed by aerial reconnaissance). Jäger's information was passed to the French divisional commander, General Ferry, who in turn passed it on to the British and French High Commands with the advice either that the men threatened be withdrawn or the gas emplacements bombarded. Both his warning and his advice were ignored. As the official British report on the affair – classed 'secret' until almost sixty years after the attack – put it:

We were aware of the fact that the Germans were making preparations for the discharge of gas for several days previously ... Nobody seems to have realised the great danger that was threatening, it being considered that the enemy's attempt would certainly fail and that whatever gas reached our line could be easily fanned away. No one felt in the slightest degree uneasy ...[4]

Neither Ferry nor Jäger profited when their predictions were proved correct. Ferry was dismissed from his post by the French High Command, furious at having their incompetence revealed. Jäger's fate was grimmer. In a memoir published in 1930, Ferry imprudently named him as the source of his information. Jäger, now a civilian, was promptly arrested, and at Leipzig in 1932 he was sentenced to ten years' penal servitude, the court deciding that his betrayal of German plans had helped cost them the war – the last and perhaps saddest casualty of the first gas attack.

The victims of Ypres were evacuated to the area around Boulogne, where they became the focus of intense scientific curiosity. What gas were the Germans using? What protection could be devised against it? The British ransacked their universities and hospitals for experts who might be able to provide the answers to these questions, and by the end of April the seaside town was filled to overflowing with wounded and dying men, attended by a small army of specialists and academics.

The largest hospital was housed in the famous pre-war Casino at Le Touquet, one of the great symbols of the Golden Era that came to an end in August 1914. Now – wrote one of Britain's leading physiologists, Joseph Barcroft – in elegant rooms which had once echoed to the sound of the roulette wheel, 'one simply wades through wounded'. Another hospital, in the Pleasure Pavilion at the end of the pier, was 'so full that it was almost impossible to move about. All the beds full and all available space on the floors. All the other hospitals are the same. Sometimes the beds are made and three cases pass through the bed in a day.'[5]

The feelings of shock and outrage were compounded by the fact that poison gas was specifically outlawed by international law. The Hague Declaration of 1899 had helped lay down the principle that there were certain methods of combat which were outside the scope of civilized warfare. The signatories, including Germany, had pledged among other things 'to abstain from the use of projectiles the object of which is the diffusion of asphyxiating or deleterious gases'.

To the gassed soldiers sixteen years later, this Edwardian gentlemen's agreement must have been as far removed from the realities of 1915 as the ornate chandeliers and paintings crated away at the Casino. With extraordinary cynicism, the Germans claimed that by not using *projectiles* but instead releasing the cloud of gas from cylinders, they had avoided breaking the Hague agreement. The German newspaper, *Kölnische Zeitung*, went so far as to claim that 'the letting loose of smoke clouds, which, in a gentle wind, move quite slowly towards the enemy, is not only permissible by international law, but is an extraordinarily mild method of war'.[6] The British Commander-in-Chief, Sir John French, did not think so. On 23 April he telegraphed London asking for the means to retaliate. On the 24th, as the Canadians were enduring the second gas attack, Lord Kitchener, the War Minister, replied. 'Before we fall to the level of the degraded Germans,' he informed French, 'I must submit the matter to the Government.' It was clear, international agreements notwithstanding, that general chemical warfare could not now be far off. While the Cabinet considered the British position with regard to gas, news of the attack was spread to the general public.

There was a great spasm of anti-German feeling. The press fuelled the anger, printing vivid accounts of the suffering of the wounded. 'Their faces, arms, hands were of a shiny grey-black colour,' wrote *The Times*, 'with mouths open and lead-glazed eyes, all swaying slightly backwards and forwards trying to get breath.'[7] Lord Northcliffe's *Daily Mail* appealed to the women of England to make respirators using a simple pattern of cotton wool in a gauze envelope. The response to the *Mail*'s call was enormous: a million of these embryo gas masks were made in a single day. Thousands unfortunately reached the front and were issued; they were useless when dry and caused suffocation when wet. A week after they arrived, the British High Command ordered them to be withdrawn; by the time the last one disappeared from the battlefield some days later, the *Mail*'s respirator had been responsible for the deaths of scores of men.

Not that the official policy was much better. The army relied on the advice of two English professors, Haldane and Baker, who visited the front on 27 April. They recommended as protection the 'use of cloths etc moistened with urine, earth folded in cloth or enclosed in a bottle from which the base has been removed'.[8] These stop-gap measures were all that the Allies had to carry them through three gas attacks on 1, 6 and 10 of May.

The last and greatest attack of the summer came on the 24th. At dawn, under cover of a heavy artillery barrage, the Germans released chlorine along a two-mile sector of the front, between the Menin Road and Sanctuary Wood, south-west of Ypres. The men who held the line – soldiers of the British 1st Cavalry, 4th and 28th Divisions – clutched hastily-issued respirators consisting of two layers of flannel (with tapes attached to tie over the mouth) which were meant to be dipped in soda solution before use, bottles of which were placed in the trenches.

The menacing cloud of greenish-white gas swirled over the British positions as it had over the French and Canadian, but this time at a totally unexpected density. The chlorine reached a concentration which proved fatal a mile and a half away; it was still strong enough to cause vomiting and smarting of the eyes nine miles from the front. Three miles back, at Ypres, houses and trees were completely blotted from view and the cellars of the hospital 'became filled with a fog'. In the trenches themselves – only a few hundred yards from the cylinders – the gas produced desperate scenes, as General Wilson recorded:

At first men used their respirators correctly, but as they became choked with gas the men re-dipped them in the solution which was distributed along the trenches.

As the gassing continued, the men became excited and could not be prevented from putting the respirators to their mouths without squeezing them dry, the result was that the men could not breathe through the saturated respirators and, thinking they were being suffocated by the gas, dipped them at shorter intervals, breathing hard between the dips instead of holding their breath, with the inevitable result that they were rendered unconscious by the gas.[9]

The attack lasted for over four hours. During the next few days, nearly three and a half thousand men were treated for gas poisoning; more than half of them had to be sent home to England. There were no figures for the number of dead.

Two days later, on 26 May, a strange figure clad in a uniform 'bearing tell-tale marks of long association with mud and barbed wire', a cap split by a shell splinter and a pistol strapped to his belt, appeared at the Advanced General Headquarters of the British Army at Hazebrouck. Major Charles Howard Foulkes of His Majesty's Royal Engineers had an appointment with General Robertson, Chief of Staff to Sir John French. It was an interview, Foulkes later recalled, of few words:

'Do you know anything about gas?' he asked, to which I replied quite truthfully, 'Nothing at all.' 'Well, I don't think it matters,' he went on; 'I want you to take charge of our gas reprisals here in France. Something is going on in London and you must cross over and find out all about it. Then come back here and tell me what your propose to do'; and with this I was dismissed.[10]

The British Army had, in Foulkes, appointed as 'Gas Adviser' a figure seemingly straight from the pages of Kipling or Rider Haggard. Foulkes was one of seven sons of a British chaplain in India, all of whom grew up to serve the Empire, and five of whom were buried overseas. By the time of his appointment in 1915 Foulkes was forty. He had spent twenty-three years in the Army, and had seen service in Sierra Leone ('The White Man's Grave' where he had twice nearly died of malaria), Gambia, the Gold Coast, South Africa, the West Indies, Nigeria and Ceylon. During the Boer War he had devised bicycle-mounted photo-reconnaissance equipment and several times narrowly escaped being shot while photographing Boer positions. In

1902, posing as a newspaperman and ostensibly covering the eruptions of the Mont Pêlee volcano, he had secretly photographed the French fortifications in Martinique for the Secret Service. In the same year, travelling on horseback and by canoe, he penetrated deep into hostile and largely unexplored country to chart the boundary between Northern Nigeria and the French Sahara. A big game hunter, a First Division football player (for the Scottish side, Heart of Midlothian), a competitor at the 1908 Olympic Games, this remarkable, archetypal son of the Empire was to crown his career as A D C to the King and die in his bed – in the same year that men landed on the moon – at the age of ninety-five.

In 1915 the task facing him was to tax even his ingenuity to the utmost. The British High Command wanted gas ready to employ in their autumn offensive. Foulkes had five months to devise a gas weapon, get it into production, recruit and train men to use it, and work out how best to employ it. Fortunately for the British, these attempts would not be hampered by further German gas attacks. After the attack on 24 May, the wind began to blow from the west, and the Germans transferred their Gas Corps to the Eastern front, where it was employed with devastating results against the ill-equipped Russian Army. Apart from two attacks against the French in October, no more gas was discharged against the Allies in France until December.

The major problem confronting Foulkes was the one which he, as a soldier, could do least about: the weakness of the British chemical industry. There was nothing in the United Kingdom, or even in the rest of the world, remotely to match the productive capacity of Germany's eight giant chemical combines huddled together in the massive concentration in the Ruhr known as the *Interessen Gemeinschaft* – the I G.

To fight a war with poison gas requires highly efficient mass-production, a demand which the I G (then capitalized at an estimated $400 million) was ideally suited to meet. Most First World War gases could be manufactured in bulk using the methods and machinery normally employed in making dyestuffs. By the start of the war, Germany had a virtual world monopoly in the production of dyes; Britain on the other hand could produce only a tenth of what she needed. The imbalance was to be a serious handicap to the Allied

8

chemical warfare effort, which right up to the end of the war lagged behind the efficiency of their enemy's. Indeed it was this unchallengeable superiority in chemical production, together with the fact that the British naval blockade was starving them of supplies of nitrate for making high explosive, that first led the German High Command to contemplate using gas.

They had introduced a form of tear gas (called *T-Stoff* after its inventor, Dr Tappen) on the Russian front in January 1915. *T-Stoff*, one of the precursors of modern riot gas, was considered just within the scope of weapons permitted by the Hague Convention. The Allies had similar weapons. In March, the French, on the initiative of a conscripted policeman, introduced tear gas cartridges and grenades. The British were developing a 'stink bomb' for clearing dugouts named 'S K' after South Kensington where it was invented. In the stress of war, it seemed but a short step from the use of gases which 'incapacitated' men by temporarily blinding or choking them, to the introduction of lethal agents.

The introduction of chemical warfare was in fact actively canvassed by the I G cartel from the outset of the war, most notably by its head, Carl Duisberg. An 'imperious Prussian who would not tolerate dissent in either his personal or his business life',[11] a man who (specificially) spoke of and believed in the 'Führer Principle' long before Hitler was ever heard of , Duisberg belonged to the scientific and industrial élite whose skill and unscrupulousness was to enable Germany to fight the world for ten out of the next forty years.

The chemical industry was the foundation of Germany's war machine. Without Duisberg's factories' discovery and mass production of synthetic nitrates, the Kaiser would have been forced to sue for peace in 1915. Now, the initiation of poison gas warfare promised both to strengthen further the I G's position in Germany, and to revive the moribund dye industry, which had been at a virtual standstill since the start of the war. Duisberg urged the employment of chemical warfare at a special conference of the German High Command in the autumn of 1914 and he personally investigated the toxicity of the various war gases. (Later he arranged for the offices of his own company, Bayer, to be decorated with a giant frieze depicting all the various aspects of the factory's war work: one panel showed gas being made, another shells being filled, a third gas masks being assembled. At the end of the war he proudly displayed this 'work of art' to a bemused Allied officer.)

To Duisberg's enthusiasm and the productive power of the I G was added the genius of Germany's leading industrial scientist. The man today generally credited as the 'father' of chemical warfare was the head of the Kaiser Wilhelm Institute in Berlin: Fritz Haber. Forty years old, a brilliant chemist, a future Nobel Prizewinner and a fervent patriot, Haber energetically set about the task of finding the world's first, practical, lethal chemical weapon. Work began in the autumn of 1914. 'We could hear,' stated a witness at the end of the war, 'the tests that Professor Haber was carrying out at the back of the Institute, with the military authorities, who in their steel-gray cars came to Haber's Institute every morning . . . The work was pushed day and night, and many times I saw activity in the building at eleven o'cock in the evening. It was common knowledge that Haber was pushing these men as hard as he could.'[12] In one of these early experiments a laboratory was blown up killing Haber's assistant, Professor Sachur.

By January Haber had a weapon ready to show the Army. Instead of filling the chemical into shells, he proposed to discharge it from cylinders. The chemical he chose was chlorine, a powerful asphyxiating gas which could be easily stored in the cylinders in liquid form; on contact with the air it evaporated into a low-hanging cloud which, with a favourable wind, could be carried into the heart of the enemy's positions. In addition, there were large stocks of chlorine to hand. Even before the war, the I G was producing forty tons per day; British production was less than a tenth of this.

The shock of the new weapon, the scale upon which an attack could be mounted, and the ability of gas to penetrate even the strongest fortifications, gave the Germans great hope that chemical warfare might end the deadlock in the west. Haber himself went to Ypres to supervise the attack. Yet despite the fact that between 22 April and 24 May, 500 tons of chlorine were discharged from over 20,000 cylinders, the Allied line held. Gas could not win the war alone – it had to be backed by a powerful offensive, which at Ypres the Germans failed to mount. Haber was bitterly disappointed. The military commanders, he wrote later, 'admitted afterward that if they had followed my advice and made a large-scale attack, instead of the experiment at Ypres, the Germans would have won'.[13]

Haber returned to Berlin where his wife Clara pleaded with him to give up his work and stay at home. Haber refused. In May he left for the eastern front where in three devastating attacks forty miles west of Warsaw the Russians lost around 25,000 men killed and wounded. Throughout the war the poorly-protected Russians suffered the worst of all the countries engaged in the chemical war: by the end of the war they were said to have suffered almost half a million casualties. In just one of the early attacks the Siberian Regiment was literally decimated – it began with thirty-nine officers and 4,310 men; it ended with four officers and 400 men.[14]

In the west, however, it was the Germans who were about to suffer. Duisberg had made a fatal miscalculation about the Allies' inability to respond with chemical weapons. Far from breaking the stalemate as he and Haber had hoped, gas was to become a major part of it. A pattern was established which was to persist to the end of the war: the Germans would initiate the use of a new gas to try to break through; it would fail, be copied by the Allies, and the cycle would repeat itself. In the summer of 1915, as work began in the Kaiser Wilhelm Institute on the next war gas – phosgene – Foulkes struggled to find the men and material for the Allies' first gas attack – using chlorine.

Haber himself was left to mourn the personal cost of his work on chemical warfare. On the night that he left for the eastern front, Clara Haber committed suicide.

And so, by a combination of industrial might, military expediency, and the skill of a handful of patriotic scientists, the world drifted into chemical warfare. Britain's poison gas offensive was waged by an élite section of the army, raised by Foulkes and known as the Special Companies (later the Special Brigade). Everyone was given extra pay and all held a rank at least equivalent to corporal. Most of them were new recruits, science graduates or industrial chemists. After the war many of them became key figures in Britain's fledgling Imperial Chemical Industries. In 1915 they carried revolvers instead of rifles, were largely excused the discipline of the parade ground, and learned instead to handle the 'oojahs', the great 190 lb cylinders of chlorine which required two men to carry them and which were to be the basis of Britain's first chemical attack.

By 25 September, 5,500 of these cylinders, containing 150 tons of gas, had been manhandled into position at Loos in Belgium ready for the British offensive. They had been shipped across the Channel in the greatest secrecy, each in an unmarked wooden box carried at a cost of twelve shillings apiece. A patrol of aeroplanes ensured that the Special Companies were not observed as they prepared the attack.

The need for surprise was paramount. In all plans for the attack distributed to company commanders, gas was referred to simply as 'the accessory', and severe penalties were imposed on anyone who accidentally described 'the accessory' as gas. The attitude of most officers to 'the accessory', and to the ill-assorted soldiers in charge of it, was well summed up by the old-school Captain Thomas in Robert Graves's *Goodbye to All That*:

Thomas said: 'It's damnable. It's not soldiering to use stuff like that, even though the Germans did start it. It's dirty, and it'll bring us bad luck. We're sure to bungle it. Take those new gas-companies – sorry, excuse me this once, I mean accessory-companies – their very look makes me tremble. Chemistry-dons from London University, a few lads straight from school, one or two NCOs of the old-soldier type, trained together for three weeks, then given a job as responsible as this. Of course they'll bungle it. How could they do anything else?'[15]

Yet, for all the suspicion, Foulkes could, on the eve of the Battle of Loos, look back on a remarkable achievement. Five months after the German initiation of gas warfare had caught the Allies by surprise, he had 1,404 men, including fifty-seven officers under his command. As they moved into position at midnight on the 25th, Foulkes waited nervously at Sir Douglas Haig's battle headquarters at a nearby château, a large-scale trench map spread out on the table in front of him, with small flags representing each of his commanders. At 5 am Haig considered calling off the attack. The wind was so slight that stepping into the grounds of the château, he asked one of his officers to light a cigarette; the puff of smoke scarcely drifted in the still morning air. Nevertheless, the attack went ahead. At 5.50 am the cylinders were opened. One gas officer, in a sector where the wind was least favourable, refused to discharge the gas. His refusal was relayed to Headquarters who instructed him to do as he was told. A few minutes later he was horrified to see the cloud drift back, gassing hundreds of British troops.

Graves was scathing about the efficiency of Foulkes's men in his sector of the front. The spanners they had been provided with for unscrewing the cocks of the cylinders were the wrong size and 'the gas-men rushed about shouting for the loan of adjustable spanners.' Only one or two cylinders were released. Warned of the attack the

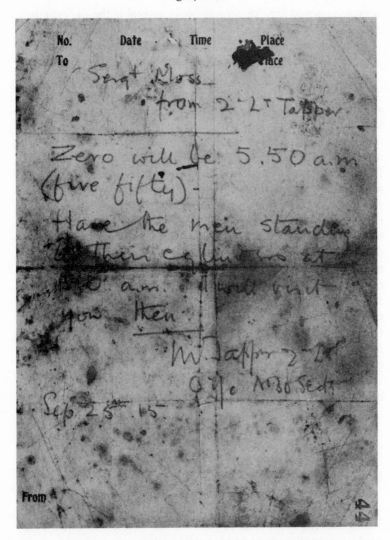

The original order given to Sergeant J. B. Moss of the Special Brigade's 'B Company' on 25 September 1915, instructing him to prepare for Britain's first gas attack (*Imperial War Museum*).

Germans opened fire: 'direct hits broke several of the gas cylinders, the trench filled with gas, the gas-company stampeded.'

Things went better elsewhere along the front. An aerial reconnaissance report handed to Haig shortly after 6 am reported that 'the gas cloud was rolling steadily over towards the German lines'. As the chlorine reached the first trenches, warning drums began to sound along the length of the German front. In the trenches themselves the scenes were a virtual replay of those at Ypres in April. Officers and men were equally unprepared. Masks had been lost or forgotten, most of the respirators they had were useless (after the attack one British sergeant reported burying twenty-three gassed Germans: all were wearing respirators). German commanders reported complete panic. Men who had been given no rations for four days as a result of the constant bombardment which had preceded the gas attack were already weak and quickly collapsed. Some men tried to crouch in dug-outs – these were at first free from gas, but gradually it accumulated and forced them out. Seventy Germans tried to come over the top to surrender but were mown down by their own machine gunners who were better equipped than the ordinary troops, with divers' helmets and oxygen cylinders. Eventually though even they succumbed: their oxygen supply lasted thirty minutes; by carefully interspersing the clouds of chlorine with waves of smoke, the British padded out the attack to forty minutes. The smoke had an additional psychological effect, blotting out the autumn morning with a fog so thick that as far back as four miles behind the German line visibility was less than ten paces.

An hour after the first discharge of gas, the British infantry charged the German line, penetrating a mile in the first rush. 'Behind the fourth gas and smoke cloud,' reported the war correspondent of the *Berliner Tageblatt*, 'there suddenly emerged Englishmen in thick lines and storming columns. They rose suddenly from the earth wear-ing smoke masks over their faces and looking not like soldiers but like devils. These were bad and terrible hours.'[16] A soldier of the 1st Middlesex Regiment, in a letter which was stopped by the censor, wrote:

I don't want to see another scene like last Saturday morning. It was just Hell with the lid off . . . The artillery bombarded them for four days and nights, never stopped, seven hundred guns behind us. At 5.45 on Saturday morning we turned the gas on the devils – it was an awful sight – and at 6.30 we climbed over the parapet and charged them. I carried a field telephone. Four of us started, I was the only one to reach the first German trench, which was full of dead, about three or four deep, all gassed. But they had the machine guns in the third-line trenches and they mowed us down, and everywhere was mud and blood. When they called the roll on the 1st Middlesex, 96 answered present out of 1020.[17]

British soldiers fought their way through German trenches that were a wasteland of dead. The 20th Brigade reported 'whole machine gun crews lying gassed to death'. Other troops described 'five men and two officers lying heaped in one place, blue in the face and undoubtedly gassed to death'. Men lay face down in the trenches; one officer reported a German still seated in his chair – gassed. Elsewhere, six dead Germans were found huddled together, as if trying to ward off the cold. Many of the dead were in the second and third lines, and in the communicating trenches where they had died trying to scramble to the rear. 'We saw the deadly effect of our gas,' wrote one officer to a London paper. 'The Germans had suffered as we too had suffered in the past.'[18]

In some places, the German line was penetrated by British troops to a depth of three miles. But, as in so many battles of the First World War, the gains were transitory and small, the sacrifices enormous. Although eighteen guns and 3,000 prisoners were captured, the Battle of Loos cost the British over 50,000 casualties. There was no breakthrough. As at Ypres, gas – unpredictable in its effects and heavily dependent upon the weather – had failed to achieve the decisive victory each side sought. Like Haber, Foulkes was left after the battle to sigh a series of 'ifs'. 'If fortune had been a little kinder, if the wind had been only slightly more favourable, there is no doubt whatever that Sir John French would have gained a smashing victory on this day.'[19] As it was, within a week the Germans had recaptured almost all the ground they had lost.

After Loos, gas was an even more unpopular weapon than it had been before. In the three weeks after the first discharge, 2,000 British troops reported as casualties of *British* gas; fifty-five cases were 'severe' and ten died. Pipes and cylinders often leaked, frequently they were damaged by enemy shells; and when a gas attack occurred, the wind often wafted the cloud over the wrong side. Even the commanders viewed it with distaste.

In the ordinary soldier there was born a hatred of gas that steadily deepened as the war progressed. For the next three years men were kept constantly on their guard. Allied anti-gas schools were set up at

Havres, Rouen, Etaples, Abbeville, Boulogne and Calais. Every soldier was put through a standard course which included an hour immersed in a cloud of gas (to give him 'confidence in his respirator') and half a minute exposed to tear gas (to give him a fright and teach him to take anti-gas precautions seriously). Masks had to be put on in a regulation six seconds – but before being allowed to do so, and while still exposed to the tear gas, men had to repeat their name, number and battalion; sometimes they were made to do it twice. 'It was,' as one historian has put it, 'a brisk business, which sent men back to the front with an aggrieved feeling of the unfairness of gas.'[20] It was believed that gas casualties were a result of slack discipline. Courts of Inquiry were held on the victims, and each gas case had to wear a 'wound stripe' – visible evidence of his neglect in allowing himself to be gassed. (This practice was only stopped after the introduction of mustard gas, when there were simply too many casualties for the system to cope with.)

The effectiveness of these stern measures is reflected in the statistics for gas casualties. Of the 180,983 British soldiers officially accounted as having been gassed in the First World War, only 6,062 are recorded as having died, giving a mortality rate of around 3 per cent[21] (although, as will be discussed later, this figure is almost certainly well below the true number).

Using these figures, advocates of chemical warfare later argued that gas was actually the most *humane* of the weapons used in the First World War, wounding far more than it killed. But the figures do not reveal either the horror or persistence of gas wounds. Nor do they show the psychological casualties. As the fighting dragged on, the constant state of gas readiness imperceptibly sapped men's strength and fighting spirit. Fear was omnipresent. Every few miles along every road, signs warned of the danger of gas. As far back as twelve miles you had constantly to carry your mask. In the event of a gas alarm a deafening racket arose along the front. Bells were rung, empty shell cases beaten, and the great Strombus horns – twenty-eight to the mile, powered by compressed air and audible nine miles away – let out warning screams. One eyewitness recalled:

With men trained to believe that a light sniff of gas might mean death, and with nerves highly strung by being shelled for long periods and with the presence of not a few who really had been gassed, it is no wonder that a gas alarm went beyond all bounds. It was remarked as a joke that if someone yelled 'gas', everyone in France would put on a mask . . . Two or three alarms a night was common. Gas shock was as frequent as shellshock.[22]

In June 1915, 2,500,000 'Hypo Helmets' were issued – bags of flannel which had been chemically impregnated against chlorine. The bags were placed over the head and tucked into the collar; two eyepieces cut into the front and made of celluloid enabled the wearer to peer out at the scene around him. In the autumn the British added modifications – the helmet was better impregnated and a rubber exhaust tube was added. Nine million of these 'P Helmets' were issued by December.

The shapeless hood, the twin eyeholes, the elephant's trunk of rubber hanging down from the mouth – the respirators gave the men a nightmarish quality as they moved around in the dense clouds of gas. To wear, the masks were extremely uncomfortable. Often they leaked around the mouthpiece, or the eyepieces cracked and let in the gas. They produced a feeling of suffocation. A dangerous concentration of carbon dioxide was likely to build up inside. They made you sweat, and when that happened the eyepieces steamed up and the chemical solution the flannel had been dipped in began to run, stinging the face and dripping down the neck. And in a long attack, the effectiveness of the helmets could come dangerously close to exhaustion; with the chemical protection worn away, the gas was able to seep through.

The P Helmet had been hastily improvised to provide protection against phosgene, another chemical used in the dye industry, whose potential as a war gas had been noticed by the Allies in the summer of 1915. The helmet arrived at the front in the nick of time.

At 5.30 am on 19 December, the German Gas Corps broke their six month silence on the British front with an attack at Ypres using phosgene for the first time. Captain Adie of the Royal Army Medical Corps recalled a loud hissing sound. 'Almost at the same moment red rockets went up from the German lines . . . I was at Headquarters drinking a cup of tea with the Colonel. At first I thought the water from which the tea was made had been over-chlorinated – a moment later I thought I smelt gas.'[23]

Travelling at great speed, the cloud – a mixture of chlorine and phosgene – outstripped the alarm system of gongs and klaxons and took hundreds of men unawares; one man was gassed five miles behind the front line. Panic set in on the dark winter morning as shell fire cut all the telephone wires to the front. It was mid-afternoon before Adie could reach the first trenches. Most of the chlorine victims were already dead, 'blue and puffed out', the wounded frothing from the mouth. The phosgene victims began to feel worse as the day progressed. Men who thought they had escaped being gassed suddenly found the slightest effort made them ill.

Some 30 or 40 men left the trench to report sick. To get to the road the men reporting sick had to go across about 100 yards of very rough muddy ground. The exertion, in heavy wet great-coats, and with all their equipment, caused great alteration in their condition, and by the time they reached the road they were exhausted and were quite unable to proceed any further. The road was strewn with exhausted men, and we did not get them all in until 7 am the next morning. The history of the men who remained at duty in the trenches was still more striking. One man, feeling fairly well, was filling sand bags when he *collapsed and died suddenly*. Two more men died in the same way that evening.[24]

One officer died suddenly in an ambulance, another collapsed while walking to report his symptoms. A third reported to a medical post at 8.30 pm. 'He said he didn't feel very well, but he did not look very bad. I gave him a cup of tea which he drank and we talked for a little while. Suddenly he collapsed in the chair he was sitting on. I gave him some oxygen but he died an hour afterwards.' 1,069 men were gassed that day; 116 died.

The appearance of phosgene greatly deepened the fear of gas. Like chlorine it had quirky side-effects – for example it made pipe tobacco taste like hay. But it was, at a rough calculation, eighteen times as powerful as chlorine, practically colourless and odourless, and much more difficult to detect. Effective in concentrations of just one part in 50,000 it had a deadly delayed action. A victim who has inhaled a lethal dose at first feels nothing more than a mild irritation of eyes and throat which quickly passes off; for up to two days afterwards a man might actually feel mildly euphoric. Throughout this period his lungs are filling with fluid. Collapse comes quickly. The slightest action – turning over in bed for instance – can send the respiration rate rocketing to 80 breaths per minute, the pulse to 120. The 'drowning period' begins. Official reports describe 'an abundant flow of thin watery fluid, often streaked with blood, which simply flows from the mouth as the dying patient loses the power to expel it. After death, the foam from this fluid may dry to a white efflorescence around the mouth.'[25] Victims were known to cough up four pints of this yellowish liquid every hour; it could take forty-eight hours to die.

The gas produced some of the most extraordinary stories of the war. Foulkes recalled a German taken prisoner after a British phosgene attack. At his interrogation, in high spirits, he ridiculed the ineffectiveness of British gas. Twenty-four hours later he was dead. One German died while writing a letter home to his family. Because of its delayed action, phosgene caused many casualties among the men of the Special Companies, unaware that they were being poisoned.

One sergeant got a slight dose of gas the day after an attack had been made, whilst disconnecting pipes from the empty cylinders: he paid no attention to it, did not even mention it at the time and carried on with his duties. He slept and breakfasted well on the following day, but an hour later he became very ill and died twenty-four hours after inhaling the gas.[26]

At the Battle of the Somme alone, fifty-seven of Foulkes's men died from the effects of their own gas.

It was at the Somme, in June 1916, that the Allies first used the new gas. In the biggest attack they had launched up to that time, chlorine and phosgene were released along a seventeen mile front, producing a massive cloud that penetrated twelve miles behind the German lines. The cloud wiped out men, horses, wildlife, insects, vegetation – virtually everything it touched. Three months before autumn, all the leaves on the trees in the nearby Monchy wood had fallen. The war correspondent of the *Frankfurter Zeitung* wrote of the hundreds of dead rats and mice that 'are found in the trenches after gas attacks. Owls are greatly excited. Behind the front, fowls and ducks are said to have become restless a quarter of an hour before the gas clouds approached; and the gas kills ants and caterpillars, beetles and butterflies. I found a hedgehog and an adder both killed by gas. The only birds that seem indifferent to the gas are the sparrows.'[27] A few weeks later, in August, a German cloud of phosgene reached a height of sixty feet and passed through a wood near Ypres, killing thousands of birds nesting in the trees.

doesn't only kill people, but /

On the Somme, phosgene killed men in their hundreds. The *Daily Chronicle* enthusiastically reported that 'British wounded brought back from the German trenches by their comrades relate that the effects of the new gases experimented with are terrible. One soldier of the Highland Light Infantry, who took part in one of the principal incursions into the enemy trenches, declares that all the Germans occupying that particular sector were dead. Two hundred and fifty corpses were counted lying huddled together.'[28]

The story was the same as in previous gas attacks: men caught unawares, panicking, and spreading the terror and confusion which enabled the gas to do its work. 'Some men,' according to a report captured from the German 12th Division, 'were taken by surprise and put on their masks too late, others ran too quickly and tore off their masks because of the difficulty of breathing. Others, again, tumbled about during the alarm and either had their masks torn off or displaced.'[29] The dead were too numerous to bury: the dug-outs where they lay were merely blown up or filled in with earth.

In the first eighteen days of the Somme Battle, the Special Brigade carried out fifty gas attacks. Phosgene became the main British chemical weapon. Over the next nine months almost 1,500 tons of it were discharged.

To the British – the public, the army, even the men of the Special Brigade – gas was universally known as 'Frightfulness'. Even after years of war and atrocity which had seen the introduction of such terrifying new weapons as the tank, the Zeppelin and the U-boat, gas was still the most hated and feared of them all, with a complete demonology to itself. Chemical weapons came to epitomise all that was most disgusting and evil about the war, a mood captured best in Wilfred Owen's famous poem:

> Gas! Gas! Quick, boys! – An ecstasy of fumbling,
> Fitting the clumsy helmets just in time;
> But someone still was yelling out and stumbling,
> And flound'ring like a man in fire or lime . . .
> Dim, through the misty panes and thick green light,
> As under a green sea, I saw him drowning.
>
> In all my dreams, before my helpless sight,
> He plunges at me, guttering, choking, drowning.
>
> If in some smothering dreams you too could pace
> Behind the wagon that we flung him in,
> And watch the white eyes writhing in his face,
> His hanging face, like a devil's sick of sin;
> If you could hear, at every jolt, the blood
> Come gargling from the froth-corrupted lungs,
> Obscene as cancer, bitter as the cud

Of vile incurable sores on innocent tongues, –
My friend, you would not tell with such high zest
To children ardent for some desperate glory,
The old Lie: Dulce et decorum est
Pro patria mori.

Foulkes tried his best to play down this image. He was tireless in
his efforts to promote gas. He acted as its ambassador, even to
neutral nations not fighting the war but who wanted to know more
about the potentialities of chemical weapons. He introduced 'Open
Days' at the Special Brigade's HQ at Helfaut. There were regular
demonstrations to convince the sceptical. 'On several occasions,'
Foulkes recalled, 'there were more than 100 Generals present at a
time, and 300 or 400 officers altogether.' Winston Churchill visited
Helfaut and came away, according to Foulkes, powerfully impressed
by chemical warfare – a conviction which was to be of crucial
importance a quarter of a century later, when Britain was next at
war. Other VIP visitors included the Duke of Westminster and
George Bernard Shaw.

This public relations exercise was useful, but in the end Foulkes
won the battle against the critics of gas warfare through simple
military expediency. A chemical arms race developed, in the rush of
which there was no time to worry about ethics. Soon, virtually every
leading chemist in Britain was at work on some aspect of gas
warfare. Thirty-three different British laboratories tested 150,000
known organic and inorganic compounds in an attempt to develop
the most poisonous war gas possible, and in 1916 this massive
research and development organization was given its focus when the
British opened an installation whose name has been synonymous
with poison gas ever since – the chemical warfare establishment at
Porton Down. Occupying a 7,000 acre site on Salisbury Plain,
Porton (whose work is described in Chapter Two) employed over a
thousand scientists and soldiers whose job it was to transform the
theories of the laboratory into actual weapons.

In a short space of time, chemical weapons moved from the fringes
of the war to its very heart. In 1915, 3,600 tons of gas were
discharged. In 1916 that figure more than quadrupled, to 15,000
tons. Chemicals and aeroplanes vied with one another as the fastest-
developing forms of warfare. Gas attacks ceased to be carefully-
planned set-piece affairs: they became an everyday occurrence. For

the British, the expansion was due in particular to two new weapons – the Livens Projector and the Stokes Mortar – which despite their prosaic titles were innovations as deadly as they were revolutionary. 'The heirs of the Livens Projector,' one expert has written, 'are the multiple rocket launchers and the aircraft cluster bombs.'[30]

Captain F. H. Livens, the inventor of the Projector, was marked by two key characteristics – a passionate hatred of the Germans, and unflagging energy. A former civil engineer and commander of 'Z' Company of the Special Brigade, 'Livens,' recalled Foulkes, 'had a strong personal feeling in the war connected, I believe, with the sinking of the *Lusitania*.' He was a 'go-getter', enthusiastically leaping in and out of gas clouds to test their effects, and prone to commandeer equipment he needed, if necessary, at the point of a gun.

His invention was crude, but so effective that it was still one of the army's main chemical weapons thirty years later. The Projector was a steel tube, generally between three and four feet long, and eight inches in diameter. It was simply buried in the ground at an angle of 45 degrees, and fired remotely by means of an electrical charge, generally in banks of twenty-five at a time. The charge sent hurtling from the tube a drum containing 30 lb of chemical, usually pure phosgene. The only warning the enemy received was the flash of the discharge. Seconds later a core of TNT burst the container over their positions, setting up an instantaneous, lethal concentration of gas. Rather than releasing the clouds of gas from cylinders which then placed them at the mercy of the wind, the Livens Projector was a means of virtually dropping the cylinders on the heads of the enemy. It was not particularly accurate, but it had a range of a mile, and was also cheap and easy to make. Livens calculated that if the Projector was mass-manufactured 'the cost of killing Germans would be reduced to only sixteen shillings apiece'.

The British first launched a full-scale attack using the Livens Projector at the Battle of Arras on 9 April 1917:

The discharge took place practically simultaneously: a dull red flash seemed to flicker all along the front as far as the eye could reach, and there was a slight ground tremor, followed a little later by a muffled roar, as 2,340 of these sinister projectiles hurtled through space, turning clumsily over and over, and some of them, no doubt, colliding with each other in flight. About twenty seconds later they landed in masses in the German positions, and after a brief pause the steel cases were burst open by the explosive charges inside, and nearly fifty tons of liquid phosgene were liberated which vaporized instantly and formed a cloud so dense that Livens, who watched the discharge from an aeroplane, noticed it still so thick as to be visible as it floated over Vimy and Bailleul villages.[31]

The terrors of the gas cloud and the artillery bombardment were combined in a weapon which the Germans came to view with particular horror. A captured German document spoke of the 'violent explosion' of a projector attack: 'volcanic sheets of flame or the simultaneous occurrence of many gun flashes, thick black smoke clouds, powerful concussion, whistling and noise of impact up to 25 seconds after the flash of discharge . . . the noise resembles that of an exploding dump of hand grenades.'[32] At Arras, the German gun crews were forced to wear their masks for hours on end; many ran out of ammunition as the gas killed hundreds of horses used to carry munitions up to the front.

It was virtually the only time the Allies took the Germans by surprise with a new chemical weapon in the entire war, and despite German attempts to copy it the Livens Projector marked a major shift in the chemical war in favour of the Allies. Its drawback was the amount of preparation which a successful projector attack required: installing, loading and camouflaging them was a risky business. Nevertheless, the British used them on an increasing scale, often in batteries of thousands at a time. New fillings of high explosive and incendiaries were developed, as well as 'stinks' like bone oil and amyl acetate whose obnoxious smell forced the enemy to don gas masks.

The Battle of Arras also saw the widespread use of the Stokes Mortar. Like the Projector, its design was extremely simple: a steel tube raised at an angle by two struts. It fired four-inch mortar bombs, each containing two litres of gas. A well-trained crew could fire fifteen bombs and have them all in the air before the first one hit its target, with pin-point accuracy, as much as 1,000 yards away.

In addition to mortars and projectors came the gas shell, whose whistling flight and thudding impact became familiar noises in the cacophony of battle. The French and the Germans used them early in 1916, and large-scale shelling by the British came in the following year. By 1918 between a third and a fifth of all shells were being filled with chemicals. The Germans actually named their gases after the markings on the shell cases: Green Cross for phosgene and chlorine, Yellow Cross for mustard gas, and White Cross for tear gas.

Gas-filled artillery weapons overcame much of the initial antagonism felt for chemical warfare among military planners. Gas could now be more easily integrated into an attack, there was less dependence on the wind, and leaking cylinders – which often gave warning of an impending attack by sending hundreds of rats fleeing across No Man's Land – were largely banished from the trenches. By 1918, 94 per cent of all the gas used was being delivered by the artillery: an over-all total for the war of 66 million gas shells. Shelling on this scale meant that chemical warfare, once an unexpected and terrifying experience, was now an ever-present threat. For in July 1917 the Germans began to use a gas weapon whose power dwarfed anything which had gone before and which was only made possible by the development of the gas shell: dichlorethyl sulphide.

Mustard gas.

The scene was once again Ypres. At 10 pm on the warm summer evening of 12 July, the British 15th and 55th Divisions came under heavy bombardment. The enemy was using 77 and 105 mm gas shells in massive numbers. But what they delivered was not 'gas' in the sense that the soldiers were used to. It was a brown liquid, rather like sherry, which gave off a smell variously described as 'unpleasant', 'oily', 'like garlic' and 'like mustard'. Apart from a slight irritation to the eyes and throat, there were no initial effects, and few men even bothered to put on their gas masks. Most quickly went back to sleep. But in the early hours of the morning they began to wake up with 'intolerable pain' in the eyes, which felt as though sand or grit had been rubbed into them. Then they began to vomit uncontrollably. As the night wore on, the pain in the eyes became so intense that many had to be given morphia. The following day the sun rose over an army that looked as if it had been stricken by some biblical plague.

When some of the milder cases were evacuated each man had to be led like a blind man by an orderly to the ambulance car.

The face was frequently congested and swollen, especially in the more severe cases, and small blisters were visible in many cases on the lower part of the face and chin, and sometimes on the neck.

A few cases had painful patches of blisters on the backs of the thighs and buttocks, and even on the scrotum, with oedema of the scrotum and penis. The vesication of the buttocks and oedema of the genitals would appear to be probably due to men sitting on the ground contaminated with the toxic substance.[33]

The hours passed and the symptoms grew worse. Moist red patches of skin affected by the vapour became massive yellow blisters up to a foot long. The gas could easily penetrate clothes, attacking the skin wherever it was most sensitive: at the bend of the elbow, the back of the knee, the neck, between the thighs. The Chemical Adviser to the Fifth Army, trying to retrieve fragments of the mustard shells for analysis, developed blisters on his wrists and on the backs of his hands. He tried to carry a portion of a shell under his arm and developed blisters on his chest, the mustard working its way through several layers of clothing. 'Owing to its high boiling point,' reported the War Office expert Sir Harold Hartley, 'some of it is scattered on the ground and continues to give off gas for some time. It could be smelt in Ypres on the day following the bombardment.'[34]

The field hospitals were choked with casualties. Two days after the attack, the first deaths occurred. Dying was a slow and agonizing process. It was not necessarily the burns that killed, but the havoc the gas wrought in the throat and lungs. 'On entering a ward full of cases gassed during the recent attack,' reported Captain Ramsay of the RAMC 'one is struck by the incessant and apparently useless coughing of the patients.'[35] The men's bronchial tubes were stripped of their mucous membrane by the gas. 'In one case,' wrote another medical officer, 'the mucous membrane formed apparently a complete cast of the trachea.'[36] The victim had died with his windpipe clogged from top to bottom.

There is no record of the precise circumstances in which Sapper Guest of the Royal Engineers was gassed on 12 July. We know only that he was admitted to hospital nine days later and 'complained of difficulty in breathing and pain in both eyes'. The following day, 'during the early morning the difficulty in breathing became more marked. He rallied slightly but relapsed in the early forenoon and died at 10 am.'

The body was examined four and a half hours after death. It was that of a well-developed man, and showed externally a slightly dusky discolouration of the skin of face and neck and vesicles on the scrotum and penis but no wounds of any kind. On opening the body, distinct irritation of the eyes, mouth, throat, nose and skin of the face was noticed by several people who were present and a faint sweetish taste was noticeable, comparable with the effect of a weak carbolic solution.[37]

Here was a gas so powerful that men standing around the dismembered corpse of a victim at an autopsy could still feel its effects ten days after the initial poisoning. And as the post mortem continued, the full extent of the damage wrought by the gas lay revealed before the doctors. The larynx and vocal chords were 'swollen and very red', the windpipe filled with 'thin frothy fluid', and 'six ounces of blood stained fluid in the left lung'; the lung itself, which was more than double its normal weight, 'felt very firm and solid', and 'portions of the lobe sank in water'; the heart weighed twenty ounces instead of the normal ten, and the veins over the surface of the brain 'contained innumerable small bubbles of gas'.

Another victim, thirty-nine year-old Lieutenant Collinge of the King's Liverpool Regiment, took ten days to die:

Brownish pigmentation present over large surfaces of the body. The forearms showed the same pigmentation, except at a place where a wrist watch had been situated, a white ring of skin being present there. Marked superficial burning of the face and scrotum. The whole of the trachea and lower part of the larynx, including the vocal chords, were covered by a yellowish membrane. The bronchi contained abundant pus. The right lung showed extensive collapse, and on section numerous patches of broncho-pneumonia, some as large as a five-shilling piece. These patches were grey in colour, and in many of them the pus could be seen to have extended beyond the limits of the bronchi to form definite abesses. Liver congested and somewhat fatty. The brain substance was unduly wet and very congested.

Collinge and Guest were only two of hundreds. The Germans had delayed their attack until they had built up enormous reserves of mustard gas and were in a position to mount a bombardment on a giant scale. In ten days Allied positions were pounded with more than a million shells containing 2,500 tons of gas. Within three weeks of introducing Yellow Cross shell, the Germans had caused as many gas casualties as had resulted from the entire gas shelling of the preceding year. By the end of the first week, the number of gassed men admitted to British Medical Units was 2,934; by the end of the second week, a further 6,476 had been added; by the end of the third week, another 4,886.

In all, from July 1917 to the end of the war, British casualties from mustard gas amounted to at least 125,000 – 70 per cent of the total number of British gas casualties for the whole war. A conservative estimate of the number of deaths was 1,859. Although the mortality rate was therefore only around 1½ per cent, the severity of the effects was enough to keep a man away from duty for two to three months, if not longer. There were frequently secondary infections of the respiratory system and the skin. First World War doctors noted that healing skin could often erupt in fresh blisters, or inflammation could occur in an area which had been previously thought not contaminated. Ramsay gave an instance of a man who 'had burns of the scrotum on the second day, and on the eighth day the skin of his back became inflamed for the first time.'[38]

Thousands of men were drawing disability pensions at the end of the war as a result of mustard gas poisoning. It was, declared a secret British assessment of gas casualties prepared in 1919, 'in a class by itself so far as casualty producing power is concerned'. It was not simply a matter of deaths and numbers wounded, it was the time it took for them to heal. 'To put the matter bluntly, mustard gas on several occasions accounted during a week or two for the prolonged removal from the sphere of active operations of casualties equivalent in number to the combatants of two or more Divisions.'[39] Thanks largely to mustard gas, in the last eighteen months of the war, one casualty in every six (16½ per cent of the total) was a victim of chemical weapons.[40]

Long after the initial bombardment had occurred, an area which had been contaminated by mustard was liable to remain dangerous. The liquid formed pools in shell craters and in the corners of dug-outs ready to trap the unwary. It polluted water. In cold weather it froze like water and stayed in the soil: mustard used in the winter of 1917 poisoned men in the spring of 1918 when the ground thawed. In this way, mustard could be used to 'seal off' whole areas of a battlefield; the only way to cross a contaminated section of ground was by laying a road of bleach. To survive in such conditions, men not only had to wear masks, but also leggings, gloves and goggles. To continue to fight it was necessary to decontaminate equipment constantly. Gas became a weapon of attrition: its military effective-ness was not to be measured merely in casualty lists. If gas never killed a man, wrote General Fries, head of the infant United States Chemical Warfare Service, 'the reduction in physical vigour and, therefore, in efficiency of an army forced at all times to wear masks, would amount to at least 25 per cent, equivalent to disabling a quarter of a million men out of an army of a million.'[41]

For the average soldier, the strain of living in this alien, chemically-polluted environment was scarcely bearable. Even the well-disciplined made mistakes. Among the rest – the shell-shocked, the careless, the raw and frightened conscripts – gas mopped up casualties. 'After July 1917,' wrote Lord Moran, 'gas partly usurped the role of high explosive in bringing to a head a natural unfitness for war. The gassed men were an expression of trench fatigue, a menace when the manhood of the nation had been picked over.'[42]

Mustard went under a variety of different names. To the Germans it was 'Lost', to the French 'Yperite', after Ypres, where it was first used; the British also code-named it HS ('Hun Stuff'). Its chemical name was dichlorethyl sulphide – a substance the British had actually turned down when it was suggested as a weapon on the grounds that it wasn't sufficiently lethal. They now had cause bitterly to regret that decision. It had taken the Germans only six months to get the gas into production. It took the French until June 1918 – almost a year. The British encountered even more difficulties in setting up bulk production. Not only was the chemical process required extremely complicated, it also proved highly dangerous.

The main English plant – capable of producing over twenty tons a day – was eventually sited at Avonmouth. Among its 1,100 workers, its Medical Officer reported in December 1918 that there had been over 1,400 illnesses directly attributable to the work.[43] In addition there were 160 accidents and over a thousand burns; three people were killed and another four had died of related illnesses in the six months that the factory was in operation. There were a vast number of complaints – blisters of the hands, scalp, shoulders, arms, abdomen, buttocks, genitals, thighs, legs and feet; erythema, iritis, scrotal dermatitis, leukodermia, conjunctivitis, pharyngitis, bronchitis, tracheitis, gastritis, pleurodynia, purulent bronchopneumonia, aphonia, acute rhinitis (bleeding from the nose); debility, gastric pain, mental inertia, chronic cough, breathlessness, memory weakness and defective eyesight. Many of the workers were old, many were women – some pregnant. There were thirty resident patients in the factory hospital, tended by a doctor and eight nurses. All in all, it added a new meaning to the phrase 'the Home Front'. Yet despite the frenzied efforts to produce British mustard gas, no supplies reached the battlefield until September 1918, two months before the Armistice.

Instead the British responded with a series of major cloud gas attacks – the last of the war – using cylinders of phosgene mounted on the backs of railway engines. Foulkes, who dreamt up the idea, called them 'beam' operations – concentrated clouds which drifted in thin columns over the enemy positions, bleaching vegetation for distances of up to 12,000 yards; at Ypres the clouds accumulated in the river valleys for hours.

The attacks caused panic among billeted soldiers in villages and towns many miles behind the lines. When a cloud was detected approaching (invariably at night) alarm bells were rung and troops and civilians, all clutching respirators, made their way to the top rooms of the houses, closing all the windows and doors. The cloud swirled by below, killing all the flowers and vegetables in the gardens. These attacks, reaching far behind the lines and for the first time affecting large numbers of civilians, were greatly feared. The Germans were so anxious to avoid revealing the casualties they incurred that – according to Foulkes – 'the greatest secrecy was always observed . . . and all burials and evacuations were carried out at night.'[44]

They were dangerous and difficult attacks to mount. Captain A. E. Hodgkin, commander of the Special Brigade's 'A' Company, left behind in his diary a striking account of what life was like in the closing months of the war: working close to the front line in the early hours of the morning, in a 'very cold and high wind', the night moonless and pitch-black, trying to manhandle tons of liquid phosgene 'brought up the line by light railway which is never repaired much and which is consequently jerky, to say the least of it. Each truck goes up separately being pushed by five or six men: every 100 yards or so it hops off the line and has to be unloaded, replaced on the line and loaded up again. My vocabulary has been improved wonderfully by the exercise, but that of the men is becoming rather threadbare.'[45]

Night after night, the men of 'A' Company would stand by to release the gas – Hodgkin by a field telephone in a tunnel full of a 'multitude of fungi and rats' – only to be told as dawn was breaking to forget about it until the next night. Often the German sentries a few hundred yards away heard them moving about and passed word to their artillery. On one occasion, Hodgkin was stranded at the front in a heavy bombardment:

The night was still uncannily quiet until 2 am when we started our return journey. When halfway down the light railway the enemy began shelling with gas shells. I have never heard so many in the air at once. So we took shelter in one of the reserve lines for about an hour and a half, by which time he seemed to have finished with Cambrin through which we had to pass. Just at this time we saw our S.O.S. signal go up and a battle begin to the north of the Canal. Then down came a barrage of gas and high explosive all along the La Bassee road. I don't know how any of us ever got back at all: we had to march all the way back to Sailly in respirators as the whole area was soaked with gas, and were pursued the entire distance with shells of all calibres.

Eventually, after weeks of waiting, Hodgkin was given the order to release the gas. The cylinders were mounted on the backs of ten 10 ton trucks, towed by four engines to within 700 yards of the German front line. At 1 am, in bright moonlight, Hodgkin watched apprehensively as the first waves of the gas drifted towards enemy positions where the night before a patrol had reported that 'loud talking and laughing could be heard at 4 am'. The discharge lasted over three hours. Hodgkin had little idea – apart from 'a good deal of promiscuous shelling for retaliation' – of what effect the attack was having. The only accurate casualty report he received was when he returned to base to be told that he had 'killed three of our own men, poor devils, who hadn't been warned by their officer to be clear of the danger area by zero time.'

Despite the riskiness of railway-mounted operations from behind the front lines, in March 1918 Foulkes was putting the final touches to what would have been the biggest cylinder discharge of all time, so great that, in his opinion, 'trench warfare would have been converted into open warfare in a day'. 200,000 cylinders of phosgene were to be opened from the backs of dozens of railway trains, releasing 6,000 tons of gas in a chemical offensive which would last for twelve hours. Few respirators – even twenty or thirty miles behind the front line – would be able to withstand such an onslaught. Casualties were estimated to be likely to be 50 per cent. In the ensuing confusion the British High Command planned to launch a mighty offensive, spearheaded by tanks, which would punch its way through the front and end the war. The sector of the front provisionally selected for the attack was that held by the 3rd Army, between Gavrelle and Gouzeaucourt.

But Foulkes's dreams of triumph were overtaken by events. In March 1918, having concluded peace with Russia, a much-strengthened German army was able to launch its own great offensive in the west. The Allies were subjected to a hurricane bombardment from over 4,000 guns. With the IG producing a thousand tons of mustard gas a month, the Germans were in a position literally to drench the British and French with gas.

On four successive nights, from 10 to 13 March, the Cambrai Salient was blanketed with 150,000 rounds of Yellow Cross shell. Later, 20,000 shells were fired in the course of fifteen hours into the village of Armentieres: liquid mustard ran like rain water in the gutters of the streets. Trying to survive for hours at a time on the stale air of the respirator was almost unendurable. The gas was everywhere. It evaporated quickly in the warm spring weather and penetrated every crevice. It waited until sweating men loosened their clothing or wiped the perspiration from their eyes – and then it struck. In the week ending on 16 March, 6,195 gas cases were admitted to medical units; the following week saw the admission of a further 6,874; and during the week ending on 13 April, the British suffered what was possibly their worst ever period, as 7,000 gassed men flooded into the field hospitals.[46]

It was the week of Field Marshal Haig's famous 'Special Order of the Day' of 11 April: 'There is no course open to us but to fight it out. Every position must be held to the last man: there must be no retirement. With our backs to the wall and believing in the justice of our cause each one of us must fight on to the end.' Over the next few weeks, 200 German divisions advanced over forty miles, capturing 80,000 prisoners and 1,000 guns. Hodgkin, retreating day after day, wrote that he felt as though he was 'living on the side of a precipice'. An enemy attack could come 'at any moment of the day or night. The bombing season has begun again with the new moon and the air has been full of enemy aeroplanes all this evening.'

The success of the attack owed much to mustard gas. Ammunition dumps later captured by the Allies were revealed to be as much as 50 per cent stocked with chemical weapons. The Americans alone suffered 70,000 casualties from mustard gas – more than a quarter of the US Army's over-all casualties for the entire war.

In advancing so far, however, the Germans had sown the seeds of their own defeat. In July and August the Allies were able to strike back at the over-extended German positions. Their armies too were heavily dependent on chemicals. By August the British and Americans were increasing the proportion of gas-filled munitions ordered from the factories to between 20 and 30 per cent of total ammunition supplied. That ratio was planned to be increased still further. By 1919 it is possible that chemicals would have come to rival, even in

some cases outstrip, high explosives. In June the French acquired
mustard gas, and in September, in the dying days of the war, the first
significant supplies of British-charged mustard shells reached the
battlefield. By then it was all nearly over.

Yet the British use of mustard gas is significant for one incident
alone. On 14 October, during the final Allied offensive, British
mustard shells rained down into a shattered Belgian village called
Werwick, causing heavy casualties among the exhausted 16th
Bavarian Reserve Infantry. A few days before the Armistice, a
trainload of the men wounded in the Werwick attack were shipped
back to Germany. Among them, blinded and humiliated, was a
twenty-nine year-old corporal, whose injuries helped determine him
to avenge the German defeat: Adolf Hitler.[47]

Fearing that he would be tried as a war criminal, Fritz Haber donned
a false beard and as the war ended took off for Switzerland: so too
did Carl Duisberg, head of the German chemical industry. Neither in
the end was tried. Indeed in 1919 Haber was honoured with the
Nobel Prize for his work on the synthesis of ammonia, a decision
which outraged the scientific world, the *New York Times* asking – if
Haber got the Chemistry Prize – 'Why the Nobel prize for idealistic
and imaginative literature was not given to the man who wrote
General Ludendorff's daily communiqués?'[48]

Between them, Haber and Duisberg had changed the history of
warfare. At least 1.3 million men had been wounded by gas; 91,000
of them had died. Germany, France and Britain had all suffered
around 200,000 casualties, and Russia more than double that figure.
An estimated 113,000 tons of chemicals had been used.[49]

Had the war gone into a sixth year, there is no doubt that these
figures would have been vastly increased. All the belligerents had
new weapons about to come into service. In the spring of 1918 a
team based at the Catholic University, Washington DC, discovered
Lewisite: faster acting than mustard gas it caused 'immediate
excruciating pain upon striking the eye, a stinging pain in the skin,
and sneezing, coughing, pain and tightness in the chest on inhalation,
often accompanied by nausea and vomiting'.[50] The first batch of 150
tons of Lewisite was at sea, on its way to Europe when the Armistice
was signed. The British had the 'M device', which generated an
'arsenical smoke' code-named DA, capable of penetrating even the
most effective German gas mask within fifteen seconds. Within a

minute the victim would be in agony. Haldane described the pain in the head 'as like that caused when fresh water gets into the nose when bathing, but infinitely more severe. These symptoms are accompanied by the most appalling mental distress and misery. Some soldiers poisoned by these substances had to be prevented from committing suicide; others temporarily went raving mad, and tried to burrow into the ground to escape from imaginary pursuers.'[51] For their part the Germans had perfected a new projector – the Gaswerfer 1918 – capable of hurling cannisters filled with phosgene-impregnated pumice granules over a distance of up to two miles. Chemical warfare had come a very long way from tear gas grenades and simple cylinders of chlorine. Weapons which four years before had been beyond the pale of civilized warfare now employed vast numbers of scientists, technicians and soldiers in large research and development installations.

At Edgewood Arsenal in the United States, the Americans had 'probably the largest research organisation ever assembled for one specific object':[52] 1,200 technical men and 700 service assistants researching into more than 4,000 potentially poisonous substances. It was a scientific project on a scale unrivalled until the Manhattan Project twenty-five years later. The entire arsenal had cost around $40 million, and within its walls were 218 manufacturing buildings, seventy-nine other permanent structures, twenty-eight miles of railway, fifteen miles of roadway and eleven miles of high tension electrical transmission lines. Its factories were capable of producing 200,000 chemical bombs and shells *per day*.

Institutions on this scale are not easily disbanded. The Americans in particular, having suffered such a high proportion of gas casualties, were not keen to turn their backs on the potentialities of chemical warfare. Victor Lefebure recorded landing in America early in 1920 to 'find New York plastered with recruiting posters setting forth the various reasons why Americans should join their Chemical Warfare Service'.[53] The strength and skill of the US pro-chemical warfare lobby in resisting disarmament, first shown at the time of the Armistice, has continued to overcome the periodic hostility of successive Presidents, senators, Chiefs of Staff and peace groups ever since; its influence is undiminished to this day.

In Britain, the Government appointed the Holland Committee to report on chemical warfare and suggest what the country's future policy should be. Its members – who included Foulkes, now promoted to General – met in May 1919 and agreed 'with no shadow of doubt' that 'gas is a legitimate weapon in war . . . and that it will be used in the future may be taken as a foregone conclusion'.[54] This decision was not accompanied by any American razzmatazz or propaganda campaign. On the contrary, British gas warfare became subject to a policy of strict official secrecy. Carefully 'weeded' files about chemical warfare in the First World War were not released to historians until 1972. An eighteen-year-old wounded in the first phosgene attack would have had to wait until he was seventy-five before he could read about it. War memoirs were also stringently vetted, and even titles were censored. Foulkes had wanted to call his account of the work of the Special Brigade either *Frightfulness* or *Retaliation*. Both were considered too provocative by the War Office and the book – which was eventually published in 1936 – was called simply *Gas!*

At the same time there appears to have been a deliberate campaign to underestimate the number of men killed and wounded by gas, possibly by tens of thousands. Officially, 180,983 British soldiers were gassed, of whom just 6,062 were killed. However the list of categories these figures *do not* include is staggering. They do not include the number of men gassed in 1915 (estimated at many thousands) for which no records exist; nor any gas victims – alive or dead – captured by the enemy; nor any who may be among the quarter of a million British soldiers described as 'missing' in the First World War; nor any of the men who died outright on the field of battle and were later recorded as having been simply 'killed in action'; nor any of the men with relatively minor injuries retained by the Field Ambulances until fit to rejoin their units; nor any gas casualties who later died after being evacuated to the UK; nor any casualties dying of illnesses brought on by their exposure to gas, etc, etc . . . One gets the impression that becoming an official gas casualty required roughly the same amount of verification as winning a medal.

Apologists for gas warfare used the statistics to argue that gas was 'humane', that it wounded rather than killed. Haldane attacked the 'group of sentimentalists who appear to me definitely to be the Scribes and Pharisees of our age'[55] who made a distinction between gas and conventional weapons. It was, he argued, certainly no worse, and possible more civilized, to kill or wound a man with chemicals rather than with shrapnel or bullets.

And what of the victims of these 'civilized' weapons? In Britain in 1920, 19,000 men were drawing disability pensions as a result of war gassing.[56] A report drawn up by the Physiology Department of Porton in June 1927 examined a group of eighteen pensioners:

In the summer time these patients are not so bad, but with early winter, their symptoms are aggravated. These patients seldom improve, but gradually get worse . . . it is only a matter of time till a cardiac condition develops in addition . . . It should be mentioned, also, that such patients have a very poor prognosis should pneumonia or other severe pulmonary conditions supervene . . . Some of these have chests like men of over sixty, chests definitely and *permanently* damaged. The evidence suggesting that Mustard is the cause appears to be conclusive. These pensioners, young and fit before the war, have a definite history of having spent some weeks or months in hospital with conjunctivitis, laryngitis, bronchitis and in some cases skin burns in addition . . .[57]

In 1929, Porton investigated a further seventy-two cases of mustard gassing and found evidence of fibrosis, TB, persistent laryngitis, TB of the spine, anaemia, aphonia, conjunctivitis and pulmonary fibrosis.[58]

These, of course, were secret reports, only recently declassified. In public, Porton maintained that the popular press 'scare-mongered' about the long-term effects of gas poisoning. Porton physiologists sat in on Medical Boards which judged the records and examined the bodies of men laying claim to war pensions. The criteria for granting them, not surprisingly, were made exceptionally harsh. A definite causal link had to be established between disability and the actual gassing – an increased susceptibility to TB or bronchitis (though admitted) was not in itself sufficient grounds upon which to claim a pension.

Many thousands of men continued to suffer from the effects of gassing in the First World War for the rest of their lives. One survivor of a phosgene attack, Fred Cayley,[59] admitted in 1980 that he had been seeing a doctor every week since 1917.* Britain is still awarding pensions to gas victims to this day. How many have never claimed but suffered and died in ignorance is not known. Modern investigations have revealed that munitions workers who are employed in the

---

* Mr Cayley died in July 1981 of chronic bronchitis. At a subsequent inquest he was recorded as having been 'killed by the King's enemies'. 'Let this be a warning,' added the Coroner, 'to anyone who plans using gas or bacterial warfare. This man suffered for more than sixty years as the result of First World War gassing.'

manufacture of mustard gas are *ten times* more susceptible to cancer than the average;[60] there are no figures for men actually gassed on the field of battle. In 1970 the World Health Organization reported that 'an examination of the mortality data on 1,267 British war pensioners who suffered from mustard gas poisoning in the 1914–18 war, and who were still alive on 1 January 1930, showed that almost all (over 80 per cent) had chronic bronchitis at that date. In subsequent years an excess of deaths attributed to cancer of the lung and pleura was observed amongst them (twenty-nine deaths found compared with fourteen expected).'[61]

Such grisly after-effects were neither foreseen nor understood in the 1920s. Porton merely admitted that 'ten years after gassing there are patients who exhibit definite residua both anatomically and clinically that are definitely due to either one or a combination of gases.'[64] The wounded and disabled were largely forgotten except in so far – as one expert put it – they provided valuable data 'which it would be impossible to obtain elsewhere'. Gradually the image of the line of blinded mustard gas victims, each with his hand on the shoulder of the man in front, shuffled away into the folk memory of the First World War. Poison gas, the once-forbidden weapon, now took its place in the world's arsenals. It has remained there ever since.

TWO

The Serpent and the Flower

... To beguile the time,
Look like the time; bear welcome in your eye,
Your hand, your tongue: look like th'innocent flower,
But be the serpent under't.

Macbeth. Act I, Scene V

The world's oldest chemical warfare installation occupies 7,000 gently rolling acres of countryside on the southern edge of Salisbury Plain, known as Porton Down. Over 700 men and women work there in labs and offices scattered through 200 buildings. There are police and fire stations, a hospital, a library, a branch of Lloyds Bank, a detailed archive with thousands of reports and photographs; there is even a cinema to screen the miles of film taken during experiments. They are the residue of more than six decades of research, generally at the forefront of contemporary scientific knowledge. Though there have been many political storms, and several attempts to close it down, Porton has survived them all – proof of the military's enduring fascination with poison gases, even in a country which now officially has no chemical weapons.

It was in January 1916 that the War Office compulsorily purchased an initial 3,000 acres of downland between the tiny villages of Porton and Idmiston, and began to clear a site for what was then known as the War Department Experimental Ground. Within two months the first scientists had arrived. At night they slept in the local inn; during the day they worked in a few ramshackle wooden huts housing a gas chamber, a laboratory and some cylinders. They were pioneers, bringing a scientific knowledge then in its infancy into a new era – and in the rush of events in the middle of the Great War seem to have been free of any ethical worries about the nature of their work. The head of the Physiology Department, Joseph Barcroft, was actually a Quaker – probably the only member of the Society of Friends ever to have had a prototype bomb named after him.[1]

In the early days there was little understanding of the long-term

37

hazards of gas, or even of how it affected the body. A complete set of experimental procedures had to be worked out from scratch – a dangerous business, and one which produced its heroes. Barcroft himself wanted to settle a dispute between the British and French about the effectiveness of hydrogen cyanide (HCN). The French had tested HCN gas on dogs, all of which died, and believed as a result that it would make an effective chemical weapon. The British conducted their tests on goats, which survived. One night Barcroft waited until everyone else had gone to bed, found a corporal to act as a witness, and without putting on a mask stepped into a gas chamber with a 1 in 2,000 concentration of hydrogen cyanide. He took a dog in with him. He recalled:

In order that the experiment might be as fair as possible and that my respiration should be relatively as active as that of the dog, I remained standing, and took a few steps from time to time while I was in the chamber. In about thirty seconds the dog began to get unsteady, and in fifty-five seconds it dropped on the floor and commenced the characteristic distressing respiration which heralds death from cyanide poisoning. One minute thirty-five seconds after the commencement the animal's body was carried out, respiration having ceased and the dog being apparently dead. I then left the chamber. As regards the result upon myself, the only real effect was a momentary giddiness when I turned my head quickly. This lasted about a year, and then vanished. For some time it was difficult to concentrate on anything for any length of time.[2]

The affair of Barcroft's Dog became one of the most famous incidents in the early history of chemical warfare. The Prime Minister, Lloyd George, wrote to Barcroft that he felt 'the most intense admiration for the gallantry and devotion which you have shown ... I desire to express personally, and as Head of His Majesty's Government, my high appreciation of your brave action, which obtained information of quite exceptional value.'[3] 'Good God,' said King George V when he heard of it, 'what a wonderful plucky thing to do.'[4]

Barcroft's phlegmatic attitude typified the early days of chemical warfare research. There were hair-raising stories. On one occasion, one of his female assistants travelled by train from his laboratory in Cambridge carrying a canister of poison gas. The canister began to leak in the compartment. She attached it to a piece of string, hung it out of the window and completed her journey to Porton.

Working methods were rough and often highly dangerous. A

circular system of trenches was dug, from the centre of which cylinders of gas were discharged. Human guinea pigs ('observers' in Porton's terminology) would station themselves in trenches and – for as long as they were capable of standing it – take detailed notes of the symptoms they felt. Indoors, the effects of chemicals were studied in the gas chambers. Ten minutes was found to be about the maximum most men could take exposed to a non-lethal gas. Observers were expected to stand in clouds of killer gases for hours wearing prototype masks to test their reliability. Later, when mustard gas made its first appearance, they rolled up their sleeves and allowed their arms to be contaminated, in order to study the progression of the terrible blisters that developed. The work, wrote Foulkes (who was himself offered the job of Commandant of Porton after the war, but turned it down) was 'unpleasant' and 'dangerous':

... but volunteers were always to be found who exposed themselves fearlessly in the chamber tests. In the case of experiments with mustard gas, experience showed that a man's skin became more sensitive after one exposure and the only satisfactory course was to use 'virgin skin'. There was, of course, no scarcity of this commodity in the country, even late in the war, but provision had to be made for a constant supply of newcomers among the experimental staff.[5]

According to Porton's own, recently declassified 'in-house' history, the demand for human beings needed in tests often far exceeded supply, 'and cooks, orderlies and clerks were frequently pressed into service for experiments'.[6] Foulkes himself made a point of personally being exposed to every war gas considered for adoption by the British.

Not all the early scientists survived. Colonel Watson, head of the Allies' Central Laboratory in France, died as a result of experiments he had conducted on himself. So too, in the final days of the war, did Colonel Harrison, Deputy Controller of the British Chemical Warfare Committee. Many more must have appreciably shortened their lives by their work. 'Risks were taken,' runs Porton's internal history, 'and sufferings were endured in a manner which was only possible by men of high morale under the urge of war.'

In their investigation into the effects of gas, the scientists at Porton had other sources of information apart from the experiments they conducted on one another. In 1917 a farm and breeding colony was added to the Establishment to provide the vast numbers of animals used

A Higher Form of Killing

in experiments. Thousands of reports of experiments made in these early years have now been released to historians.[7] They give some idea of the scale and substance of the grim research which has made Porton a top target for anti-vivisectionists. Cats, dogs, monkeys, baboons, goats, sheep, guinea pigs, rabbits, rats and mice were variously tethered and caged outdoors in the trench system and indoors in the gas chambers for exposure to gas clouds. Chemicals were squirted into their faces and injected into them, and bullets, sprays and bombs fired into, over and at them. With the discovery of mustard gas, bellies and backs were shaved and the chemical rubbed in; some animals were opened up and their organs smeared with mustard, the wound then stitched back together and the symptoms which developed noted. The Establishment became such a prominent centre of vivisection that it later developed its own strain of 'Porton mice', now a standard laboratory animal in use throughout the world.

These animal experiments were as unpopular among most non-scientists then as they are today. Haldane records that the physiologists at Porton 'had considerable difficulty in working with a good many soldiers because the latter objected so strongly to experiments on animals, and did not conceal their contempt for the people who performed them'.[8] And Sir Austin Anderson – at that time a junior member of Porton's staff – recalled 'a highly intelligent and friendly little monkey that the men loved so much that they gave him a little khaki coat with corporal's stripes, christened him the A P M, and gave him the free run of the animals' quarters. He never went into the gas chamber and I think survived the war.'[9]

The hours at Porton during the First World War were long, the number of experiments almost more than the system could cope with. 'It was not uncommon for the Officer-in-Charge to spend four to six hours each evening, seven days a week, in writing up and assessing accumulated results.'[10] And always, a few hundred miles away in France, was the pressure of battle, the scientists' main source of raw data. 'We had,' wrote Foulkes, 'in the theatre of war itself a vast experimental ground . . . Human beings provided the material for these experiments on both sides of No Man's Land.'[11]

The bodies and organs of gassed soldiers were regularly shipped back to Porton for microscopic examination by the physiologists of the Royal Army Medical Corps – 'the body snatchers' as they were known at Porton. For the scientists' records, oil paintings were made of organs taken from post mortems. In some cases the bodies themselves were preserved: a scientist's report of October 1923, five years after the end of the war, speaks of 'a score of human cases gassed by H S in France, which I have recently had an opportunity of studying.'[12]

As the war progressed and work intensified, Porton underwent rapid expansion. Its testing ranges were doubled in size. The early collection of huts grew into a small village, housing five separate sections. Eight rows of barracks accommodated more than a thousand troops, ballistics experts, army doctors and scientists. These were backed up by a civilian workforce of five hundred. To the system of trenches and dug-outs was added a new firing range, a mile and a half long, manned by wounded artillery men; they claimed that with their pay topped up by Porton's 'danger money', they earned more carrying out test shoots on Salisbury Plain than they did under fire from the Germans on the Western Front.

The outbreak of peace in Europe in 1918 was only a minor hiccup in Porton's routine. On Armistice night the animal keepers got drunk and released the monkeys who spread considerable alarm and confusion in the Salisbury area; apart from that it was business as usual. Professor A. E. Boycott, an ardent pacifist who had decided to work at Porton only as long as the war lasted, was one of the very few to leave: 'the day after the Armistice he flatly refused to have anything more to do with gas warfare'.[13]

At the end of the war, Porton was not closed down. Instead, in 1919, the Government set up the Holland Committee. They unanimously recommended that Porton continue in action, and went on to lay down many of the principles upon which the Establishment is run today. In view of the 'large degree of risk' entailed in the work, 'a very liberal allowance of leave' – three months a year – was granted to the staff. Everything possible was done to attract 'the best brains in the country' to Porton. As long as 'secrets of national importance' were not disclosed, the scientists employed were given the right to publish their work and to attend the meetings 'held by the Learned Societies'. Salaries were generous, particularly for the senior positions, and the Committee 'expressed the feeling that nothing under £2,000 a year could be relied upon to induce a man of the first rank to accept the post of Director of Research at Porton' – making it one of the most highly paid scientific jobs in the country. The Committee also concluded:

. . . that it is impossible to divorce the study of defence against gas from the study of the use of gas as an offensive weapon, as the efficiency of the defence depends entirely on an accurate knowledge as to what progress is being or is likely to be made in the offensive use of this weapon.[14]

This was a crucial admission. No matter how loudly the British, or any other nation, renounced gas warfare in public, in secret they felt bound to give their scientists a free hand to go on devising the deadliest weapons they could, on the grounds that they had first to be invented, before counter-measures could be prepared.

Porton Down made use of this logic between 1919 and 1939 to carry out a mass of offensive research, developing gas grenades and hand contamination bombs; a toxic air smoke bomb charged with a new arsenic codenamed 'DM' was tested; anti-tank weapons were produced; and Porton developed an aircraft spray tank capable of dispersing mustard gas from a height of 15,000 feet. At the same time the weapons of the First World War – the Livens Projector, the mortar, the chemical shell and even the cylinder – were all modified and improved.

There was extensive human testing, often involving scores of men at a time. Some of the tests were so drastic, one wonders what could possibly have motivated men to go through with them. In 1922, for example, twenty 'observers' were placed in a gas chamber for ten minutes' exposure ('the limit of tolerability') to the arsenic gas 'DA' and suffered

. . . a disagreeable sense of pressure over the head, dull aching in the roots of the teeth and sense of pressure in the ears; salivation is also marked. Gnawing pain at the back of the face, numbness and cold of the fingers and feet. Dryness of the throat, pain and cough. Retching and nausea are observed. On removal from the chamber all symptoms increase in intensity at once. The men feel definitely ill: in the higher concentrations they lie down, sigh and roll about: in the lower concentrations there is a tendency to keep moving, in both an attempt to find a place of relief . . .[15]

Mustard gas, 'the King of Gases', employed the most human volunteers. Just one experiment in 1924 involved forty men. In April 1928 large numbers of human observers were contaminated in five separate aerial spray tests. In the same year bricks were coated with mustard; after a fortnight men handled them and the vapour given off was found to be still powerful enough to cause burns 'of a severe character'. In October 1929 'two subjects received copious applications of crude Mustard which practically covered the inner aspect of the forearm. After wiping the liquid mustard off roughly with a small tuft of grass the ointment (seven weeks old) was lightly rubbed with the fingers over the area . . .'[16]

This is just a random selection of the sort of work which was done in Britain. Similar research was being carried out throughout the world. Italy established a Servizio Chemico Militare in 1923 with an extensive proving ground in the north of the country. The main French chemical warfare installation was the Atelier de Pyrotechnie du Bouchet near Paris. The Japanese Navy began work on chemical weapons in 1923, and the Army followed suit in 1925. In Germany, despite the fact that Haber's Kaiser Wilhelm Institute had been closed down in 1919, limited defensive work continued, later to form the basis of Germany's offensive effort. And in 1924 the Military-Chemical Administration of the Red Army was established and Russian chemical troops were stationed at each provincial army headquarters.

Chemical weapons were not merely researched and developed – they were used. At the beginning of 1919 the British employed the 'M' device (which produced clouds of arsenic smoke) at Archangel when they intervened in the Russian Civil War, dropping the canisters from aeroplanes into the dense forests. The anti-Bolshevik White Army was equipped with British gas shells, and the Red Army are also alleged to have used chemicals.

Later in 1919, Foulkes was dispatched to India, and in August urged the War Office to use chemicals against the Afghans and rebellious tribesmen on the North-West Frontier: 'Ignorance, lack of instruction and discipline and the absence of protection on the part of Afghans and tribesmen will undoubtedly enhance the casualty producing value of mustard gas in frontier fighting.'[17] Many of the Cabinet were dubious, including the Secretary of State for India. Foulkes had little time for their scruples:

On the question of *morality* . . . gas has been openly accepted as a recognised weapon for the future, and there is no longer any question of stealing an unfair advantage by taking an unsuspecting enemy unawares.

Apart from this, it has been pointed out that tribesmen are not bound by the Hague Convention and they do not conform to its most elementary rules . . .[18]

Foulkes had his way. Stocks of phosgene and mustard gas were sent out, while in the scorching heat of the Khyber Pass in midsummer, British troops trained in anti-gas suits. Large supplies of smoke shells were stored at Peshawar near the Afghan frontier for use in flushing-out rebellious tribesmen from their mountain hideouts. Major Salt, Chemical Adviser to the British Army in India, wrote that after 'the usual talk about "clean hands" and "low-down tricks against the poor ignorant tribesman" . . . the Government have decided they will adopt a policy of using gas on the frontier.'[19] The RAF is alleged to have used gas bombs against the Afghans. It would have been a murky episode in Britain's imperial history, and records were either not kept or were destroyed: there are today no operational accounts in the British archives.

Used against poorly-armed and trained insurgents, the imperial powers rapidly learnt that gas was a devastating weapon. Persistent agents like mustard could make favourite ambush positions untenable for weeks. Tear gas and smoke weapons, especially if used from the air, forced the enemy into the open where he could be more easily picked off. By 1925 the French and Spanish were employing poison gas in Morocco, and it had become clear that chemical warfare had found a new role, as a tool by which major powers could 'police' rebellious territories.

Yet despite its widespread development and use in the years following the First World War, gas warfare was still technically illegal. The Allied Powers described it as a 'prohibited' form of warfare at Versailles in 1919 and banned the importation and manufacture of poison gas in Germany for all time. Three years later, the Washington Treaty went even further: the 'civilised Powers' decreed that the banning of chemical warfare should 'be universally accepted as part of international law binding alike to the conscience and practice of nations'.

Finally, in May 1925, under the auspices of the League of Nations, a conference on the international arms trade was convened in Geneva. Led by the United States, the delegates agreed to try and tackle the problem of poison gas, 'with,' as the Americans put it, 'the hope of reducing the barbarity of modern warfare.' After a month of wrangling in legal and military committees – during which the Polish delegation far-sightedly suggested that they also ban the use of germ weapons, then little more than a theory – the delegates came together on 17 June to sign what remains to this day the strongest legal constraint on chemical and biological warfare:

The undersigned Plenipotentiaries, in the name of their respective Governments:

Whereas the use in war of asphyxiating, poisonous or other gases, and of all analogous liquids, materials or devices, has been justly condemned by the general opinion of the civilized world; and

Whereas the prohibition of such use has been declared in Treaties to which the majority of Powers of the world are Parties; and

To the end that this prohibition shall be universally accepted as a part of International Law, binding alike the conscience and practice of nations;

Declare:

That the High Contracting Parties, so far as they are not already Parties to Treaties prohibiting such use, accept this prohibition, agree to extend this prohibition to the use of bacteriological methods of warfare and agree to be bound as between themselves according to the terms of this declaration . . .[20]

Thirty-eight powers signed the Geneva Protocol, among them the United States, the British Empire, France, Germany, Italy, Japan and Canada; the fledgling USSR did not attend.

'The signing of the Geneva Protocol of 1925,' as one expert has put it, 'was the high-water mark of the hostility of public opinion towards chemical warfare.'[21] Unfortunately, the anti-gas lobby had underestimated the strength of the interests ranged against them. Merely signing the Protocol was not enough to make it binding – individual governments had to ratify it. In many cases this meant a time lag of at least a year, and it was in this period that the supporters of chemical weapons struck back.

The United States Chemical Warfare Service launched a highly effective lobby. They enlisted the support of veterans' associations and of the American Chemical Society (whose Executive declared that 'the prohibition of chemical warfare meant the abandonment of humane methods for the old horrors of battle'). As has often happened since, the fight for chemical weapons was represented as a fight for general military preparedness. Senators joined the CWS campaign, among them the Chairman of the Committee on Military Affairs who opened his attack on ratification in the Senate debate with a reference to the 1922 Washington Treaty: 'I think it is fair to say that in 1922 there was much of hysteria and much of misinformation concerning chemical warfare.' Other Senators rose to speak approvingly of resolutions which they had received attacking the Geneva Protocol – from the Association of Military Surgeons, the American Legion, the Veterans of Foreign Wars of the United States, the Reserve Officers Association of the United States and the Military Order of the World War. Under such heavy fire, the State Department saw no alternative but to withdraw the Protocol, and reintroduce it at a more favourable moment. It was not to be until 1970, forty-five years after the Geneva conference, that the Protocol was again submitted to the Senate for ratification; it took another five years for this to be achieved.

Japan followed America's example and refused to ratify (they finally did so in May 1970). In Europe, the various countries eyed one another cautiously. France ratified first, in 1926. Two years later, in 1928, Italy followed suit and a fortnight after her, the Soviet Union declared that she, too, considered herself bound by the Protocol. Only after Germany ratified in 1929 did Britain feel able at last to accept the Protocol: on 9 April 1930, five years after the Conference, Britain at last fell into line.

Many of the states which ratified the Protocol – including France, Great Britain and the USSR – did so only after adding two significant reservations: (1) that the agreement would not be considered binding unless the country they were fighting had also ratified the Protocol; (2) that if any other country attacked them using chemical or biological weapons, they reserved the right to reply in kind.

'Justly condemned by the general opinion of the civilised world' chemical weapons might be; abandoned they certainly were not. The Geneva Protocol was, effectively, a ban only on the *first use* of poison gas or germs. There was certainly no ban on researching and stockpiling chemical weapons. While the British Government stressed that Porton Down was only concerned with defensive work, full scale research into new weapons actually accelerated. *A Brief History of the Chemical Defence Experimental Establishment Porton*, the slim, forty-four page house history of Porton, is quite frank about the cynical way in which the public were deceived:

On the offensive side of chemical warfare, the Government's pronouncement following ratification of the Geneva Protocol meant that any actual
development of weapons had to be done 'under the rose'. As a gesture, the
Offensive Munitions Department at Porton changed its name back to
'Technical Chemical Department' and in 1930 the term 'Chemical Warfare'
was expunged from official language and titles and 'Chemical Defence' was
substituted. Thereafter all offensive work was done under the heading
'Study of chemical weapons against which defence is required'.

This 'defensive' work included 'improvements to many First World
War weapons, including gas shells, mortar bombs, the Livens
Projector and toxic smoke generators' and the development of
'apparatus for mustard gas spray from aircraft, bombs of many
types, airburst mustard gas shell, gas grenades and weapons for
attacking tanks'. The various inventions were tested in north Wales,
Scotland, and in installations scattered throughout the Empire,
notably northern India, Australia and the Middle East.

The commitment by most of the world's governments never to
initiate the use of poison gas did not stop research: it simply made the
whole subject that much more sensitive, and thus more secret. In
1928, the Germans began to collaborate with the Russians in a series
of top secret tests called 'Project Tomka' at a site in the Soviet Union
about twenty kilometres west of Volsk. For the next five years,
around thirty German experts lived and worked alongside 'a rather
larger number of Soviet staff', mainly engaged in testing mustard gas.
The security measures surrounding Project Tomka 'were such that
any of its participants who spoke about it to outsiders risked capital
punishment'.[22]

In Japan, experimental production of mustard gas was begun in
1928 at the Tandanoumi Arsenal. Six years later the Japanese were
manufacturing a ton of Lewisite a week; by 1937 output had risen to
two tons per day. Extensive testing – including trials in tropical
conditions on Formosa in 1930 – resulted in the development of a
fearsome array of gas weapons: rockets able to deliver ten litres of
agent up to two miles; devices for emitting a 'gas fog'; flame throwers
modified to hurl jets of hydrogen cyanide; mustard spray bombs
which released streams of gas while gently floating to earth attached
to parachutes; remotely-controlled contamination trailers capable
of laying mustard in strips seven metres wide; and the 'Masuka Dan',

a hand-carried anti-tank weapon loaded with a kilogram of hydrogen cyanide. Defensive preparations were equally thorough, and ran right down to masks for horses and camels (two feet long and eight inches in diameter) and masks, leggings and shoes for dogs.[23]

The Japanese set about the study of chemical warfare with a dedication that at times bordered on fanaticism. The Army Chemical Warfare School was established in 1933 at Narashino, twenty-one miles east of Tokyo. It had a forty acre site and impressive facilities. The School Commandant, Major General Yamazaki, promised 'just and severe punishment' for those who failed to adhere to its code:

1. The training must give the students skill in combat, tactics and conducting warfare, so as to bring the war to a final victorious conclusion.
2. The school must build up in the students an unfailing spiritual power and firm conviction in final victory.
3. Students will practice thoroughgoing obedience and complete execution of their duties.[24]

The students were all carefully selected officers. Most took an eleven month course. In twelve years the school turned out 3,350 chemical warfare experts.

There is now little doubt that from 1937 onwards the Japanese made extensive use of poison gas in their war against the Chinese. In October 1937 China made a formal protest to the League of Nations. In August 1938 they accused the Japanese of using mustard gas, and produced a variety of witnesses, including a British surgeon who had treated nineteen gas casualties wounded while fighting on the Yangtze front. Chinese peasants are said to have been driven from caves and tunnels by gas and then massacred by waiting Japanese troops.

Like the British and French before them, the Japanese discovered that gas was a superb weapon when used against poorly trained and largely ignorant opponents. Operations in China became text book examples of the use of chemical weapons – so much so that the Japanese actually turned the accounts of their gas attacks into a series of pamphlets entitled *Lessons From the China Incident*, and distributed them among the students at the Narashino school. One Soviet authority estimated that a third of all Japanese munitions sent to China were chemical, and that 'in several battles up to 10 per cent of the total losses suffered by the Chinese armies were due to chemical weapons'.[25]

The Italians made use of chemicals in their invasion of Abyssinia in much the same way. In 1935 and 1936, 700 tons of gas were shipped out, most of it for use by the Italian air force. First came torpedo-shaped mustard bombs. Then, in early 1936, the Italians tried out the new technique of aerial spraying. In a speech to the League of Nations, Abyssinian Emperor Haile Selassie described how 'groups of nine, fifteen and eighteen aircraft followed one another so that the liquid issuing from them formed a continuous fog ... soldiers, women, children, cattle, rivers, lakes and pastures were drenched continually with this deadly rain.'[26] According to the British, the Italians were using 500 lb 'spray type' bombs filled with mustard gas. They functioned by means of a time fuse. When the bomb was 'about 200 feet above the ground' it burst open – 'the liquid contents were scattered in the form of spray over a considerable area'.[27]

Reports filtering out of Abyssinia gave some idea of the appalling suffering which mustard gas was capable of inflicting on defence-less natives. The liquid lingered on the ground and on foliage, contaminating not only troops but peasants passing through the bush. Walter Holmes of the London *Times* wrote of men 'injured in the legs and lower parts of the body. In several cases, large areas of skin had been removed from the legs and thighs; some of these men had also suffered extremely painful burning of the genital organs.' Italian planes, Holmes reported, flew low over the countryside spraying mustard in a 'fine rain of corrosive liquid'. There was no protection and no escape, and large numbers of natives 'received ghastly injuries to the head, face and upper parts of the body'.[28] Blinded victims could not make their way into the hills where the Red Cross had first aid posts; untreated skin wounds were infected with gangrene. Dr John Kelly, Head of the British Red Cross in Abyssinia treated 150 cases of 'severe burns' from mustard gas in three days at the end of February 1936: 'many of the patients were women, children and infants'. In the course of two weeks in March he treated a further 200–300 victims, many too blind to make their way to his ambulance. 'A large number of the burns treated were of a terrible nature.'[29] The reports of Holmes and Kelly – including photographs of the victims – joined the bulging file on Italian use of gas held by the League of Nations.

This was not war, but slaughter. Abyssinia was little more than a proving ground for the murderous modern gas weapons which had been developed (in Porton's words) 'under the rose' of the Geneva Protocol since the end of the First World War. Just as the German bombing of Guernica a year later warned how the bomber could be used against civilians, so Abyssinia showed how effective gas warfare had become. Around 15,000 Abyssinian soldiers were killed or wounded by chemical weapons – almost a third of the total casualties for the entire war.

In the disintegrating peace of 1936, the Italian use of gas was described by the British Prime Minister, Stanley Baldwin, as a 'peril to the world' and he voiced the question which was now in the minds of most of the world's governments: 'If a great European nation, in spite of having given its signature to the Geneva Protocol against the use of such gases, employs them in Africa, what guarantee have we that they may not be used in Europe?'[30]

The answer, obviously, was none. After Abyssinia British Intelligence was in no doubt about Italian intentions. 'It may be concluded,' wrote MI 3 in August 1936, 'that in a future war she would employ the gas weapon unless special circumstances render such a course inadvisable.'[31] Three months later, in November, the British Government announced that everyone in the United Kingdom was to be issued with a gas mask. In September 1938, at the time of the Munich crisis, over thirty million were issued to the public. There were 'cot respirators' for babies, and specially designed 'invalid hoods' for the sick and elderly. Official Government films warning of the dangers of gas were shown in cinemas, while signs in buses and on underground trains exhorted the population to carry their masks at all times. In homes throughout Europe the same scenes were repeated as families tried on gas masks. The French even developed protective measures for pigeons.

While their civilians trained in defence, the world's major powers embarked upon large-scale chemical rearmament. In 1936 the French built a factory to produce phosgene at Clamency, at a cost of eighteen million francs.[32] A year later, First World War mustard gas and phosgene plants at Edgewood Arsenal in the United States were put back into action. New factories were opened by the Soviet Union at Brandyuzhsky, Kuibyshev and Karaganda. The British – with the 'whole-hearted co-operation' of Imperial Chemical Industries (ICI) – began building a new mustard gas factory at Sutton Oak near St Helens in Lancashire in 1936; two more factories were planned. On 2 November 1938, the Cabinet ordered the creation of an industrial productive capacity of 300 tons of mustard gas per week and a reserve of 2,000 tons.

British Intelligence conjured up a frightening picture of a Europe swarming with scientists and chemists at work on war gases. German research on chemical warfare was said to have 'been pursued unremittingly' since the First World War. Laboratories were at work in Berlin and in the Ruhr, and three experimental centres were said to exist – one near Munster and two others at Wunsdorf and List. Six aircraft at a time, flying 'simultaneously or in relays' were believed to take part in low-altitude spray trials. Over-all, capacity was estimated to be greater than that attained during 1918. The Italians were reported to be capable of producing twenty-five tons of mustard and five tons of Lewisite a day, as well as possessing an 'unstated capacity for phosgene, chloropicrin and DM'. In the USSR training of chemical troops was said to be pushed to 'almost fanatical limits': 'Of all countries, Soviet Russia appears to devote the greatest effort to developing the chemical arm.' (The Germans shared British misgivings, and estimated the number of Soviet scientists directly involved in chemical warfare at over 6,000.) The report concluded: 'Massive bombardment may be anticipated with concentrations of all available supplementary chemical weapons and close co-operation of aircraft. In retiral, use will be made of large-scale contamination of areas by chemical lorries and low flying aircraft, together with heavy contamination by mines, etc, of bridges and traffic centres. Aerial attack with HE [high explosive] and incendiary bombs may be followed by gas.'[33]

Faced with this alarming assessment, and with war only a few months away, in May 1939 the British and French began to collaborate on a joint chemical warfare policy. According to a 'Most Secret' report[34] by the head of the British delegation, the attitude of the two governments was broadly similar. 'The French think that the chemical industries in Germany and Italy are so highly developed that the use of gas by these countries may be regarded as certain. Their delegation had not considered the possiblity that either Germany or Italy might refrain from using gas in the early stages to avoid retaliation in kind.'

Against this certainty, the French had ready a considerable arsenal, including four and a half million *grenades oeuf* – grenades resembling large eggs filled with mustard gas to be dropped in clutches of fifty at a time; they had no fuses, being designed simply to break on impact. The French were shown to have placed far greater reliance than the British on phosgene, using it as a filling 'for projectors, for artillery shell and for large aircraft bombs'. One ingenious device was 'a 200 kg bomb filled with phosgene. This contains a bursting charge designed to blow out any earth which may have fallen in behind the bomb after penetration.'[35]

On their side, the British offered the French an unrivalled expertise in a method of chemical warfare which Porton had made its own: high altitude spraying of mustard gas. British bombers were now able to accurately release spray from a height of 15,000 feet, out of danger from anti-aircraft guns. With no warning, enemy troops could be drenched in a drizzle of mustard gas which the British calculated would contaminate '100 per cent of the personnel in the area affected who are not under cover'.[36] The secret was a variant of conventional mustard (HS): three times as powerful, it was code-named 'HT', and had a very low freezing point. The French were greatly excited by the discovery: it was regarded as of 'the first importance'. The British gave the French one of their 250 lb spray tanks and a series of joint trials was arranged – first with a harmless substitute for mustard gas at Bourget in France, and then with the real thing at the vast French proving ground in the Sahara.

French scientists were invited to Porton, and their British counterparts permitted to visit France's gas factories 'to witness manufacture'. After a 'complete and frank pooling of information' the two sides parted on 12 May. A variety of sub-committees were established; offensive weapons were dealt with on Sub-Committee E. By the time its members met again in September, the war with Germany had already begun. Few doubted that general chemical warfare would take place and that – as a Secret Intelligence Summary put it – 'if the Germans deem it expedient to introduce gas warfare it will be pursued with their characteristic vigour, ingenuity and ruthlessness'.[37]

Even fewer are likely to have questioned another of the Summary's conclusions: *'it is not thought that any important new war gas has been discovered'*. In fact the Germans had secretly developed a new series of gases dozens of times more deadly than anything the Allies possessed. Had Hitler known of his enemies' ignorance, the Second World War might well have taken a different course.

THREE
Hitler's Secret Weapon

Towards the end of 1936, Dr Gerhard Schrader, a German scientist researching into possible new insecticides, made a remarkable discovery. He had been methodically working his way through an enormous range of organic phosphorus compounds when he suddenly stumbled upon a series of poisons of extraordinary power. On 23 December he managed to prepare some of the chemical for the first time, and tested it by spraying a concentration of just one part in 200,000 on some leaf lice. All of the insects were killed. A few weeks later, in January 1937, Schrader began the first manufacturing trials. Immediately he discovered that what he had at first considered a promising insecticide had side-effects upon man which were 'extremely unpleasant'.

'The first symptom noticed,' he later recalled, 'was an inexplicable action causing the power of sight to be much weakened in artificial light. In the darkness of early January it was hardly possible to read by electric light, or after working hours to reach my home by car.'[1] The slightest drop of the substance spilt on the laboratory bench caused the pupils of his eyes to contract to pin-points, and he suffered acute difficulty in breathing. After a few days of this, Schrader and his assistant were forced to stop work for three weeks in order to recover. They were lucky to escape with their lives. Inadvertently they had discovered, and become the first victims of, the world's most powerful chemical weapon, the original 'nerve gas': tabun.

It was obvious that there could be no question of using Schrader's discovery as an insecticide: in tests that spring almost all the animals exposed to even tiny quantities of it were dead within twenty minutes. Instead, under a Nazi decree of 1935 requiring German industry to keep secret any invention with military potential, Schrader was summoned to Berlin to demonstrate tabun to the Wehrmacht.

Its value as a war gas was quickly recognized. Dogs or monkeys poisoned by tabun seemed to lose all muscular control – their pupils shrank to dots, they frothed at the mouth and vomited, they had diarrhoea, their limbs began to twitch and jerk; finally, within ten or fifteen minutes, they went into convulsions and died. In addition to its potency, tabun had other advantages. It was colourless and practically odourless, and it could poison the body not merely by inhalation, but also by penetrating through the skin. The so-called nerve gases were as great an advance over the chemical weapons of the First World War as the machine gun was over the musket.

It was not until the early 1940s that the Nazi scientists began to understand exactly why tabun was such a lethal agent. Unlike the gases of the First World War, which have a general effect, the nerve gases inhibit the action of a specific chemical in the body called cholinesterase. Cholinesterase's function is to control the muscles by breaking down the chemical which causes muscular contraction, acetylcholine. If this is not done, the level of acetycholine in the body builds up to a disastrous level, sending all the muscles of the body into contraction. The body thus poisons itself, as it loses control of all its functions. The muscles of the arms and legs along with those which control respiration and defecation go into a state of violent vibration. Death comes as a result of asphyxiation.

The Wehrmacht was impressed. Colonel Rüdriger, head of the Army's poison gas installation at Spandau, ordered the construction of new laboratories to produce sufficient quantities of tabun to begin field trials. Schrader, who worked for the IG Farben chemical conglomorate, was moved to a new factory at Elberfeld in the Ruhr 'to pursue the study of organic phosphorus compounds undisturbed'.[2]

A year later, in 1938, he discovered a compound related to tabun – isopropyl methylphosphonofluoridate – whose potential 'as a toxic war substance' he found to be 'astonishingly high'. The new agent was named sarin, a title invented by Schrader as an acronym of the names of the four key individuals involved in its production: Schrader, Ambros, Rüdriger and van der Linde. In June 1939 the formula for sarin was passed on to the Wehrmacht's laboratories in Berlin. Tests on animals showed it to be almost ten times as poisonous as tabun.

In September 1939, as scientists in Berlin prepared the first samples of sarin, the German army launched its invasion of Poland. For the second time in a generation, German chemists were at the heart of their country's war effort. On 19 September, after almost three weeks of uninterrupted victory, Adolf Hitler rose to address a tumultuous audience in Danzig. He told them – in a speech clearly designed for Allied ears – of fearsome new German weapons, against which his enemies would be defenceless. It is conceivable that he had in mind the new nerve gases. At any event, that same month the German chemical industry was ordered to put in hand plans to build a new factory capable of producing a thousand tons of tabun a month.

Construction work began in January 1940 in the forests of Silesia in western Poland. The factory was built close to the Oder River, forty kilometres from Breslau, at a place called Dyhernfurth. Its Wehrmacht code-name was 'Hochwerk'. By 1943 it had cost 120 million reichsmarks. The money came in the main from the Wehrmacht and was funnelled through specially-created companies with only a nominal connection to I G Farben (one of 'the many ruses attempted and plans entered into for the purpose of enabling the company to disclaim in the post-war period any responsibility whatsoever in providing these outlawed instruments of war'[3]). The companies included Anorgana, Luranil, Monturon and Montana. Anorgana was the largest, and its managing director, Otto Ambros, one of the most powerful industrialists in Germany, with direct access to Hitler. Six years later at Nuremburg he was sentenced to eight years in prison for 'slavery and mass murder'. Through Anorgana, Ambros provided the chemists and technicians needed to build and run the Nazi war gas plants.

Dyhernfurth was one of the Third Reich's largest and most secret factories. It covered an area over a mile and a half long and half a mile wide. Had they won the war, the Nazis planned to turn it into Europe's largest chlorine factory. It had a monthly capacity for producing 3,000 tons of nerve gas – 500 tons from each of its six separate units. The factory was completely self-contained. It made the intermediate products needed in the manufacture of tabun; it made the tabun itself; and it had a cavernous underground shell-filling plant, where the liquid nerve gas was loaded into aircraft bombs and shells. This last area was one of the most closely-guarded parts of the site. It was artificially ventilated and 'in the charge of one Dr Kraz'. Under his supervision 'the shells were sent out from Dyhernfurth in trucks and by train. The cargoes were always secreted under coverings so that specific markings were not easily detected'.[4] The charged munitions were stored in a subterranean arsenal at Krappitz in Upper Silesia. Altogether, the factory employed a workforce of 3,000 – all German – who were housed in a vast barracks built in a clearing in the forest.

From the outset the Nazi nerve gas project was beset by difficulties, and it took over two years, until April 1942, to get the factory operational. Many of the chemicals needed to make the liquid nerve gases were found to be exceptionally corrosive and all iron and steel equipment had to be plated with silver. The nerve gas itself was so highly toxic that the whole of the plant 'was enclosed in double glass-lined chambers with pressurized air circulating between',[5] and all apparatus had to be decontaminated with steam and ammonia. The workers wore respirators and special protective suits made of cloth sandwiched between two layers of rubber which were discarded after every tenth wearing. If anyone was suspected of having been contaminated, their clothes were torn off and they were immersed in large baths of sodium bicarbonate solution.

Being drafted to work at Dyhernfurth was a grim prospect. The experience of Dr Wilhelm Kleinhans, a young IG Farben scientist, was fairly typical. In August 1941 he was one of a team of chemists and engineers assembled by Ambros in Ludwigshafen. They were, he informed them, to work for the Reich, in return for which they would be exempted from military service. Before leaving for Dyhernfurth in September, Kleinhans was let into the secret of tabun and sarin by Schrader himself, who told him that the gas mask was not much protection against agents which could penetrate through the skin. Life at Dyhernfurth itself, far from home and in the oppressive forests of Silesia, was both unpleasant and dangerous:

All members of the staff working in the Dyhernfurth plant were never free at one time from the effects of tabun; some of the members were labouring to a greater or lesser degree under the influence. Those affected could be easily recognised because of the contracted condition of their eyes' pupils and at varying intervals each member found it necessary to remain outside the plant for two to three days in order to throw off the effects of the tabun.[6]

It was discovered that resistance to low concentrations of tabun 'was increased by a higher than average amount of fats' and all the workers at Dyhernfurth were given extra rations of milk and fatty foods.

Even before production got underway at the factory there were over 300 accident cases. In the two and a half years that it was operational at least ten men were killed. Kleinhans recalled four pipe fitters who died when a large quantity of tabun drained onto them from pipes they were trying to clean. 'These workmen died in convulsions before the rubber suits could be torn off.' Schrader knew of a man who had half a gallon of tabun poured down his neck; death occurred in two minutes. In one of the most serious accidents, seven workmen were hit in the face by a stream of liquid tabun which forced itself between the face and the respirator. 'They became giddy, vomited, and so then removed their respirators thus inhaling more of the gas. On examination they were all unconscious (one or two were still excited but not conscious) had a feeble pulse, marked nasal discharge, contracted pupils and asthmatic type of breathing. Involuntary urination and diarrhoea occurred.'[7] Despite intra-muscular injection of atropine and heart drugs, artificial respiration, cardiac massage and the use of oxygen masks, only two of the seven survived: the moment they both recovered consciousness they had a second bout of convulsions and had to be sedated for ten hours. The bodies of the dead men were autopsied and their organs sent back to Berlin, where their brains and lungs were found to be thickly congested.

If the Germans had any doubts at all about the potency of their nerve gases, the Dyhernfurth accidents must have completely dispelled them. If this was the effect of tabun in a factory, with every modern medical facility to hand, what might its effects prove to be on the battlefield, against unprotected and unsuspecting Allied soldiers? By the middle of 1943, as the rush of German victories began to turn into an ebb tide of defeats, Hitler started seriously to consider employing his *Siegwaffe*: his Victory weapon.

By the middle of the war, the Nazis had acquired a vast, hidden armoury of chemical weapons. Despite all the other burdens involved in fighting the war, the Wehrmacht still found hundreds of millions of marks to pump into the production and testing of poison gas. According to a team of experts from Porton Down who investigated the German chemical warfare programme after the war:

The total effort put by the Germans into chemical warfare research was considerable, the scientific staffs employed as far as can be ascertained being about double the numbers employed in Great Britain. The buildings and equipment provided were on a lavish scale, and it was clear that not only was no expense grudged in providing laboratory space and apparatus ample for the immediate programme, but that reserve stocks and space were available for accommodating a large expanse of research staff.[8]

The Germans had a score of factories capable of producing around 12,000 tons of poison gas every month. The British and Americans believed around 70,000 tons to have been stockpiled; the Soviet estimate was 250,000 tons. In addition to tabun, the Germans had two types of mustard gas (*Somer-Lost* and *Winter-Lost*) for warm and cold climates, and a terrifying incendiary gas, *N-Stoff* (or chlorine trifluoride) produced exclusively by the SS, which could cause clothes, hair and even asphalt to burst into flames. There was also small-scale production of sarin – the second nerve agent discovered by Schrader – in a closely-guarded compound at Dyhernfurth known simply as 'Building 144'; by the end of the war a whole factory devoted to the manufacture of sarin, with a capacity of 500 tons a month, was nearing completion at Falkenhagen, south-east of Berlin.

Research and testing was carried out at laboratories at Spandau and at the *Truppenhubuengsplatz* or training area at Raubkammer, fifty square miles of forest and heath just north of Munster. Between them, the two installations employed around 1,200 people.

The Germans developed a series of ingenious weapons and devices which give some idea of the way Hitler might have been able to use his chemical arsenal. To slow up an enemy advance, for example, Raubkammer produced various methods of ground contamination. One was

to pour mustard into a hole in the ground lined with paraffin wax, cover the top over and wait for the advancing enemy to break the crust . . . A second method consisted of glass bulbs holding approximately 250 cc of mustard which were painted half yellow and half green. These were emplaced in shallow holes in the ground and lightly covered if necessary. It was stated that troops passing over an area mined with these *Bodenkugeln* broke 80 per cent of them . . . A chemical mine which acted like a concertina was also being considered. The pressure of the foot ejected mustard from a nozzle into the air and, it was hoped, onto the unsuspecting walker.[9]

A separate team of scientists at Raubkammer known as 'Group X' worked specifically on anti-personnel weapons.

Important industrial premises were to be protected by means of a grenade filled with hydrogen cyanide which would function when the wire fence was cut . . . Hand grenades filled with cyanide solution would be given to guards

... Some experiments had been carried out on the introduction of gases into narrow openings by means of a hand spray of 5–10 litres capacity. The weapon proposed had to be actually introduced into the opening, and there was no question of any attack being made from a distance. The gases considered were lachrymators, hydrogen cyanide, cyanogen chloride, mustard and chlorine trifluoride.[10]

A machine gun was tested capable of firing 2,000 rounds of ammunition a minute charged with tabun or sarin 'with the object of attacking tanks by creating a concentration of gas round the air inlets'. Another anti-tank weapon was the gas grenade. Tests on captured tanks produced good results: 'it was thought that even if death did not take place, the crew would be rendered unconscious for sufficient time to enable the tank to be captured intact or destroyed.'[11]

The Luftwaffe had almost half a million gas bombs, ranging from 15 kg anti-personnel devices up to 750 kg phosgene bombs. Copying the design of captured Russian spray tanks, German pilots learnt to spray columns of marching men so effectively that 50 per cent of the troops were contaminated, even if they managed to get into their gas masks and capes in time – 'this was found even with troops who had been attacked and knew they were likely to be attacked again.'[12] Hydrogen cyanide, mustard and tabun were the best agents. The Germans also tried spraying concentrated acids and alkalis: 'fuming nitric acid was thought to be of some value in a low spray owing to the painful burns produced'.[13]

The Nazis carried out a successful series of tests, charging their flying bombs and rockets with poison gas. In 1939, Hermann Ochsner, the General in command of all German chemical troops, advocated the use of gas 'against industrial concentrations and large cities' as a weapon of terror. 'There is no doubt that a city like London would be plunged into a state of unbearable turmoil which would bring enormous pressure to bear on the enemy Government.'[14] Now, in the V-weapons, the scientists had the means to deliver the terror which Ochsner – and Hitler – desired. According to the Porton scientists, 'plans were in hand to fill the V-1 with phosgene in place of the normal 800 kg of hexa-TNT'.[15] The Raubkammer experts had also made plans to use the V-weapons to deliver nerve agents into the very heart of London; the British standard civilian respirator would have offered little protection against tabun. Considering the fact that on some days during 1944 the Nazis were able to send flying bombs over the English coast in waves of 200 at a time, Hitler had here a terror weapon of horrifying dimensions.

Like the British and Americans, the Germans made extensive use of animals and human 'observers' in their testing of poison gases. Men crawled over contaminated ground on their hands and knees; others, wearing bathing costumes and oxygen cylinders, sat in gas chambers filled with hydrogen cyanide. 'Chemicals were fired into woods and human subjects entered the area to see how long they could remain there without adjusting their respirators.' For testing mustard gas rabbits' ears were used, as was shorn horse skin; 'the skin between a dog's toes' was found to be particularly good 'for comparison with humans'.[16]

The Allied investigators' most grisly find at Raubkammer was a Black Museum whose exhibits included the organs of animals gassed with tabun, and 'some 4,000 photographs mounted in albums and folders'. The photographs were of men wounded or killed by gas in accidents or experiments. 'Due to the gruesome appearance of some half-dozen fatal cases,' reported the Allied scientists, 'political prisoners might have been used in these experiments.'[17]

They might indeed. Although thousands of files on chemical warfare were destroyed by the Nazis between 1944–5, enough survived to show that with the start of the mass-extermination programme in the middle of the war, drastic experiments using lethal agents had begun to be carried out directly on human beings. At Natzweiler Concentration Camp, for example, in 1943, Professor Wimmer of the University of Strasburg 'contaminated the forearms of twelve habitual criminals' with mustard gas.

The men were then put to bed. The next day, there were deep areas of necrosis on the forearms, and also burns on the side of the body where the contaminated arms had come into contact. The men also suffered a severe conjunctivitis and about three days later bronchitis, which developed into broncho-pneumonia.[18]

Each of the victims was photographed daily; three of them died. Later in the same year at Natzweiler, a second Strasburg scientist, Professor Picker, carried out tests on a further ten 'habitual criminals', exposing them in gas chambers for periods of three minutes at a time to ever-increasing concentrations of phosgene.[19]

Three scientists, led by SS *Oberführer* Dr Mrugowsky, tested poison bullets on 'five persons who had been sentenced to death'. The chemical was aconitine, a substance closely related to the nerve gases, which had already been considered as a possible agent by the British and Canadians. Mrugowsky's account of the experiment, stamped top secret and dated September 1944, was sent to the Reich-Surgeon of the SS:

Each subject of the experiments received one shot in the upper part of the left thigh, while in a horizontal position. In the case of two of the persons, the bullets passed clean through the upper part of the thigh. Even later no effect from the poison could be seen. These two subjects were therefore rejected...

The symptoms shown by the three condemned persons were surprisingly the same. At first, nothing special was noticeable. After 20 to 25 minutes, a disturbance of the motor nerves and a light flow of saliva began, but both stopped again. After 40 to 44 minutes a strong flow of saliva appeared. The poisoned persons swallowed frequently; later the flow of saliva is so strong that it can no longer be controlled by swallowing. Foamy saliva flows from the mouth. Then, a sensation of choking and vomiting starts... One of the poisoned persons tried in vain to vomit. In order to succeed, he put 4 fingers of his hand, up to the main joint, right into his mouth. In spite of this, no vomiting occurred. His face became quite red.

The faces of the other two subjects were already pale at an early stage. Other symptoms were the same. Later on the disturbance of the motor nerves increased so much that the persons threw themselves up and down, rolled their eyes and arms. At last the disturbance subsided, the pupils were enlarged to the maximum, the condemned lay still. Massetercramp and loss of urine was observed in one of them. Death occurred 121, 123 and 129 minutes after they were shot.[20]

Tabun and sarin were also almost certainly tested on the inmates of the concentration camps. As the British investigators put it at the end of the war: it was extremely unlikely that the Nazi leadership 'would have agreed to the diversion of considerable effort, in difficult circumstances, to the production of a chemical warfare agent which had not been shown unequivocally to be capable of killing men.'[21]

The experiments on human beings were not the isolated acts of a handful of SS sadists. After the war, Baron Georg von Schnitzler, a leading Nazi supporter and a prominent member of the board of IG Farben, swore that Ambros and other board members were aware of what was happening. British Intelligence reported that one of the IG Farben directors was said to have 'justified the experiments not only on the grounds that the inmates of concentration camps would have been killed anyway by the Nazis, but also on the grounds that the experiments had a humanitarian aspect in that the lives of countless German workers were saved thereby.'[22]

Most of the scientists working on poison gases loudly protested that they knew nothing of the experiments. Their denials were frequently unconvincing: some certainly had proven links with the SS As the Allied interrogators drily observed, 'The profession of such complete ignorance, advanced with wholly unnecessary vehemence left us with some doubts regarding their veracity.'[23]

In the 'night and fog' of Hitler's Germany, where any slight suspicion of disloyalty might lead to arrest by the Gestapo, few scientists seem to have had the will to resist such perversions of their profession.

By the end of 1944, Germany had a formidable nerve gas arsenal dispersed around the country. Poison gas shells were stored at Krappitz in Upper Silesia; others were said to have been hidden in old mine shafts in Lausitz and Saxony. In all, the various top secret munitions dumps contained around 12,000 tons of tabun – 2,000 tons loaded into shells, 10,000 into aircraft bombs.

As greater and greater tonnages of nerve gas weapons were stockpiled, the temptation to use them was correspondingly increased. Hitler himself – wounded by mustard gas in the First World War – was known to have a marked aversion to using chemical weapons: Raubkammer was the only major military trials ground he never visited.[24] Nevertheless, as Germany's military plight became more desperate he began to hope that the nerve gases – like the V-weapons and the Nazis' prototype jet engine – would ultimately turn the war in his favour. Shortly before D-Day, in 1944, he boasted to Mussolini of secret weapons that would 'turn London into a garden of ruins' and referred specifically to a deadly new war gas being developed by German chemists.[25] At the same time, stocks of tabun were moved south into Bavaria in case – as was at one time planned – Hitler should leave the *Führerbunker* in Berlin and put up a last-ditch stand amid the natural fortresses of the Alps.

Three of the most fanatical Nazi leaders, Bormann, Goebbels and Ley, repeatedly urged Hitler to unleash nerve gas. Goebbels wanted to use it against British cities in revenge for the destruction of Dresden. Albert Speer, Minister for Armaments in the Third Reich, recalled a secret conversation with labour leader Robert Ley 'by profession a chemist' held in his special railroad car. Ley's 'increased stammering betrayed his agitation: "You know we have this new poison gas – I've heard about it. The Führer must do it. He must use it. Now he has to do it. When else! This is the last moment. You too must make him realise it's time." ' Speer remained silent.

Hitler, to be sure, had always rejected gas warfare; but now he hinted at a situation conference in headquarters that the use of gas might stop the advance of Soviet troops. He went on with vague speculations that the West would accept gas warfare against the East because at this stage of the war the British and American governments had an interest in stopping the Russian advance. When no one at the situation conference spoke up in agreement, Hitler did not return to the subject. Undoubtedly the Generals feared the unpredictable consequences.[26]

By 1945 it would have been suicidal for Hitler to have embarked upon chemical warfare. Even though there were thousands of tons of tabun available, there were simply not enough bombers left to deliver it. If he had issued the necessary orders Speer, aware that Germany would court massive retaliation, was fully prepared to sabotage them. Already, according to his testimony at Nuremberg, Speer was going to great lengths to divert raw materials and supplies of intermediates away from Germany's chemical warfare factories: a claim which was corroborated by Karl Brandt, the head of chemical warfare defence in Germany. According to Brandt, he, Speer and General Kennes (Assistant Chief of the General Staff) 'had an agreement that, if some order had been forthcoming to start gas warfare against the Allies, they would themselves ensure that the initiation would not occur, as they proposed to hold up transport of supplies.'[27]

A year earlier, however, and things might have been very different. The British were so certain that the Nazis had no new war gas that during the Allied landings in Normandy in June 1944, Montgomery left all his troops' anti-gas equipment behind in England; none of his men even carried gas masks.[28] Used against the fragile beach-heads, tabun might well have stopped the D-Day landings in their tracks. 'When D-Day finally ended,' wrote General Omar Bradley after the war, 'without a whiff of gas, I was vastly relieved. For even a light sprinkling of persistent gas on Omaha Beach would have cost us our footing there.' Gas, in Bradley's view, could have 'forced a decision in one of history's climactic battles'.[29] With the extra six months that such a successful attack might have brought him, Hitler's V-weapons might have seriously crumbled British commitment to the war; at the same time, the absence of the long-promised second front could have led Stalin to seek a separate peace. Had Hitler ordered its use, tabun could conceivably have saved Germany from defeat.

The reason he failed to do so probably had much to do with a conversation at the Wolf's Lair, his headquarters in East Prussia, back in May 1943. After the collapse at Stalingrad, both Speer and his chemical warfare expert, Otto Ambros, were summoned to a special conference by Hitler to discuss using gas to stem the Russian advance. Ambros began by saying that the Allies could out-produce Germany in chemical weapons. Hitler interrupted to say that he understood that might be true of conventional gases – 'but Germany has a special gas, tabun. In this we have a monopoly in Germany.' Ambros shook his head. 'I have justified reasons to assume that tabun, too, is known abroad.'[30] According to Ambros, the essential nature of tabun and sarin had been disclosed in technical journals as long ago as 1902, and like many other German scientists he could not believe that the chemical warfare experts of Porton Down or Edgewood Arsenal had failed to develop them. Whether Ambros genuinely believed that the Allies had their own nerve gases, or whether he was merely trying to put off Hitler, the result was the same: Hitler turned on his heel and abruptly left the meeting. From that moment on, no matter how tempted he felt to use his secret gases, Hitler had always to balance in his mind the conviction of his scientists that the Allies had them too.

Had he known how flimsy the evidence was which supported these convictions he might have thought again. Nazi scientists, for example, read great significance into the fact that references to compounds related to nerve gases suddenly ceased to be mentioned in American scientific journals at the beginning of the war. They correctly deduced this was a result of censorship by the US authorities. What they did not know was that this was to protect the secrecy of the insecticide DDT then under development, not the secrecy of any new war gas. In other words, the Führer had been misled. Neither the Americans nor the British possessed a chemical weapon remotely capable of matching nerve gas.

Although it is generally the British who are hailed as the masters of secrecy and deception in the Second World War, the Germans must take a great deal of credit for the skill with which they deceived the Allies over nerve gas. It was one of the greatest secrets of the Third Reich, known only to a handful, and it was protected by labyrinthine security measures. Both the main nerve gases were given code names. Tabun was initially known as 'Le 100', then as 'Gelan', then as 'Substance 83'; sarin as 'Stoff 146'. Just as the Allies code-named the atomic bomb 'Tube Alloy' after a relatively innocuous war material, so eventually the nerve gases came to be known respectively as 'Trilon 83' and 'Trilon 146' after a common German detergent.

All chemicals needed in the manufacture of nerve gas were transported under false names, names which were often changed a second or third time on arrival at their destination. The shipments were recorded in cipher in the so-called 'Black Book', a volume the size of a warehouse ledger, an inch and a half thick. At the end of the war it was secretly buried by the Nazis.

The result was records which would be largely unintelligible if captured. Even senior scientists were kept in ignorance of the various stages of nerve gas manufacture; they knew the details only of the particular part they worked in. Schrader himself was kept away from certain vital areas of research. In Nazi Germany even the most intellectually curious were too intimidated to ask questions. 'It was,' concluded an Allied report at the end of the war, 'safer to know little . . . Many of the technically-trained plant operators wore "blinkers" and dared allow their gazes to sweep only in the most restricted arc.'[31]

By such methods the Germans kept the secret of their nerve gases intact for more than eight years – one of the greatest triumphs of Nazi counter-espionage. The security precautions were breached only once, by complete accident, and so successful had the Nazis been in disguising the existence of tabun, that the British apparently refused to believed what they heard.

Throughout the war, unsubstantiated rumours did circulate between Washington and London of a new German poison gas. In 1941, United States and British chemists held a series of top-level talks. Did the Americans, the British asked, believe in rumours of a new Nazi gas? The Americans said that they did.

Stories of the German nerve gases have had such wide circulation from so many sources, some of which appear to be reliable that it is judged that the Germans do have some gas which can be used in this manner.[32]

The intelligence coup which should surely have finally convinced the Allies came two years later. On 11 May 1943, the British Army in Tunisia captured an important German prisoner. The man – whose name does not appear in the official records – was a chemist from the main Nazi chemical warfare laboratory at Spandau. He told the British everything he knew of a super gas called 'Trilon 83'. The information was passed back to London by MI 19 (the branch of Military Intelligence responsible for the interrogation of prisoners) where it formed the basis of a 'Most Secret' report dated 3 July 1943.[33]

The unknown informant told of a 'clear colourless liquid with little smell' which 'cannot be classed with any of the other war gases as it is a nerve poison' causing the eyes to shrink 'to a pin-head and asthma-like difficulties in breathing. In any heavier concentrations death occurs in about a quarter of an hour.' The prisoner, continued the report,

... when engaged on research work on these chemicals was under continued treatment... One chemist lost his life in spite of constant injections of lobelin to excite the respiratory centre. Tests with this gas are extremely dangerous as there is no perceptible threshold of irritation as is the case with other gases ... by the time one is aware of the gas through its physiological effects (the only means of detection) it is too late to put on the respirator ...

The gas does not lend itself to spraying but will be used in gas shells etc especially against fortified positions and towns. In the latter case panic will be caused by its blinding effect without its being necessarily in fatal concentrations.

The chemist passed on details of the chemicals involved in manufacture and advice on defensive measures. All his information, advised the report, 'may be classified as reliable'. Twenty-five copies were produced and circulated throughout Whitehall and Porton. Astonishingly, nothing happened.

The failure to act on the MI 19 report is all the more remarkable considering that the British, in their development of DDT, had tested compounds similar to tabun as potential war gases. They actually had a small production plant making a chemical called 'PF-3' which had similar effects on the body to tabun. Nerve gas had been accepted as a *theory*. Now, faced with the evidence that the Nazis had turned it into a workable weapon, the men at Porton chose to dismiss it. While German stocks of tabun mounted, they continued to concentrate their energies on time-consuming and futile attempts to produce a better version of mustard gas.

April 1945 was Porton's moment of truth. A German ammunition dump was captured and a mysterious shell shipped back to the United Kingdom. Gingerly dismantled with the help of a nearby American field laboratory, the scientists discovered Hitler's secret weapon. It was a terrible shock. Thirty-five years later it is still a source of embarrassment. 'The one time we were really caught with our trousers down,' says one senior Porton man today.

In classic bureaucratic manner, Porton at once tried to shift the blame on to someone else: it was not their fault, but the result of a failure in intelligence. The dismantled shell, claims Porton's internal history, 'was our first intimation that the Germans had this gas . . . no Intelligence Report from the year 1937 when Germany started working on it as a war gas had given any tangible clue to its existence.'[34]

This has remained Porton's excuse ever since. The yellowing MI 19 report – discovered amid a pile of recently declassified Government documents entitled 'Chemical Warfare Intelligence 1939–44' – enables this part of the record at least to be set straight. The British were 'reliably' warned of the existence of nerve gas almost *two years* before the end of the war. If Hitler had decided to use tabun in 1944, the decision to disregard the report might have gone down in history as one of the costliest intelligence blunders of the Second World War. Thanks in part to the Allied chemists' stubborn belief in their own superiority, Hitler's secret weapon stayed a secret till the end.

FOUR

A Plague on your Children

The noise of fourteen thousand aeroplanes advancing in open order. But in the Kurfurstendamm and the Eighth Arrondissement, the explosion of anthrax bombs is hardly louder than the popping of a paper bag.

Aldous Huxley, *Brave New World* (1932)

The history of chemical and biological warfare has thrown up some strange stories, but few are as bizarre as those which surround a small island off the north-west coast of Scotland. It lies in its own well-protected bay, close to the fishing village of Aultbea – an outcrop of rock, well-covered with heather, three hundred feet high, one and a half miles long and a mile wide.

It takes about twenty minutes to reach by fishing boat from Aultbea. As you draw closer it's possible to make out the shapes of hundreds of sea birds nesting on its craggy shore-line. Their calls are the only sounds which break the silence. Once upon a time the island is said to have supported eleven families. Today, the only sign of human habitation is the ruin of a crofter's cottage.

This utterly abandoned island is Gruinard. Thanks to a series of secret wartime experiments – the full details of which are still classified – no one is allowed to live, or even land here.

In 1942, the hillsides around Aultbea bristled with military activity. It was here that the Russian convoys used to form up, prior to making the dangerous and terrifying run to Murmansk. It was a restricted area. There were military checkpoints on the roads. The local population – mainly crofters and fishermen – had to carry special passes. They grew used to the sight of uniforms, and avoided asking questions. It is not surprising, therefore, that in the summer of 1942, few paid any attention to the arrival in Gruinard Bay of a new military contingent. In a sheltered spot, just half a mile from Gruinard, on the mainland on the farthest side of the bay, they pitched camp. A couple of Nissen huts were built. Lorries arrived carrying fuel and food and cases of scientific instruments. Finally, the soldiers – perhaps twenty-five in all, commanded by Captain Dalby of the Royal Artillery – were joined by a party of nine civilians. They carried with them, and handled with great care, a set of large glass flasks, which were taken straight into one of the huts.

The new arrivals seemed distinctly ill at ease in these primitive surroundings. A photograph, taken at the time, shows a group of them standing stiffly in front of the camp. One of them, his hands stuffed deep into his pockets, is Dr David Henderson, a brilliant bacteriologist and a leading member of the Lister Institute. To his left stands Donald Woods, a long way now from his usual location in the unit for bacterial chemistry at London's Middlesex Hospital. Next to him is another leading bacteriologist, W. R. Lane. Standing closest to the camera, arms akimbo and with a pipe clamped (as usual) between his teeth is the most scientifically renowned, and in many ways most significant member of the party – Graham Sutton, normally in charge of all experimental work at Porton Down.

Their leader does not appear in the photograph. Dr Paul Fildes, at that time in his early sixties, was arguably Britain's top bacteriologist: a Fellow of the Royal Society, founder of the *British Journal of Experimental Pathology* and editor of the great nine-volume *System of Bacteriology* published by the Medical Research Council in 1931.

The presence of these famous scientists at Gruinard Bay in the summer of 1942 was a closely guarded secret. They had been given orders by the Highest Authority – a euphemism for the Prime Minister – to investigate the practicability of a biological bomb. Supervised directly by a top secret Whitehall committee chaired by a member of the War Cabinet, Lord Hankey, the tests this little group conducted on Gruinard were the beginnings of a massive research project, costing millions of pounds and employing thousands of people, which would ultimately give the Allies a weapon with a destructive power equivalent to the atomic bomb.

Its first victims were to be sheep. Porton's agents had scoured the local hillsides, paying the crofters good prices for their highland sheep. Around thirty were collected and set to graze in a field close to the scientists' base camp. As the date for the experiment approached, they were herded into a landing craft and ferried across the half mile stretch of water to Gruinard.

In one of the Nissen huts, Dr Henderson prepared the weapon itself. It was a 25 lb chemical bomb, eighteen inches high and six inches in diameter; normally it contained mustard gas. To help him prime it, Henderson called in the Porton team's young explosives expert, Major Allan Younger. Neither man wore a gas mask, as Henderson uncorked one of the flasks. 'I was asked to hold the bomb,' recalled Younger, 'whilst he poured this mixture in. It turned out to be a brown, thick gruel, and with great trepidation I held on to the thing making sure I wouldn't spill it, as he poured this thick stuff in.'[1]

The 'thick stuff' was a slurry of concentrated anthrax spores.

After the bomb had been filled, it, too, was ferried across to Gruinard. With it went Sutton, Henderson and Younger. Each man was now clad like some science fiction monster, in a rubberized suit, gas mask, high rubber boots and thick gloves. The anthrax weapon was placed on a small mound of earth. Around it, tethered in concentric circles, were the sheep. An explosive charge was carefully attached to the bomb and a fuse laid. While the sheep grazed un-concernedly, the scientists retreated to a safe distance down wind.

Anthrax had long been considered the most practicable filling for a biological weapon. A decade earlier, Aldous Huxley had predicted a war involving anthrax bombs. Even before that, in 1925, Winston Churchill wrote of 'pestilences methodically prepared and deliberately launched upon man and beast ... Blight to destroy crops, Anthrax to slay horses and cattle, Plague to poison not armies only but whole districts – such are the lines alone which military science is remorselessly advancing.'[2]

Anthrax is an acutely infectious and deadly disease. In nature it generally occurs in cattle or sheep, but it can be equally deadly to man. If contaminated meat is accidentally handled it can produce coal-black malignant skin ulcers which lead to blood poisoning. Inhaled it is even more deadly. The tiniest of doses can produce, in a matter of hours, a choking cough, difficulty in breathing, and a high fever; in nine cases out of ten, death will follow soon after. It was this latter form of the disease which most interested Porton.

Its other advantage as a weapon was its exceptional toughness. Left for two hours at a temperature of 20° centigrade, the bacteria of anthrax turn into spores – virtually indestructible organisms which can lie dormant for years, waiting to infect any living tissue with which they may come into contact. The technique for cultivating the spores, once mastered, could be harnessed for mass-production. At Porton the anthrax was prepared in metal containers resembling milk churns.[3] Henderson's development of a kind of refined vacuum cleaner which could then suck the spores off the cultures where they had been grown was the breakthrough which enabled the Gruinard test to take place. The 'harvested' anthrax had been filled into flasks and driven north to Scotland. Now the scientists had to wait to see whether the weapon would work in practice as well as it promised to in theory.

The bomb exploded. Billions of spores formed an invisible cloud which wafted over the terrified sheep and gradually dispersed over the testing site and the sea. Then silence returned once more to Gruinard. At the end of the test, the scientists made their way to a nearby beach where each was stripped to his underpants by an army sergeant (who burnt the contaminated suits) and given a thorough shower. They then gathered their everyday clothes and were rowed back to the camp.

A day later, the sheep began to die. The pile of carcasses grew steadily throughout the week. They were incontrovertible proof that biological warfare was no longer just a nightmare science-fiction fantasy: it could be made a reality. The Gruinard tests proved that germs could be produced, transported, loaded into munitions and exploded over target areas without necessarily destroying the fragile living organisms which spread the infection.

In further tests that year, and in the summer of 1943, more bombs were exploded. The climax came when a Wellington bomber made a low-level run over the island and neatly deposited the world's first biological payload in the target area. 'The bombs exploded,' remembers Younger, 'with a sharp crack, quite unlike the "crump" of high explosive.'[4] At the end of each round of tests the sheep were dragged to the edge of some nearby cliffs and flung over. Younger dug a trench, filled it with 1,000 lb of explosives, and brought the hilltop crashing down on the carcasses.

There was little regard for safety. At the end of one year's experiments, Younger was entrusted with the job of transporting the flasks of anthrax from Gruinard to Porton for winter storage – a journey of six hundred miles. He was given an eight hundredweight van, a driver, a road map and instructions to avoid major highways and at all costs not to stop if confronted by suspicious circumstances.

In southern Scotland, we drove around a corner and found a woman lying apparently dead on our side of the road just ahead of us. She'd probably been run over. It was a tremendous moral dilemma, but I felt I couldn't afford to stop. I knew just how dangerous this stuff was, and that it was top secret. It was my responsibility to ensure that things didn't go wrong. That's why I passed by. Ever since, I have had it on my conscience.[5]

Further south, Younger was less cautious. When his driver suggested they stop for the night he agreed. They chose the large industrial city of Leeds. Younger headed for the central police station and handed over the van and its cargo to the bemused station sergeant for safekeeping. 'I told him it was a top secret war material and had to be guarded overnight. He didn't ask any questions.'[6] Relieved of their responsibility, Younger and his driver went off in search of the nearest pub, while the world's first biological bomb lay in the back of a van in the centre of one of England's most densely populated towns. Fortunately for Younger there was no air raid on the centre of Leeds that night.

Younger's final visit to Gruinard was equally eventful. There was an outbreak of anthrax on the Scottish mainland when a dead sheep floated across to the mainland in a heavy storm. Younger now believes that he used too high a charge of explosives and that one infected carcass was thrown clear by the force of the blast that brought down the clifftop. A government scientist was installed at a hotel in Aultbea to handle compensation claims.

The anthrax outbreak, and the possibility of a security leak, sent a collective shudder running down the spines of the members of the Bacteriological Warfare Committee in London. Younger and Fildes immediately took off from Porton in a Beaufort torpedo bomber to fly to Gruinard. It developed an oil leak half way and crash landed in a ploughed field near Liverpool. The two men were taken to hospital, but the only injuries suffered were some cuts to Dr Fildes's hand, which he sustained from a bottle of whiskey he was drinking from as the plane skidded across the ground. They completed the remainder of the journey by train and car.

Once on Gruinard, they donned protective suits and decided to try to rid the island of contamination by burning off the heather, which in some parts of the island was chest-high. Gruinard went up like tinder. One of Younger's most vivid wartime memories is of overlooking Gruinard Bay from a hotel on the mainland that evening, and watching as 'a line of fire ate its way up the side of the island'. The huge cloud of dense black smoke, heavily contaminated with anthrax, drifted out over the sea, while the fires made a spectacular display in the gloomy northern night.

Fildes's apocalyptic attempt to rid Gruinard of contamination was a failure. The charred island was sealed off. Today dramatic warning signs still ring its beaches at 400 yard intervals:

GRUINARD ISLAND
THIS ISLAND IS
GOVERNMENT PROPERTY
UNDER EXPERIMENT
THE GROUND IS CONTAMINATED
WITH ANTHRAX AND DANGEROUS
LANDING IS PROHIBITED

Porton's scientists make regular pilgrimages back to Gruinard in the hope that one day they may be able to re-open it to the public. It is an exercise in good public relations Porton would desperately like to perform: 'Anthrax Island', as it is popularly known, is a grave embarrassment, a reminder of a past the scientists would prefer to play down.

For Fildes's successors at Porton Down, the problem is now beginning to look insoluble. As Rex Watson, the present Director of Porton Down, put it in an interview in 1981: 'The attraction of anthrax when it was used was that it was thought to be sufficiently resistant an organism to withstand being dispersed by a munition . . . I don't think at that time perhaps they understood as much as we do now about its persistence over very long periods.'[7] Porton 'would expect there to be an area of contamination for the next tens, perhaps even hundreds of years.' Until that area is clear, Gruinard will remain closed to the public. At the moment, to be sure of being safe, the Porton men who go back still have to wear protective suits and take a seven and a half month course of injections. 'I doubt,' added Dr Watson, 'that we would do such an experiment now if we had to in those conditions.'

Schemes to render Gruinard safe have included plans to remove thousands of tons of top soil, and even to encase it in concrete. In the meantime the island has reverted to nature. The heather which Fildes and Younger burnt off has now returned and is six feet deep in places. Rabbits are said to have turned black as genetic changes have rendered them immune to the anthrax spores, now estimated to lie buried nearly a foot underground.

The wartime testing of anthrax did not end with the burning of Gruinard. The final experiment on the island – in which the bomber dropped the anthrax bomb – was a failure; the bomb fell into what proved to be marshy ground, making it impossible to measure the spread of the spores. This experiment was subsequently repeated on a beach in Wales. The precise location of this test site is still classified.[8]

Gruinard is the most startling reminder of the power of biological weapons, and of the high priority which their development was given in the 1940s. The exact nature and extent of that wartime programme remains one of the last great secrets of the Second World War. Now, with the recent release of some vital official documents, and the increased willingness of some of the participants to reveal at least a little of their work, that secret can at last begin to be told.

Mankind has practised primitive forms of biological warfare for thousands of years: the poisoning of enemy wells with the bodies of dead soldiers and animals in order to spread disease is a practice as old as war itself. In the fourteenth century the Crimean town of Kaffa was captured when the beseiging Tartar army catapulted the bodies of plague victims into the city; the Russians are said to have used similar techniques against the Swedes in the eighteenth century. The British used blankets infected with smallpox in an attempt to wipe out whole tribes of North American Indians.

There were a number of allegations of germ warfare during the First World War. The great strides in medical knowledge of the previous fifty years enabled individual types of bacteria to be identified and isolated. The Germans were accused of having innoculated horses and mules with glanders (a highly infectious animal disease), cattle with anthrax, and German spies were caught supposedly trying to spread plague bacteria in Russia in 1915 and 1916. These were not necessarily just propaganda stories. A top secret American report describes accounts of German biological warfare sabotage as 'confirmed and undoubted'.[9] Foulkes paid a visit to the Lister Institute in 1915 when he was casting around for means of retaliating against the German chlorine attacks, but quickly dismissed germ warfare as a practicable possibility. The nations of Europe had difficulty enough in fighting off the natural ravages of disease without deliberately introducing it onto the battlefield.

Nevertheless, by 1925 it was considered sufficiently feasible for the prohibition of 'bacteriological methods of warfare' to be included within the scope of the Geneva Protocol. No nation at this time is recorded as having had a biological weapon, or even a single laboratory researching into the possibility of developing one. But the search for a new gas to replace mustard inevitably edged scientists towards the consideration of the possibility that the next generation of 'indiscriminate' weapons might be biological rather than chemical. At the same time, the development of mass-immunisation techniques offered the chance of overcoming the major disadvantage of using disease as a weapon: the 'boomerang' effect on your own troops and civilian population. 'CBW' – military jargon for Chemical and Biological Warfare – gradually began to enter the vocabulary of war. It was natural that the two types of weapon should be lumped together: they were 'unconventional', relied upon highly sophisticated scientific and medical skills, were abhorrent to the majority of the population, and had to be developed in conditions of great secrecy.

Ironically it was the Geneva Protocol's ban on biological warfare that led to the start of the biological arms race. In 1932, a Japanese army major, Shiro Ishii, returned home from a European tour convinced that biological weapons were an effective means of fighting a war: with flawless logic he concluded that they must be, otherwise the statesmen at Geneva would not have gone to the trouble of banning them. Major Ishii's conviction became an obsession. A small, thin, bespectacled man in his early forties – his outwardly scholarly appearance belied a powerful personality. 'This individual,' wrote the Americans in 1946 'was the compelling force behind the scenes throughout the whole period of Japanese investigation into the field of biological warfare.'[10]

Despite receiving little official encouragement, by 1935 Ishii had persuaded the Japanese authorites to let him set up a germ warfare research centre at the Harbin Military Hospital. Bombs were designed and tested and cultures of germs prepared and evaluated. In the same year, the Japanese military police, the *Kempai*, arrested five Russian 'spies' in the Kwangtung region of China. All were said to be carrying glass bottles and ampoules containing biological agents – dysentery, cholera and anthrax – for sabotage missions. After the war, Ishii claimed that the Russian attacks were successful: according to the *Kempai*, 6,000 Japanese soldiers died of cholera in the Shanghai area, while 2,000 of the army's horses were killed by anthrax.

True or not, the allegations spurred the Japanese War Ministry into taking a far keener interest in biological warfare. In 1937, with his work at the Harbin Military Hospital yielding promising results, Ishii was given permission to build the world's first major biological warfare installation.

The site chosen was near a small village called Pingfan, about forty miles south of Harbin, close to the South Manchuria Railroad. By 1939 when it was almost completed, Ishii was a general. The Pingfan Institute, as it was known, had a garrison of 3,000 scientists, technicians and soldiers, and was completely self-supporting. The Institute raised its own vegetables and livestock; it had a flock of 50,000 hens. Within its closely guarded walls was a school and a hospital, and a separate compound for plague research. An attached air base provided lavish transport facilities for the senior scientists as well as aircraft for field trials. 'Perhaps no better indication of the magnitude of the Pingfan project', wrote American Intelligence after the war

can be gained than consideration of the fact that in addition to various offensive activities, the vaccine production capacity of the plant was of the order of twenty million doses annually. Furthermore, the spectrum of vaccines ranged from typhoid to typhus.[11]

For offensive use, Pingfan opened a Pandora's Box of disease: typhus, typhoid, anthrax, cholera, plague (the ancient Black Death), salmonella, tetanus, botulism, brucellosis, gas gangrene, smallpox, tick encephalitis, tuberculosis, tularemia and glanders. The bacteria were grown in vast numbers in aluminium tanks designed by Ishii. Each strain had its own 'growing time', at the end of which it was 'harvested' by being scraped from the surface of the tank with a small metal rake (Ishii demonstrated the technique to the Americans a few months after the end of the war). Diseases of the intestine, like dysentery and typhoid, were harvested after a growth period of twenty-four hours; plague, anthrax and glanders took forty-eight hours; anaerobes (bacteria which can live without oxygen), a week.

In August 1945, with the Russian army only a few miles away, the Pingfan Institute was destroyed: every piece of machinery systematically smashed to bits, every scrap of incriminating paper burned. There are therefore no records of just how much biological agent was made at Pingfan. Colonel Tomosada Masuda, head of 'Section Three' at Pingfan, claimed after the war to have 'no figures on this'. The quantities were almost certainly huge. His American interrogators calculated that for each set of bomb experiments, 900 tanks were used, each yielding a harvest of 40 grammes of bacterial scrapings.[12] In 1949 Russian investigators put the productive capacity of Pingfan at *eight tons* of bacteria a month.*

Like the British a year later, Masuda quickly came to the conclusion that anthrax was the most practical bomb filling. Its spores were found to live for three months in Pingfan's carefully prepared suspensions. This compared with a mere three days for cholera, and a week for dysentery and plague.

The Japanese spent at least seven years trying to perfect an anthrax bomb. Over 2,000 'Uji' bombs were filled with anthrax and tested experimentally. It was a substantial programme: the Uji bomb was one of nine types of aircraft bomb which had been tested at Pingfan by 1940. The deadliest munition developed was the 'Ha' bomb, designed to shatter into thousands of pieces of shrapnel, spreading the anthrax spores to murderously good effect. A single scratch wound from a piece of contaminated shrapnel was estimated to cause illness and death in 90 per cent of its victims. The standard Japanese heavy bomber could carry twelve Ha bombs.

In just two years, in addition to thousands of guinea pigs and mice, at least 500 sheep and 200 horses were killed in biological tests. By 1939, over 4,000 bombs had been produced. Other weapons tested included shells, aerial sprays and sabotage devices for poisoning wells.

As in every chemical and biological warfare installation throughout the world there were stringent safety precautions. All workers wore a completely rubberized anti-plague suit, together with a respirator, surgical gloves and rubber boots. After every experimental trial they were required to strip completely 'and bathe themselves in 2 per cent creosol or mercuric chloride'.[13] All enlisted men received extra rations of food; officers were given danger pay of an extra 60 yen ($25) a month.

But there were accidents and deaths. At least twenty men a year working in the laboratories contracted infections from the material they handled. In 1937, two died from severe cases of glanders. In 1944 there were two deaths from plague. Anthrax was a constant

---

* The main American germ warfare factory, at Vigo in Indiana, would – at peak production – have been capable of producing twelve times this amount: 100 tons of bacteria per month.

source of danger. Masuda recalled the example of two soldiers:

... one of the two individuals had been ordered to cut the grass at the experimental site a day after an anthrax trial. He contracted pneumonic anthrax and passed away after a short course of the disease. The second fatality was the first soldier's room mate and he died from anthrax septicemia, the result of contact infection.[14]

At Pingfan the Japanese also devoted considerable time to perfecting sabotage techniques. Scientists devised one particularly unpleasant poison for contaminating foodstuffs: christened 'fungu toxin', it was made of an extract from the livers of blow fish. Masuda himself supervised experiments in the poisoning of water supplies using cholera, typhoid and dysentery in over a thousand wells in Manchuria. Evidence later collected by the Russians suggested that the Japanese also cultivated the plague-infected flea as a biological weapon. Pingfan was said to be capable of producing 500 million fleas a year. In 1941 these were tested by being dropped in porcelain aircraft bombs; later the Japanese carried out successful experiments in spraying the fleas from high altitudes.

Like the Nazis with their nerve gas programme, the Japanese struggled to restrict the secret of the Pingfan project to the tightest possible circle. Each scientist laboured in his own particular field and was refused access to other areas. Despite the large capital investment in Pingfan – it cost between six and twelve million yen (up to $5 million) a year to run – even the Emperor was not informed of the existence of the germ warfare programme: 'Biological warfare,' Ishii told the Americans in 1946, 'is inhumane and advocating such a method of warfare would defile the virtue and benevolence of the Emperor.'

Radiating out from Pingfan were eighteen other biological warfare out-stations, each staffed by around 300 people; many were on mainland China. 'Ishii,' wrote the Americans, 'developed a biological warfare organisation that at its height extended from Harbin to the Dutch East Indies and from the island of Hokkaido to the Celibes.'[15] The whole programme was administered by an organisation called Boeki Kyusuibu, whose innocuous title is translated as 'Anti-Epidemic Water Supply Unit'.

When the war ended and the Americans began to piece together the scale of the Japanese germ warfare project, Ishii topped the list of scientists they wished to interrogate. It took U.S. Intelligence almost five months to locate him, living in seclusion at his country home and suffering from chronic dysentery – an unpleasant legacy of his career in germ warfare. He was taken to Tokyo and grilled solidly for a month.

At the end of that time he was still denying any knowledge of what the Americans suspected was the criminal aspect of his work: the use of human guinea pigs in biological warfare experiments. It was to be almost two years before the full story emerged; the US Government promptly suppressed the facts for the next quarter of a century. (The story of the immunity from prosecution granted to Ishii, and the subsequent cover-up is told in Chapter Seven.)

Pathological material and specimens from five hundred human victims were turned over to the Americans. The number of people actually experimented upon was far higher, and almost certainly ran into four figures.

The Japanese infected prisoners – mostly Chinese, but possibly including American, British and Australian POWs – with the full range of diseases under study at Pingfan. Ishii admitted feeding five prisoners with a two-day old culture of botulism; another twenty were injected with brucellosis. Bombs designed to produce gas gangrene were exploded next to tethered prisoners – an experiment confirmed by a witness at the Khabarovsk War Crimes Trial two years later:

In January 1945 . . . I saw experiments in inducing gas gangrene, conducted under the direction of the Chief of the 2nd Division, Colonel Ikari, and researcher Futaki. Ten prisoners . . . were tied facing stakes, five to ten metres apart . . . The prisoners' heads were covered with metal helmets, and their bodies with screens . . . only the naked buttocks being exposed. At about 100 metres away a fragmentation bomb was exploded by electricity . . . All ten men were wounded . . . and sent back to the prison . . . I later asked Ikari and researcher Futaki what the results had been. They told me that all ten men had . . . died of gas gangrene.

There were similar experiments with anthrax bombs. Victims were injected with tetanus, smallpox, plague and glanders, as well as being exposed to aerosol clouds of disease in gas chambers. The infections were not always allowed to run their full course: victims would be killed with massive doses of morphine, and then dissected to check the progress of the disease up to the point of death. Of the human remains studied by the Americans in 1947, anthrax accounted for 31 deaths, cholera 50, dysentery 12, glanders 20, mustard gas 16, tetanus 14, plague 106, salmonella 11, tuberculosis 41, typhoid 22, typhus 9.*

Concurrent with these human experiments, there is strong – almost conclusive – evidence to suggest that the Japanese were also waging actual biological warfare in China.

On 4 October 1940, according to the Chinese Ambassador in London, a Japanese plane visited the town of Chuhsien in the province of Chekiang. 'After circling over the city for a short while it scattered rice and wheat grains mixed with fleas over the western section of the city',[16] and the resulting plague epidemic killed twenty-one townspeople. Three weeks later 'Japanese planes raided Ningpo and scattered a considerable quantity of wheat grains over the port city'. Ninety-nine people were killed by plague.[17]

On November 4th 1941 at about 5 am a lone enemy plane appeared over Changteh in Hunan Province, flying very low, the morning being rather misty. Instead of bombs, wheat and rice grains, pieces of paper, cotton wadding and some unidentified particles were dropped. There were many eyewitnesses, including Mrs E. J. Bannon, Superintendent of the local Presbyterian hospital, and other foreign residents in Changteh. After the 'all clear' signal had been sounded at 5 pm, some of these strange gifts from the enemy were collected and sent by the police to the local Presbyterian hospital for examination which revealed the presence of micro-organisms reported to resemble P. pestis (plague bacteria). On November 11th, seven days later, the first clinical case of plague came to notice, then followed by five more cases within the same month, two cases in December, and the last to date on January 13th 1942 . . . Changteh had never been, as far as is known, afflicted by plague.[18]

In another attack on Kinghwa, three Japanese planes

. . . dropped a large quantity of small granules, about the size of shrimp eggs. These strange objects were collected and examined in a local hospital. The granules were more or less round, about 1 mm in diameter, of whitish-yellow tinge, somewhat translucent with a certain amount of glistening reflection from the surface. When brought into contact with a drop of water on a glass slide, the granule began to swell to about twice its original size. In a small amount of water in a test tube, with some agitation it would break up into whitish flakes and later form a milky suspension.[19]

* Taken from a 'Summary Report on B W Investigations' submitted to the Chief of the US Chemical Corps in Washington on 12 December 1947. Released in 1981 under the Freedom of Information Act.

A Plague on your Children

Traces of plague bacteria were found. Finally there were another 600 cases of plague in three other Chinese provinces which the Chinese ascribed to an 'inhuman act of our enemy'. The detail certainly suggests that the incidents were more than mere propaganda stories. Whether they were isolated events or part of a systematic biological attack on China is unknown.

In July 1942 the Chinese allegations were passed on to Winston Churchill. Two days later he had them placed on the agenda of the Pacific War Council.

The growing alarm in London and Washington that the Japanese were on the verge of initiating biological warfare gave an added urgency to the first anthrax bomb tests on Gruinard that summer. Up to then the Allied germ warfare effort had lagged significantly behind the Japanese, but from 1942 onwards the Anglo-American biological programme began to vie with the Manhattan Project for top development priority.

The British biological warfare project was born on 12 February 1934 at a meeting of the Chiefs of Staff. For two years, a Disarmament Conference in Geneva had been discussing means of finally ridding the world of chemical weapons. Germ warfare had also been included, and in view of this, Sir Maurice Hankey told the Service Chiefs, he 'was wondering whether it might not be right to consider the possibilities and potentialities of this form of war'.[20] The Chiefs of Staff agreed, and authorized Hankey to put out discreet and 'very secret' feelers to the Medical Research Council to see if they would help. Like the Japanese, the British were prompted to begin work on germ weapons as a result of a peace initiative aimed at banning them.

For Hankey it was the beginning of a long involvement with biological weapons. At the age of fifty-seven this *doyen* of civil service mandarins was cast as the unlikely counterpart to General Shiro Ishii: just as the Japanese owed their venture into the field of biological warfare to Ishii, Britain owed hers to Hankey. He was entirely suited, both in character and position, to the task. 'Short, spare of figure . . . a dedicated dietician, almost a non-smoker and teetotaller, he lived, and enjoyed, a spartan existence,' recalled a subordinate. He had 'little or no sense of humour' and was 'too intense and taut to be a social success, and had no "small talk"'.[21] In 1934 he was a uniquely powerful Whitehall official, Secretary to both the Cabinet and the Committee of Imperial Defence, 'a man

81

whose advice, over a period of 25 years, no Prime Minister or Service Chief could afford to disregard in matters of Defence.'[22] His career and temperament are neatly summed up in the four word title Stephen Roskill chose for his official biography: *Hankey: Man of Secrets.*

Amid the prevailing policy of appeasement in the 1930s, Hankey at first made little progress. Edward Mellanby, the secretary of the Medical Research Council, refused to have anything to do with a project which used advances in medicine for destructive purposes. Hankey had more success with Paul Fildes, the pugnacious head of the MRC's Bacteriological Metabolic Unit, who agreed to take up a watching brief on the subject. In September 1936 Hankey proposed to the Committee of Imperial Defence that 'an expert official body' should be set up to 'report upon the practicability of the introduction of bacteriological warfare and to make recommendations as to the counter-measures'.[23] In October the CID approved, and Hankey became Chairman of the newly-created Microbiological Warfare Committee.

In March 1937 the Committee submitted its first report, specifically on plague, anthrax and foot-and-mouth disease. Though they concluded that 'for the time being ... the practical difficulties of introducing bacteria into this country on a large scale were such as to render an attempt unlikely' they urged that stocks of serum be built up to meet any potential threat.[24] From 1937 to 1940, Britain began to stockpile vaccines, fungicides and insecticides against biological attack.

In April 1938 the Committee produced a second report, and in June Hankey circulated 'Proposals for an Emergency Bacteriological Service to operate in War': the emphasis was on defence, the tone still low-key. It was only in the following year, with the outbreak of war, that the tempo began to quicken. An emergency Public Health Laboratory was set up; linked to the normal laboratory services it covered the whole of the country. Its primary function was to investigate suspicious outbreaks of disease, and to act as the distributing centre for the stocks of vaccine and sera.

In September 1939, Hankey – now with a seat in the House of Lords – was brought into the War Cabinet as Minister Without Portfolio. His influence over Neville Chamberlain had never been greater, and to Hankey the Prime Minister 'confided' the job of Britain's biological warfare overlord with the proviso, recalled

Hankey, 'not to authorise any preparations for the offensive use of bacteria without his approval'.[25] But within a matter of days – as the Wehrmacht smashed through Poland's defences and Hitler at Danzig warned of his 'secret weapons' – the brief changed. The Chiefs of Staff met on 25 September and heard from Sir Cyril Newall, the Chief of the Air Staff, that attention had been drawn

to a form of attack which cannot be regarded as beyond the bounds of possibility – namely, the deliberate and indiscriminate dropping of bacteria with the object of spreading disease. The fact that the German Government have notified us of their intention to observe the Geneva Protocol is, of course, no reason to imagine that they will in fact observe those provisions a moment longer than is necessary.[26]

A sabotage attack by enemy agents using bacteria was 'not impossible in the very near future'. The matter was referred to the War Cabinet and within a few days Hankey had been ordered to step up research into germ warfare.

Towards the end of September [wrote Hankey in 1941] Mr. Chamberlain gave his approval to a proposal that I should authorise experimental work in order to discover what are the possibilities of infection being transmitted by various forms of micro-organisms through the air, so as to give us greater knowledge as to how to protect ourselves against such methods. The work was to be conducted in this spirit and not with a view to resort to such methods ourselves.[27]

Whatever the 'spirit' in which the work was conducted, Britain now began researching in earnest into offensive biological weapons.

A new and highly secret laboratory was established at Porton Down in 1940. It was, one of its early members has recently said, 'a primitive affair – little more than an old wooden army hut'. The tiny biological warfare team, never more than a few dozen strong, was presided over by Paul Fildes. He was detached from the Medical Research Council, which was 'reluctant to associate itself with even defensive work on what was regarded as a morally indefensible perversion of medical knowledge',[28] and 'by an informal compromise' placed on the staff of Porton. Throughout his life Fildes had no qualms about his work. *The Times*, in its curiously unsympathetic obituary of him in 1971, described him as 'by nature and upbringing conservative in outlook' and 'a little vain' about his achievements:

Some found him difficult; to most he was reserved and rather uncompromising in manner, with a quiet, ruminative way of speaking that never varied, even in anger or when, as sometimes happened, he was being devastatingly rude. Those who got to know him had for him a lasting, if occasionally rueful, affection . . .'[29]

In 1940 he was fifty-eight and a confirmed bachelor. Allan Younger, the young explosives expert who accompanied him to Gruinard in 1942, recalls him as small in stature, with a powerful sense of purpose and a passionate belief in the work he was doing.

He gathered around him men with a similar determination. The eminent British biologist Lord Stamp, for example, joined the team in 1941: earlier, in April of that year he succeeded to the family title when his father, mother and brother were all killed in the Blitz. 'I felt useless where I was, at the Public Health Laboratory,' he remembers today, 'and I was determined to pay back the Germans for what they did, and to see that our country was not left defenceless as London was when my family was killed.'[30]

All Fildes' team were convinced – and repeatedly reminded in briefings – that they were in a desperate race against the Nazis. In November 1939, R. V. Jones – in a memorandum after Hitler's Danzig boast – put 'bacterial warfare' first, 'new gases' second and long-range rockets only fifth on his list of German secret weapons 'which must be considered seriously'.[31] According to British Intelligence '. . . the Germans and Russians appear to have carried out considerable research on bacteriological methods of attack. Spraying of the virus of foot and mouth disease, dispersal of anthrax spores, and pollution of water supplies by enemy agents are specifically mentioned.'[32]

In 1940–41 these fears were greatly increased by the threat of invasion. Hankey and the Bacteriological Warfare Committee actually went so far as to recommend the compulsory pasteurization of milk and the chlorination of all supplies of drinking water. Only after the Ministry of Food pointed out the massive cost and administrative difficulties involved were the schemes dropped.[33] Later in the war, the Allies feared that the Germans planned to use the V-weapons to deliver biological agents into the heart of London: the Canadians sent the British 235,000 doses of an antidote to botulinus toxin, the most feared of biological weapons. 'When the V-1 attack was launched in June, 1944,' recalled a Canadian general, Brock Chisolm in 1957, 'and the first flying bomb went off with a big bang, showing that it only contained normal high explosives, the general staffs all heaved an immense sigh of relief.'[34] 117,500 British, American and Canadian troops were issued with self-inoculating syringes to protect them against biological attack during the Normandy landings.[35]

In fact in this, as in so many of its evaluations of German chemical and biological warfare, Allied intelligence was hopelessly wrong. According to evidence presented at Nuremburg, the German decision to investigate biological warfare was not taken until a secret conference of the Wehrmacht High Command in *July 1943*:

It was decided that an institute should be created for the production of bacterial cultures on a large scale, and the carrying out of scientific experiments to examine the possibilities of using bacteria. The institute was also to be used for experimenting with pests which could be used against domestic animals and crops, and which were to be made available if they were found practicable . . . aircraft were to be used for spraying tests with bacteria emulsion, and insects harmful to plants, such as beetles were experimented with . . .[36]

The German biological warfare programme was literally years behind that of the Allies. Work centred on the Military Medical Academy at Posen, under the supervision of a Professor Blome. Experiments were carried out on concentration camp inmates at Natzweiler, Dachau and at Buchenwald, where prisoners were deliberately covered with typhus-infected lice.

Horrific though the experiments were, the Nazi biological project itself never got very far. There is no evidence to sugggest that in two years' work at Posen the Nazis ever managed to produce a feasible weapon. In March 1945 the Military Academy was evacuated in the face of the oncoming Red Army, and Blome attempted to have the whole site destroyed in a Stuka attack. All he salvaged were some plague cultures, which in the event proved unusable: the Russians were already on German soil, and the Germans themselves – none of whom had been inoculated – would have suffered as much as the enemy.

At the end of the war, the Soviet Union pressed for the death penalty for one of the Nuremburg defendants, Hans Fritzsche, on the grounds that he had first suggested the possibility of germ warfare to the German High Command. For Britain and America it was an acutely embarrassing moment. By 1945 they were aware that they had invested vastly more time and effort in producing these 'forbidden weapons' than the Nazis. They insisted – to the fury of the Russians – that Fritzsche be acquitted. To avoid tarnishing their wartime honour, all American, British and Canadian records on their wartime biological weapons programmes remained in the 'Most Secret' category; the British closed their archives to historians until the end of the twentieth century.[37]

Since the war, Britain has categorically stated that she has never possessed any biological weapons. As recently as 1980, at the Review Conference of the Convention on Biological and Toxin Weapons, the British delegation firmly stated: 'The United Kingdom has never possessed and has not acquired microbial or other biological agents and toxins in quantities which could be employed for weapon purposes.'[38] On at least two other occasions in 1980 – on 5 March and 11 March – the same assurance was repeated.

The United Kingdom's declaration is hard to reconcile with the facts.

Although the bulk of the official records are closed, even a department as efficient at 'weeding' out embarrassing secrets from the public archives as the Ministry of Defence lets the odd paper slip through. Documents now show that it was the *British* who mass-manufactured the West's – probably the world's – first biological weapon.

The breakthrough was made by Dr Fildes and his team after a series of open air experiments at Porton in the autumn of 1941. The information went first to a seven-man 'Sub-Committee' (of whose records there is today no trace) consisting of Air Vice-Marshal Peck and representatives from the Army, the Medical Research Council, the Agricultural Research Council, Porton, the Lister Institute and the Ministry of Agriculture and Fisheries. The Sub-Committee's composition suggests that at this stage British interest was confined largely to anticrop and livestock weapons, and this is further confirmed by a 'Most Secret' memorandum to Winston Churchill from Lord Hankey, dated 6 December 1941:[39] 'Most of the work,' he wrote, 'has related to diseases of animals and is continuing.' After three paragraphs giving the background to his involvement in germ warfare, Hankey went on:

The Sub-Committee reports that if ever we should desire, e.g. for purposes of retaliation, to take offensive action, the only method technically feasible at the moment is the use of anthrax against cattle by means of infected cakes dropped from aircraft. The experiments which have been made for the Sub-

Committee give good ground for supposing that considerable numbers of
animals might be killed by this method if it were used on a sufficient scale at
the time of the year when cattle are in the open ... There is, as yet, no
satisfactory experimental basis for other methods, although the possibilities
of certain virus diseases of animals are being actively examined.
5. Readiness to use anthrax as a weapon would involve the following
preliminary preparations:–
(a) The production of adequate quantities of bacteria and their storage in the
laboratory ...
(b) The manufacture of two million cakes. These would be made ostensibly
for an ordinary agricultural purpose without risk of leakage of information,
and then delivered to Porton by an indirect channel for storage until
required.
(c) The provision of machinery for filling the cakes with bacteria ...
(d) Determination of the method of discharge of the cakes from aircraft and
other details for operational use. No special difficulty is expected in this.
6. The above preliminary preparations would take about six months from
the date of authority to proceed. At the end of six months it would be
possible to take offensive action at short notice if that should be decided
upon, e.g. as a measure of retaliation.
7. At the outset of the war both the Allies (French and British), and the
Germans, re-affirmed their intention to abide by the terms of the Geneva
Protocol of 1925 prohibiting the use in war of asphyxiating or poisonous or
other gases and bacteriological methods of warfare. Nevertheless, I would
not trust the Germans, if driven to desperation, not to resort to such
methods. It is worthy of mention that a few specimens of the Colorado
Beetle, which preys on the potato, were found in some half a dozen districts
in the region between Weymouth and Swansea a few months ago: although
these are not important potato districts and no containers or other
suspicious objects were discovered, there were abnormal features in at least
one instance suggesting that the occurrence was not due to natural causes.

'I ask for permission to authorise the preparatory measures mentioned in paragraphs 5 and 6 above,' concluded Hankey, 'as an
essential preparation for possible retaliation.'

Churchill received Hankey's memo on Sunday, 7 December – the
day the Japanese attacked Pearl Harbor. Two weeks later he flew to
the USA for the first Washington Conference leaving the whole
subject in the hands of the Chiefs of Staff. On 2 January 1942 the
Defence Committee met in Churchill's absence and discussed biological warfare. The minutes are a model of official discretion: 'Lord
Hankey was authorised to take such measures as he might from time
to time deem appropriate to enable us without undue delay to

retaliate in the event of resort by the enemy to the offensive use of bacteria.' However, the Defence Committee ruled, there were conditions: 'There must be no operational resort to this method of warfare for purposes of retaliation, *or otherwise*, [authors' italics] without the express approval of the War Cabinet or Defence Committee.' In addition, Hankey was to make sure that the stockpiling of biological weapons 'would not recoil upon ourselves or our Allies' or 'lead to an appreciable diversion of scientific or industrial effort'. The Defence Committee also directed that 'all possible precautions must be taken to avoid publicity on the subject'.[40]

In the event the British did not produce two million anthrax-filled cattle cakes, but five million.[41]

The scale of the project is startling. To have been capable of filling five million cakes, Porton must have been producing anthrax on a large scale. Half a dozen filling machines were installed, operated by female munition workers. The cakes were not the large blocks we are used to today, resembling instead large pellets. Each had a small hole bored into it which was filled with anthrax spores and then sealed; they were all stored at Porton.

It was by any standards a crude weapon. It appealed to Fildes's sense of humour, and one of his favourite jokes was to picture the RAF strewing millions of cakes over the moonlit German countryside, with thousands of them ending up in gardens and streets and 'rattling on the Burgomeister's roof'.

Bizarre though the project was, it would certainly have caused widespread suffering if it had been used against Germany. In addition to the serious food shortages which an anthrax outbreak would have caused, there would also have been human casualties. Cutaneous anthrax, which produces skin ulcers and can lead to septicaemia, is caught by handling contaminated animals. Intestinal anthrax results from eating contaminated meat and is fatal in 80 per cent of cases. British policy on biological weapons had moved a long way since Chamberlain had initially 'confided' it to Hankey. It was to move much further.

According to his own account, Paul Fildes made his most spectacular contribution to the Second World War on 27 May 1942 on a street corner in Prague in Czechoslovakia.

Ever since the establishment of the biological warfare wing at Porton, Fildes had been working on 'BTX' – the botulinal toxins, recently described in a World Health Organization report as 'being among the most toxic substances known to man'.[42] BTX, more commonly known as botulism, generally appears as a particularly virulent form of food poisoning, with an average mortality rate of 60 per cent. Although there is no official confirmation, by 1941 it appears that Fildes had succeeded in turning BTX into a weapon; the British code-named it 'X'.

Chemical and biological weapons have long been favourite tools of spies: the ties between Porton, Camp Detrick in America, and the wartime Special Operations Executive (SOE) and Office of Strategic Services were extremely strong (see Chapter Nine). Both Polish and Russian partisans used biological weapons in sabotage operations against the Germans.[43] In December 1942, for example, the Gestapo discovered a germ warfare arsenal in a four-roomed Warsaw house used by the Polish underground. They reported to Himmler the discovery of 'three flasks of typhus bacilli, seventeen sealed rubber tubes presumably containing bacteria, and one fountain pen with instructions for use for spreading bacteria.' 20 lb of arsenic had also passed through the house.[44] A few days later, Himmler showed Hitler a captured NKVD order instructing the Russian partisans to use arsenic to poison German occupation troops.[45] The raid on the Warsaw house apparently failed to prevent the Poles from continuing to use germ weapons. The Combined Chiefs of Staff learned from the Polish Liaison Officer in Washington, Colonel Mitkiewicz, that in the first four months of 1943 426 Germans had been poisoned by the Polish underground; that seventy-seven 'poisoned parcels' had been sent to Germany; and that 'a few hundred' Nazis had been assassinated by means of 'typhoid fever microbes and typhoid fever lice'.[46]

Against this background it is therefore not surprising that the British Secret Service should have turned to Fildes for help when, in October 1941, they began to plan Operation Anthropoid. Its object: the assassination of Reinhard Heydrich.

It was an almost suicidal mission for those who undertook it, but one which the British regarded as of overriding importance. Heydrich had already acquired a fearsome reputation as the ruthless head of the *Sicherheitsdienst* (SD), the Nazi security service, through which he ran the counter-intelligence operation against British agents in occupied Europe. He was said to be Hitler's personal choice as the man to succeed him as *Führer*, and in

September 1941 he appointed him *Reichsprotektor* of Bohemia and Moravia.

Heydrich was remarkably successful in his new job. By means of the stick and the carrot he turned the Protectorate, with its extensive arms industries, into an important component in the German war economy: with the stick he broke the back of the resistance movement, terrorizing its supporters and eliminating its leaders; with the carrot he enticed the Czech workers into greater productivity by increasing their rations and shortening their working hours. As General Frantisek Moravec, head of Czech Intelligence in London, put it, the autumn of 1941 'was a triumph for Heydrich: the armament industry hummed, a bumper crop was harvested and, with the elimination of the heroes of the resistance, peace and prosperity reigned in Bohemia and Moravia.'[47] The British Secret Service, in conjunction with the S O E and the Czech exiles in London decided to have Heydrich killed.

At ten o'clock on the night of 29 December 1941, a four-engined Halifax bomber took off from Tempsford aerodrome. To help it make the long, hazardous flight over occupied Europe, the R A F laid on a diversionary bombing raid to draw off German radar and fighter squadrons. Four and a half hours after take-off, seven Czechs, in semi-moonlight, parachuted into the snow-covered hills near the small Bohemian town of Lidice.

The men had all been trained at Cholmondely Castle in Cheshire and in an S O E Special Training School in Scotland. With them they carried British arms, wireless and cipher equipment. Two weapons in particular were handled with extra care. They were British No. 73 Hand Anti-tank grenades. Normally these were 9½ inches long and weighed 4 lb. The grenades the Czechs carried were special conversions, consisting of the top third of the grenade, with adhesive tape thickly binding the open end. The grenades each weighed just over 1 lb. It now seems likely that they had been personally prepared by Fildes at Porton, and each contained a lethal filling of X.

The 'Anthropoids', led by Jan Kubis and Josef Gabcik, went to earth with the help of the Czech underground for five months, building up a detailed picture of Heydrich's movements. Astonishingly for so high a Nazi leader he rarely travelled with an armed escort. On 23 May 1942, by a stroke of great good fortune, the Anthropoids learned where Heydrich would be in four days' time. At 9.30 am on the morning of the 27th they took up positions on a hairpin bend near the Troja Bridge in a suburb of Prague on the busy route to Heydrich's fortress HQ at Hradcany Castle. Precise details of what followed differ, but in all there were probably six assassins: four men armed with sub-machine guns and grenades, one with a mirror to flash a signal when Heydrich's car rounded the bend, and Rela Fafek, Gabcik's girlfriend, who was to drive a car ahead of Heydrich: if he was coming along unescorted she would wear a hat.

At 10.31, complete with hat, she drove round the corner. Seconds later came the mirror signal. Gabcik strode into the middle of the road and aimed his sub-machine gun at the bend. Heydrich's open-topped green Mercedes came sailing round the corner, but as Gabcik tried to open fire his gun jammed. As the car slowed, Heydrich screamed at his chauffeur to put his foot on the accelerator, but the driver, a last-minute replacement, kept slamming on the brakes. It was at this point that Kubis hurled one of Fildes's grenades.

Heydrich had just risen to his feet in the now-stationary car when the grenade exploded with a force powerful enough to shatter all the windows in a passing tram. Although it missed the Mercedes, the blast tore off the door. Splinters from the grenade embedded themselves in Heydrich's body. Like 'the central figure in a scene out of any Western'[48] Heydrich leapt into the road, shouting and screaming, then suddenly dropped his revolver. Clutching his right hip he staggered backwards and collapsed. The gunmen escaped.

Heydrich, in considerable pain and bleeding from his back, was driven, fully conscious, in a commandeered van to the nearby Bulovka Hospital. The doctor on duty in the surgery department was Vladimir Snajdr.

Heydrich [he recalled] was alone in the room, stripped to the waist, sitting on the table where we carry out the first examination.

I greeted him in Czech; he raised his hand but did not answer. I took forceps and a few swabs and tried to see whether the wound was deep. He did not stir, he did not flinch, although it must have hurt him. Meanwhile a nurse had telephoned Professor Dick, a German, asking him to come to the theatre.

At first sight the wound did not seem dangerous . . . Professor Dick hurried in. He was a German doctor whom the Nazis had appointed to our hospital.

'What's the matter?' he asked. It was only at that moment that he caught sight of Heydrich. He cried '*Heil!*' clicked his heels and began to examine him. He tried to see whether the kidney was touched: no, all seemed well for Heydrich. And the same applied to his spinal column. Then he was put into a wheelchair and taken off to the X-ray room. Heydrich tried to behave courageously and he walked from the chair to the X-ray machine himself. The X-ray showed something in the wound, perhaps a bomb splinter. Or a piece of coachwork. In short, there was something there inside. Dr Dick thought the splinter was in the chest wall and that it could be extracted by a simple local operation. We had a theatre in the basement for operations of that kind. Dick tried it, but without success. The patient's state called for a full-scale surgical operation: one rib was broken, the thoracic cage was open, a bomb splinter was in the spleen, the diaphragm was pierced.

'Herr Protektor,' said Dick to Heydrich, 'we must operate.'

Heydrich refused. He wanted a surgeon to be brought from Berlin.

'But your condition requires an immediate operation,' said Dick. They were speaking German, of course.

Heydrich thought it over and in the end he agreed that Professor Hollbaum, of the German surgical clinic in Prague, should be called in. He was taken to the aseptic theatre: I was not there; I had to stay in the room where the instruments were sterilized. Dr Dick was the only one who helped Professor Hollbaum during the operation. The wound was about three inches deep and it contained a good deal of dirt and little splinters . . .

After the operation Heydrich was taken to Dr Dick's office on the second storey. The Germans had emptied the whole floor, turning the patients out or sending them home; and they transformed the dining room into an SS barracks. They set up machine guns on the roof and SS, armed to the teeth, paced about the entrance below.

No Czech doctor and no Czech member of the staff was allowed on the floor where Heydrich was. I tried to go up there to ask how he was doing; I said I was on duty and that I was looking for Dr Puhala, but they told me openly that I had no business there.

So I have no exact information on Heydrich's condition after the operation. Perhaps they had to remove his spleen. I did not see him again. But Dr Dick said that he was coming along very well. His death surprised us all . . .[49]

Heydrich's sudden collapse – from apparently only minor injuries to coma and subsequent death – may have baffled the doctors, but in retrospect matches completely the symptomatology of BTX poisoning. After an initial period of calm, lasting perhaps for a day or so, the victim lapses into a progressive paralysis which fails to respond to treatment. As X went to work on Heydrich's central nervous system, the doctors could only stand by helplessly as their famous patient succumbed to the classic symptoms of poisoning by BTX:

a combination of extreme weakness, malaise, dry skin, dilated and unresponsive pupils, blurred vision, dry coated tongue and mouth, and dizziness when upright. As the patient becomes worse, he develops a progressive muscular weakness with facial paralysis, and weakness of arms, legs and respiratory muscles. He may die of respiratory failure unless artificial respiration is applied. There may be associated cardiac arrest or complete vasomotor collapse.[50]

The patient generally either dies or recovers within seven days. A week after the ambush, on 4 June 1942, Heydrich died. Dr Snajdr recalled that the official diagnosis of the cause of Heydrich's death was septicaemia.

Blood transfusions could do nothing. Professor Hamperl, head of the German Institute of Pathology, and Professor Weyrich, head of the German Institute of Forensic Medicine, drew up a joint report on their medical conclusions. Among other things it said, 'Death occurred as a consequence of lesions in the vital parenchymatous organs caused by *bacteria and possibly by poisons carried into them by the bomb splinters* [authors' italics] and deposited chiefly in the pleura, the diaphragm and the tissues in the neighbourhood of the spleen, there agglomerating and multiplying.'
That is all I can tell you.[51]

Heydrich's coffin was borne in state in a black-crêped train into Berlin, escorted by Adolf Hitler's SS guard. The Führer laid a wreath on the grave of 'the man with the iron heart'. 'The German intelligence service,' one historian has written, 'would never really recover from the murder of Heydrich.'[52]
Even so, the mission failed in one of its most vital objectives: to awaken Czech resistance to the Nazi regime. The Germans launched a period of terror. The entire town of Lidice was razed in reprisal: its male population shot, its women and children carried away in trucks. 10,000 Czechs were arrested. The Anthropoids were hunted down and eventually trapped in the crypt of a Greek Orthodox Church in Prague. Kubis and Gabcik were both killed. Yet, wrote General Moravec, one of the planners of the mission, 'our hope that the Czech people would react to the German pressure with counter-pressure did not materialise. Indeed that had been our problem throughout the war and we were never able to solve it.'[53] On the day that Heydrich died 'fifty thousand Czech workers demonstrated against the British-inspired act in Prague.'[54]

Why would the British have sanctioned the use of a biological weapon? Partly they must have wanted to ensure that the assassination of Heydrich, once embarked upon, would be almost certain to succeed: what they knew of X must have convinced them that it was the perfect fail-safe weapon. Certainly there would have been few moral qualms. Those in MI 6 who plotted the killing probably felt that making Heydrich the first victim of a poisoned weapon was a fitting end for so despised an enemy. And it was, also, an opportunity for Fildes to see whether X really would work as a weapon.

There is no *written* evidence of Fildes's involvement in Heydrich's death. The relevant official files are still closed. When asked to comment, Porton Down could only reply that they had no record of this incident; if Fildes was involved, they added, they thought it highly unlikely that any record would have been made.[55] We have therefore only the circumstantial evidence which points to the use of a biological weapon – and the claims of Fildes himself.

The secret of X in Heydrich's murder might have died with the Anthropoids themselves had it not been for Fildes. *The Times* was right when it spoke of a streak of vanity in his character: he made a point of telling a number of colleagues what he had done. Two senior scientists involved in Allied germ warfare have privately confirmed that Fildes told them he 'had a hand' in the death of Heydrich. To a young American biologist, Alvin Pappenheimer – later Professor of Microbiology at Harvard – Fildes was even more melodramatic. Heydrich's murder, he told Pappenheimer, 'was the first notch on my pistol'.[56]

The development of X and its use in Operation Anthropoid was little more than an adventurous interlude in the routine of Fildes's work. The centre of the British germ warfare programme was still anthrax, and how best it could be turned into a weapon of mass-destruction. Tests continued at Porton throughout the spring of 1942, and it was in that summer that Fildes and his team first went up to Gruinard Island in northern Scotland to test the prototype anthrax bomb.

Other biological warfare work continued in Canada. In 1941 a former Superintendent of Porton together with three scientists travelled to Canada to advise on the setting up of a joint gas and germ weapons testing area. The site chosen was at Suffield in Alberta – a vast, bleak tract of prairie between Medicine Hat and Calgary. The cost of opening up and running Suffield was shared by the British and Canadians.

The work of the two countries was to be transformed by the entry into the war of the United States. Ever since the mid-1930s American intelligence had been aware of the growing world interest in biological warfare. In 1940 the US Health and Medical Committee of the Council for National Defense began to consider 'the offensive and defensive potential of biological warfare'. In August 1941 a 'Special Assignments Branch' was formed at Edgewood Arsenal to pursue researches further: in November, with the attack on Pearl Harbor less than a month away, the War Department formed the WBC Committee headed by Dr Jewett of the National Academy of Sciences to evaluate the threat of germ warfare. Its report, still classified today, eventually landed on the desk of the Secretary of War, Henry L. Stimson, in February 1942. It spelt out clearly that America stood in serious danger of biological attack. Stimson felt obliged to act, and on 29 April 1942 he wrote to President Roosevelt outlining the committee's findings:

This committee has made an extensive study and a very thorough report in which it points out that real danger from biological warfare exists for both human beings and for plant and animal life. The committee recommends prompt action along a number of lines, some involving the development of vaccines, some dealing with scientific techniques of defense. Others involve protective measures such as water supply protection, and still others require further research. The matter which the committee considered as requiring the most immediate attention is the great danger of attacks on our cattle with the disease 'Rinderpest' which has been at times most destructive in the Philippines.

Biological Warfare is, of course, 'dirty business' but in the light of the committee's report, I think we must be prepared. And the matter must be handled with great secrecy as well as great vigor ...

Some of the scientists consulted believe that this is a matter for the War Department but the General Staff is of the opinion that a civilian agency is preferable, provided that proper Army and Navy representatives are associated in the work ... Entrusting the matter to a civilian agency would help in preventing the public from being unduly exercised over any ideas that the War Department might be contemplating the use of this weapon offensively. To be sure, a knowledge of offensive possibilities will necessarily be developed because no proper defense can be prepared without a thorough study of means of offense. Offensive possibilities should be known to the War Department. And reprisals by us are perhaps not beyond the bounds of possibility any more than they are in the field of gas attack for which the Chemical Warfare Service of the War Department is prepared ...

Having asked for the report and having now received the disturbing warnings to which I have made reference and especially in view of the recommendation for immediate action, I should appreciate it if you would advise me of your wishes in order that such action as you wish may be promptly taken.[57]

Two weeks after receiving Stimson's letter, on 15 May, Roosevelt gave his approval to the creation of a biological warfare research organization. The following month, Stimson appointed George W. Merck as Director of the War Research Service.

Like Britain, the US feared that enemy agents would use biological weapons in sabotage operations. The scientists at Edgewood Arsenal told their opposite numbers at Porton in a secret meeting of their worry that botulism, for example,

might be used by sabotage agents for the wholesale poisoning of foods ... Mosquitoes and other insects impregnated with bacteria which produce communicable and infectious diseases is another possibility which has caused some argument in this country.[58]

From 1942 onwards the British and the Americans pooled their resources on biological warfare in much the same way as they did on the atomic bomb. In the spring of 1942, for example, an American liaison officer arrived at Porton Down. American officers attended the trials on Gruinard and even made a film of the successful experiment. (The film is still held in Porton's archives.)

The war-strained British economy could probably never have withstood the massive investment in raw materials and scientific skill that a full-scale biological weapons programme would have entailed. The American economy could. Between 1942 and March 1945 the US invested over $40,000,000 in plant and equipment. Almost 4,000 people were eventually employed in biological warfare research, testing and production.

Lord Stamp, who had an American wife he had not seen for three years, was chosen by Fildes as Britain's representative on germ warfare in the United States. Stamp entered Canada and visited scientists working on biological weapons at Ottawa and Kingston before travelling south and crossing into the US in March 1943. He went straight to the National Academy of Science in Washington, avoiding the normal channels of scientific liaison, and joined 'the inner circle of bacteriological warfare'. For the next two years he had a unique opportunity to move across wartime America, travelling between the numerous university laboratories at work on germ weapons, and the four great American centres of biological warfare production: the parent research and pilot plant at Camp Detrick in Maryland (known as 'The Health Farm'); the Field Testing Station at Horn Island, Pascagoula, Mississippi; the large-scale production plant at Vigo, near Terre Haute, Indiana; and the Field Testing Station at Granite Peak near Dugway in Utah.

Churchill was fond of quoting the words of Edward Grey, a former British Foreign Secretary, who once described the United States as a 'gigantic boiler. Once the fire is lighted under it there is no limit to the power it can generate.' So it was with biological weapons. In October 1943, the cloud chamber project was begun at Camp Detrick, in which small laboratory animals had concentrations of biological agent passed over them. For the first time a mass of data began to be obtained about the spread of disease by inhalation: as one expert has pointed out, 'at this time in history, it was not yet widely accepted that the airborne transmission of pathogens was an important factor in the spread of natural disease.'[59]

Like the Gruinard tests, the cloud chamber project proved that a biological bomb or aerosol was perfectly feasible. Among the potential agents studied at Camp Detrick were anthrax, glanders, brucellosis, tularemia, meliodosis, plague, typhus, psittacosis, yellow fever, encephalitis and various forms of rickettsial disease; fowl pest and rinder-pest were among the animal viruses studied; various rice, potato and cereal blights were also investigated.[60] Large-scale freeze-drying methods were pioneered in order to dispense with the less easily stored forms of liquid suspensions. At one point there is said to have been a flourishing Entomological Warfare Department, producing Colorado Beetles, fleas and other insects for use as possible weapons.

America provided the money and resources; Britain provided the brains. One of the best examples of this partnership in action is the little-known story of the development of anti-crop warfare: the destruction of the enemy's food supply by either chemical or biological agents.

In 1940 researchers at Britain's great chemical combine, ICI, discovered a number of substances 'showing powerful growth retarding properties'.[61] Extensive aerial spray tests were carried out over the east of England, and eventually two chemicals were chosen as anti-crop agents. One, codenamed '1313' acted against cereal crops like wheat, oats, barley and rye; the other, '1414', destroyed sugar beet and root crops. They laid waste everything they touched. '1 lb per acre of either substance would result in almost complete destruction of the vulnerable crops under ideal conditions,' reported the scientists.

'In 1941,' according to a highly secret Cabinet paper written after the war, 'their use by aerial distribution over Germany was envisaged. The size of such an operation was however in terms of our resources at that time rather formidable and for this reason and because of the early extension of the war into the corn growing areas of South Eastern Europe, active development was discontinued.'[62] Churchill turned the scheme down because it would have taken the RAF 7,000 sorties 'all made within a month, to reduce the German home-produced supplies of food by one-sixth'.[63] The British chemical industry was under such strain that it would have taken three years, until 1945, to build up sufficient stocks to enable operations to be launched against Germany.

Two years later the merits of 1313 and 1414 were re-examined by Sir John Anderson, the Chancellor of the Exchequer and the Minister responsible for anti-crop warfare. By this time the Americans were also at work on similar compounds; 'but,' wrote Anderson to Churchill in March 1944, 'so far as we know, they do not realise that they can destroy crops, such as clover and sugar beet (with 1414) under ordinary farming conditions'. Nor did they appreciate 'that laboratory trials indicate that 1313 has some action on rice'. Anderson recommended that ICI hand their factory designs and flowsheets over to the Americans to enable them to use anti-crop warfare against the Japanese. British research, meanwhile, should continue. In an ominous aside, which foreshadowed the American 'defoliation' of Vietnam by twenty years, he suggested that 'these substances may have a part to play later on, in connection with arrangements for keeping world peace'.[64]

Churchill agreed. In April 1944 Britain turned over all her technology to the United States. The following year she went one stage further and allowed the Americans to use Porton's tropical research stations in Australia and India for large-scale testing.

A top secret paper prepared for the Joint Technical Warfare Committee in November 1945 on 'Crop Destruction' reveals just how far the American programme eventually progressed. 'In addition to the substances already examined (in the UK) approximately 800 chemical substances have been examined in America'. The weapons eventually produced by pooling the two countries' work were code-named 'LN' – LN8, LN14, LN32 and LN33. LN32 was the only agent produced in Britain; later, in very low concentrations, it was marketed as a weedkiller. One low-flying aircraft loaded with LN could destroy six acres of crops. A large cluster bomb was developed which burst at a height of 3,000 feet and rained down a concentration of 5 lbs of agent per acre. Within twelve hours all the contaminated crops would be utterly destroyed. With 20,000 tons of LN8 the Americans reckoned they could destroy the entire Japanese rice crop; 10,000 tons of LN33 would destroy the corn crop; 1,000 tons of LN32 would destroy all roots.

The American authorities had actually built up a stock of material and were planning an attack on the main islands of Japan early in 1946, calculated to destroy some 30% of the total rice crop. Expert opinion had confirmed that there is no bar under international law or agreement to the use of these substances in war in this way.[65]

By 1945 the Americans also had a range of *biological* anti-crop agents which they were capable of mass-producing: exotic-sounding fungi like *Sclerotium rolfsii* (Agent C) which rots the stems of tobacco plants, soya beans and sugar beets, sweet potatoes and cotton; *Phytophtera infestans (Mort) de Bary* (Agent LO) which causes 'late blight' in potatoes; *Piricularia oryzae* (Agent IE) a fungus which attacks rice; and *Helminthosporium oryzae van Brede de Haan* (Agent E), the cause of 'seedling blight' and 'brown spot' on young rice plants.[66]

In little over a year, incorporating British discoveries, the Americans were in a position to launch a potentially catastrophic attack on their enemies' food supplies. On a couple of occasions the US may have employed some sort of anti-crop agent. In Germany in the autumn of 1944 there was a widespread plague of Colorado Beetles so severe that Schrader, the inventor of nerve gas, was pulled off war work and put on a project to find an insecticide to save Germany's potato crop. From the dock at Nuremburg Göring accused the Allies of deliberately dropping the insects over Germany. In 1945, the Japanese rice harvests were stricken with blight after attacks from

American aircraft, and they were forced to design an ingenious scheme of plot rotation to salvage something of their crops.

The idea of bringing a country to its knees by inducing wholesale starvation was not original. The British, for example, had used a naval blockade against the Germans in the First World War with just such an intention. But, as the authors of the post-war paper pointed out, here was a weapon 'which would be more speedy than blockade and less repugnant than the atomic bomb'. They also foresaw '. . . their possible use for the purposes of internal security within the Empire, e.g. for the destruction of food supplies of dissident tribes in order to control an area . . .'[67]

Britain did indeed employ anti-crop weapons in Malaya soon after the war, but as the Empire dissolved, the opportunities for the British to use them declined. In the post-war world, the use of anti-crop agents as a weapon of world policing would fall increasingly to America rather than the United Kingdom. The story of the Anglo-American biological programme is part of the wider picture of an enfeebled and failing imperial power reluctantly giving way to a rising one: anti-crop agents were one of the tools of the job Britain bequeathed to America.

In the winter of 1943, a year and a half after the first sheep had died on Gruinard, the Allies began to manufacture a biological bomb. It weighed 4 lb and was filled with anthrax spores which were given the code-name 'N'. Its design was largely British, its manufacture exclusively American.

At the time, N was probably the greatest Allied secret of the war after the atomic bomb. All documents connected with it carried the highest security classification: 'Top Secret: Guard' (which the Americans jokingly translated as 'Destroy Before Reading'). In February 1944, when Lord Cherwell, Churchill's scientific advisor, wrote the Prime Minister an account of N, the official typist left blanks in the typescript which Cherwell went through and filled in by hand.

N spores [he told Churchill] may lie dormant on the ground for months or perhaps years but be raised like very fine dust by explosions, vehicles or even people walking about . . . Half a dozen Lancasters could apparently carry enough, if spread evenly, to kill anyone found within a square mile and to render it uninhabitable thereafter . . .

. . . This appears to be a weapon of appalling potentiality; almost more formidable, because infinitely easier to make, than tube alloy [the code-name for the atomic bomb]. It seems most urgent to explore and even prepare the counter-measures, if an there be, but in the meantime it seems to me we cannot afford not to have N bombs in our armoury.[68]

From its small beginnings in a wooden hut at Porton, the biological warfare programme – only four years old – now promised to produce the most potent weapon of mass-killing yet devised. N obviously carried enormous implications for the future of the war, and Churchill immediately invoked security procedures similar to those which surrounded the Manhattan Project. Instead of raising the subject with the full Defence Committee, the Prime Minister initialled Cherwell's minute and passed it on to his trusted liaison officer, General Ismay, instructing him to keep it 'in a locked box' and to raise it personally with the three Chiefs of Staff.

One day later, on the morning of 28 February, Ismay read Cherwell's paper to a secret session of the Chiefs of Staff Committee. 'They feel', he told Churchill that afternoon, 'that Hitler would not hesitate to indulge in this form of warfare if he thought that it would pay him to do so, and that the only deterrent would be our power to retaliate. The Chiefs of Staff accordingly agree with Lord Cherwell that we cannot afford not to have N bombs in our armoury.'[69]

Lord Hankey had by now left the chairmanship of the Bacteriological Warfare Committee (although he would return to it after the war). In his place was Ernest Brown, the Chancellor of the Duchy of Lancaster. On 8 March, after what he described as 'the most secret consultations with my military advisors', Churchill ordered Brown to place an order with the Americans for half a million anthrax bombs: 'Pray let me know when they will be available. We should regard it as a first instalment.'

I should also like [continued Churchill] to have an early report from you as to what would be involved in producing the material on a considerable scale in this country. It might be preferable to fill our bombs over here.[70]

It was clearly galling for the Prime Minister to see what had once been a British project swamped by the larger American one. Yet there was no alternative. In May Brown wrote back to tell him that a full-scale biological programme was simply beyond the scope of the British economy:

The existing small pilot plant in America requires 500 men (bacteriologists, laboratory assistants, chemical engineers and skilled operators), so that we

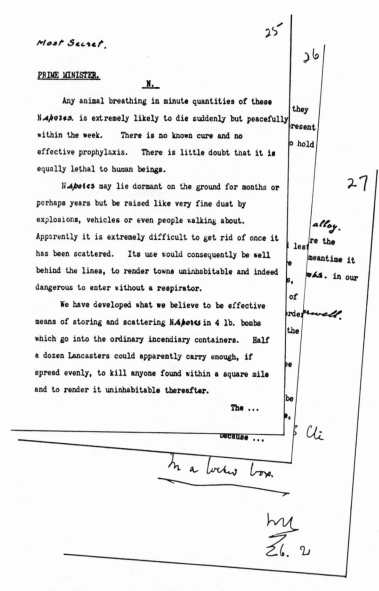

Lord Cherwell's minute to Churchill about the 'appalling potentiality' of anthrax. As a security precaution, the typist left blanks in the text which Cherwell filled in by hand (*Public Record Office*).

A Plague on your Children

should require not less than 1,000 men for a plant of even moderate size. Even if enough skilled workers capable of handling the highly dangerous work could be obtained, there would be serious interference with existing work on medicine and the fermentation industries. Also, any plant erected in this country would be susceptible to danger of air attack, with the particular risks likely to result from a dispersal of the product.[71]

Britain would have to take whatever the Americans chose to give her.

In May 1944 an initial batch of 5,000 anthrax-filled bombs came off the experimental production line at Camp Detrick. In July the first full-scale production is believed to have got under way at a factory whose precise location has not been disclosed. It had a capacity for producing 50,000 Porton 'Type F' 4 lb bombs a month, and its entire production was turned over to the British. This would mean, estimated Brown 'that up to a quarter of a million bombs should be made and filled on our behalf by the end of the year.'[72] The bombs were to be shipped to Britain for storage in case they were needed quickly for 'operational use' in the European theatre. It was a project with obvious hazards. 'Consideration,' wrote Brown to Churchill, 'is being given to the questions of what information as to the contents of the bombs should be given to transport authorities; what instructions should be given to those who will have to handle the bombs; and also what information should be given to certain categories of Intelligence Officers and to the Medical Services.'[73]

The main centre for the production of the Americans' biological bombs was at Vigo in Indiana. Built at a cost of $8,000,000 it employed around 500 people. The disease organisms were designed to be cultivated over a four-day cycle in twelve 20,000 gallon tanks, harvested and then filled into the Americans' own modified version of the Porton 'Type F' bomb, the 'E48R2'. Vigo was capable of producing over 500,000 anthrax bombs a month,[74] or 250,000 bombs filled with botulinus toxin. 'Both of these agents,' wrote one US expert, 'store well and could be stockpiled on a large scale.' The raw materials required for a month's output at Vigo were 300,000 lb of glucose or cerelose, 625,000 lb of corn steep liquor, 1,000,000 lb of yeast, 50,000 lb of casein, 20,000 lb of peptone and 190,000 lb of phosphates. The Vigo plant was highly dangerous to operate and although it was ready to go into production early in 1945 it was never actually used. At the end of the war the factory was leased to an industrial concern for the production of antibiotics. It could, however, have been put back into production in an emergency within three months, although 'only with great hazard to the operators'.[75]

Biological warfare as envisaged during the war would have had one simple aim: to wipe out such a huge proportion of the enemy's population that his whole war machine would cease to function. Accordingly, as Paul Fildes put it in a top secret memo after the war, N was 'designed for strategic bombing'.[76] Individual 4 lb anthrax 'bomblets' were loaded – 106 at a time – into 500 lb cluster bombs designed to burst in mid-air and scatter the spores over as wide an area as possible.

A contingency plan to use N against Germany was drawn up by the British during the war. Rough calculations based on 'results from actual field trials and experiments on monkeys' suggested that if six major German cities – the ones selected were Berlin, Hamburg, Stuttgart, Frankfurt, Wilhelmshafen and Aachen – were simultaneously attacked by a heavy bomber force carrying 40,000 500-lb bombs, '50 per cent of the inhabitants who were exposed to the cloud of anthrax might be killed by inhalation, while many more might die through subsequent contamination of the skin'.

The terrain will be contaminated for years, and danger from skin infection should be great enough to enforce evacuation . . .
    There is no satisfactory method of decontamination. There is no preventative inoculation . . .[77]

It would have taken the Americans eight months to have built up the stock of four and a quarter million 4-lb bombs necessary to mount the attack; 2,700 heavy bombers would have been used in the operation. The death toll in Germany would have been around three million.

We cannot be sure when this plan was drawn up. As one of the target cities – Aachen – fell to the Allies in October 1944 it is reasonable to assume that it was composed before then, possibly in the summer of 1944. We now know that if the war had gone badly for the Allies N might well have been used.

The development of biological weapons was accelerating as the war ended. Attempts were made to develop a method of spraying anthrax from aircraft. Anti-personnel mines were designed. 'The mines,' according to Fildes, 'would contain preformed pellets coated with some suitable biological agent.'[78] Looking ahead, he foresaw a role for germ weapons in the rocket age.

According to another British expert, Brigadier Owen Wansbrough-Jones, in evidence to a top secret sub-committee of the Chiefs of Staff shortly after the end of the war, anthrax 'was 300,000 times more toxic than phosgene'. He predicted that germ weapons would be a hundred times more efficient within ten years.[79] In confirmation of his view, in December 1945, Dr Henderson, Fildes' deputy, reported 'that as a result of continued research the potency of N has been stepped up to the order of ten times. In Dr Fildes' judgement this confirms his statement that continued research by good men may produce important improvements.'[80]

Judged by today's standards, anthrax is a crude weapon. It not only destroys populations wholesale, it renders the cities in which they live uninhabitable for generations. The conquerors would inherit little more than a poisoned desert. According to the Director of Porton Down, speaking in 1981, if anthrax had been used against Berlin in the war, the city would still be contaminated today.[81]

Near the end of the war, the Americans, aware of N's limitations, went on to develop 'US', a weapon designed to spread brucellosis. Like mustard gas, brucellosis has the attraction of a low mortality rate (around 2 per cent) but at the same time a tremendous capacity to inflict casualties. It causes 'chills and undulating fever, headache, loss of appetite, mental depression, extreme exhaustion, aching joints and sweating'.[82] In severe cases, it can put a man out of action for a year. It is also highly infectious: whereas only 200 workers were claimed by the Americans to have been affected by their work on anthrax during the war, virtually everyone associated with the brucellosis programme is said to have felt its effects for a time. The bomb-load required to attack a city was found to be less than one-tenth that of anthrax; the target itself would be contaminated for only a matter of days. By 1945, according to Fildes, US was 'in an advanced stage of development'.[83] As the war ended, the stocks of anthrax-filled cattle cake stored at Porton Down since 1942 were incinerated.[84] From its crude beginning, the Allied biological warfare programme had, in three years, reached a position in which it was being considered in the same breath as the atomic bomb. In his evidence to the Chiefs of Staff Technical Warfare Committee in December 1945, Wansbrough-Jones described the two types of warfare as 'complementary' and suggested that in future germ weapons might be used 'in minor wars on which it was not worth using atom bombs; or major ones in which they were being barred'. The development of brucellosis in particular offered a role for germ warfare in the future.

Biological warfare need not remain a method of warfare repugnant to the civilised world. The further development of types such as US coupled with *a certain amount of informed guidance of the public* [authors' italics] might well result in its being regarded as very humane indeed by comparison with atom bombs.[85]

There was no longer any talk of a weapon which had been acquired 'solely for defensive purposes'. By the end of the war, the programme to develop germ warfare had picked up a momentum of its own: work went on long after it was obvious that Hitler and the Japanese were in no position to mount such an attack. The result was a hidden arsenal of anti-crop sprays, poison gas and germ weapons which the British and Americans have been at pains to play down ever since. On at least one occasion, in 1944, the British very seriously considered using them. Far from being 'a study in re-straints' as one writer has described it,[86] the story of chemical and biological warfare in the Second World War is one of massive stockpiling, subterfuge, blundering, bluff and secret preparation. The world was spared the horrors of germ and gas warfare not by any noble desire to obey international law, but by a chapter of historical accidents.

FIVE

The War That Never Was

. . . it may be several weeks or even months before I shall ask you to drench Germany with poison gas, and if we do it, let us do it one hundred per cent. In the meanwhile, I want the matter studied in cold blood by sensible people and not by that particular set of psalm-singing uniformed defeatists which one runs across now here now there.

Winston Churchill in a 'Most Secret' minute to the Chiefs of Staff. 6 July 1944.[1]

Hours after war was declared, in September 1939, the British ambassador in Berne paid a brief visit to the Swiss Foreign Ministry. He delivered a short message from the British and French governments to be passed on to Hitler. The two countries promised to abide by the Geneva Protocol and refrain from using poison gas and germ warfare, provided the Nazis undertook to do the same. A few days later the German ambassador signalled his country's agreement.

Neither side placed much faith in the bargain. Mention the word 'gas' to any British man or woman over the age of fifty and you are likely to trigger off a series of memory associations: the voice of Neville Chamberlain at the time of the Munich crisis, the sight of children and babies in respirators, the suffocating feeling of first trying on the standard civilians gas mask, the inconvenience of having constantly to carry this strange metal and rubber object in its fragile cardboard box. Crouched in the dark, through innumerable air raids, they waited for a gas attack which in the end never came. At the end of the war, the British alone had manufactured 70 million gas masks, 40 million tins of anti-gas ointment and stockpiled 40,000 tons of bleach for decontamination; 10 million leaflets had been prepared for immediate distribution in the event of chemical attack, and by a long-standing arrangement the BBC would have interrupted programmes with specially prepared gas warnings.[2] Contingency planning ran down to the smallest details. Civilians 'lightly contaminated by gas spray or mustard gas bombs' would have been advised 'to go home, discard their clothes, take a bath and put on a complete change of clothing'. More serious casualties would be sent to special clearing stations, undressed and 'issued with a simple form of garment to enable them to reach home and would be given a small bag in which to take their personal valuables'. Their contaminated clothes would be sent to dry cleaners – specially requisitioned for the purpose – decontaminated and returned.[3]

Over forty years later it is difficult to appreciate just how great the fear of gas was. It was not a fanciful 'terror weapon' – virtually everyone in the country knew someone who had been gassed in the First World War, and knew also that the modern bomber now made it possible for the frightfulness of Ypres to be delivered into the living room. In the early months of enemy bombing, when no one knew what to expect, gas was the most dreaded horror of all.

Chemical warfare loomed equally large in military minds. Right from the start each side worked on the assumption that the other would initiate chemical warfare. When the British Expeditionary Force went to France at the beginning of the war, the General Staff reckoned the Germans would use 160 heavy bombers to deliver 18,000 gallons of mustard gas every twenty-four hours; a third of the entire force was expected to be contaminated daily.[4] Throughout the war, chemical weapons and stocks of anti-gas equipment were moved on to every major battlefield: there were gas dumps in France in 1940, in North Africa, in the Far East, the Middle East, in Italy, on the Russian Front and finally in 1944 in France once again. For six years the introduction of gas warfare continued to be regarded as a day to day possibility by both sides. As a result, poison gas factories swallowed up the war effort of tens of thousands of scientists, technicians and skilled workers. Production never slackened, and by 1945 the world's major powers had amassed around half a million tons of chemical weapons, five times the amount used in the whole of the First World War. Why these enormous reserves were never used has intrigued soldiers and historians ever since. Contrary to most expectations, in this one aspect of warfare – often by the thinnest of margins – the world managed to preserve a precarious peace.

The success of the German *Blitzkrieg* through the Low Countries and northern France in May 1940 at first made worries about gas warfare irrelevant. It did not fit into the strategy of rapid armoured thrusts supported by air strikes which the Germans used to win the

Battle of France: gas slows down armies by forcing them to don respirators and decontaminate their vehicles constantly. Using chemical weapons would in fact have favoured the British and the French, but there is no evidence to suggest that they ever considered doing so. Their stocks could not have lasted for more than a few days, and their commanders – still reeling in shock at the scale of the Wehrmacht's successes – were in no state to add further to the chaos by introducing gas. The campaign ended in four weeks without either side resorting to gas. Only against the stricken British army on the beaches of Dunkirk would an aerial attack using mustard have made sense, but by then Hitler was eager to arrange a peace treaty; gassing helpless soldiers would have destroyed the chances of any negotiations before they even started.

It was the British, in the summer of 1940, who drew up the first serious plans for using gas. On 15 June 1940, only two days after Dunkirk, the Chief of the Imperial General Staff, Sir John Dill, circulated one of the most explosive memoranda of the war. Restricted to a few of the country's top military commanders, shrouded in secrecy for over thirty years, it was entitled 'The Use of Gas in Home Defence'[5] – a brief and cogent military argument in favour of spraying an invading German army with mustard gas.

'So far during this campaign,' began to Dill, 'Germany has not used gas. We may assume that this omission is not from humanitarian reasons but because up to the present it would not have been to her advantage to do so . . .' In the event of an invasion this might well change, and Dill suggested that the War Cabinet be asked to allow the armed forces 'to anticipate the use of the gas by the enemy, by ourselves taking the initiative in our defence against invasion, even if Germany or Italy has not by that time started chemical warfare.'

There are strong military arguments in favour of such action. Enemy forces crowded on the beaches, with the confusion inevitable on first landing, would present a splendid target. Gas spray by aircraft under such conditions would be likely to have a more widespread and wholesale effect than high explosives. It can moreover be applied very rapidly, and so is particularly suitable in an operation where we may get very little warning.

. . . Besides gas spray, contamination of beaches, obstacles and defiles by liquid mustard would have a great delaying effect. The use of gas in general would have the effect of slowing up operations, and we believe that speed must be the essence of any successful invasion of this country.

There are of course grave objections to taking this step . . .

Dill mentioned two 'grave objections' in particular. 'We have bound ourselves not to use gas except in retaliation. To break our word may tend to alienate American sympathy.' In addition, British use of gas would 'immediately invite retaliation against our industry and civil population.' Dill nevertheless considered the risks worth taking and he ended his advocacy of the initiation of gas warfare in ringing tones:

While the probable repercussions must be fully realised I consider that the military advantages to be gained are sufficient to justify us in taking this step. We must expect the Germans to spring one or more surprises on us as part of their invasion plan. We may be sure that every detail of that plan has been meticulously worked out. Some unexpected action on our part, taken promptly and vigorously, might throw all their arrangements out of gear. At a time when our National existence is at stake, when we are threatened by an implacable enemy who himself recognises no rules save those of expediency, we should not hesitate to adopt whatever means appear to offer the best chance of success.

Desperate though the British plight was in June 1940, Dill's proposal ran into a wall of opposition from the military establishment. The Director of Home Defence, on the same day he received the memorandum, scrawled Dill a curt handwritten note:

I do *not* agree that this is a sound suggestion.
We should be throwing away the incalculable moral advantage of keeping our pledges and for a minor tactical surprise; & the ultimate effects of retaliation by the enemy would be very serious in this overcrowded little island.[6]

Even stronger condemnation came from one of Dill's own staff, Major-General Henderson, who described it as a 'dangerous' proposal: 'such a departure from our principles and traditions would have the most deplorable effects not only on our own people but even on the fighting services. Some of us would begin to wonder whether it really mattered which side won.'[7]

In the face of such strong opposition, Dill withdrew his memorandum. But two weeks later, on 30 June, his views suddenly found the backing of the most powerful man in the country – Winston Churchill. After the war, in considering what might have happened if the Germans had invaded, Churchill wrote: 'They would have used terror, and we were prepared to go to all lengths.'[8] 'All lengths', recently declassified documents show, would have included initiating gas warfare:

> Let me have [he instructed General Ismay] a report upon the amount of mustard or other variants we have in store, and whether it can be used in air bombs as well as fired from guns. What is our output per month? It should certainly be speeded up. Let me have proposals. Supposing lodgements were effected on our coast, there could be no better points for application of mustard than these beaches and lodgements. In my view there would be no need to wait for the enemy to adopt such methods. He will certainly adopt them if he thinks it will pay. Home Defence should be consulted as to whether the prompt drenching of lodgements would not be a great help. Everything should be brought to the highest pitch of readiness, but the question of actual employment must be settled by the Cabinet.[9]

It is conceivable that Churchill's instruction was the result of a private approach from Dill; at any rate, the anti-gas lobby were immediately swept aside. Within a week, Britain had scraped together her meagre stocks of gas and had them loaded into aircraft spray tanks and bombs at more than twelve RAF bases from Scotland to the South Coast: all were operationally ready to mount a chemical attack by the end of the first week of July.[10]

Had the German invasion come it would have been met by squadrons of Lysander, Blenheim, Battle and Wellington bombers loaded with spray tanks holding between 250 and 1,000 lb of mustard. 'Low spray attacks,' wrote the Inspector of Chemical Warfare, 'on an enemy approaching our shores in open boats or after landing are likely to be effective if frequently repeated, and will ultimately result in 100 per cent casualties among the men hit by the spray. If the enemy are not wearing eyeshields, a considerable number will be blinded unless they cover their eyes. They cannot do this and use their weapons at the same time. Low spray attacks are therefore likely to reduce the risk to other low-flying aircraft in bombing and machine gunning.'[11]

Britain had only 450 tons of mustard gas in stock (less than one-twentieth of the amount held by the Germans) and the effort would have been concentrated on trying to deliver the whole amount in a single day, to drive the invading Germans straight back into the sea. It was thought that the Germans would not be coming ashore with any spare clothes: 'repeated low spray attacks will leave him defenceless against blistering'. The RAF thus planned to mount the maximum possible number of sorties in a single day. Having made its bombing run over the beach-head and released its gas, it was calculated that each aircraft 'should be able to return the empty tanks to a landing ground near the charging station, and pick up full tanks without delay. Refilling of tanks should only be a matter of hours.'[12]

In addition to spray, 30 lb and 250 lb gas bombs would have been used against 'quays or other areas where stores are being landed'. Although there would be some shelling using gas, and there were 6,000 Livens drums ready to be fired, the main effort would have been delivered by air. 'I consider the results to be obtained from air attack to be so much greater than any other method that, with the limited quantities of gas now available, every gallon should be used for the air arm.'[13]

Dill told Churchill that from the 5 July onwards Britain would be able to mount an aerial gas attack 'on a considerable scale for a limited period' – in all, Bomber Command could carry enough mustard 'to spray a strip 60 yards wide and some 4,000 miles long'. Apart from around 50 tons of phosgene, this represented the whole of Britain's offensive capability, and Dill estimated the spring of 1941 as the earliest possible date on which the country could wage a chemical war using land weapons.[14] In other words, had an invasion actually been mounted by the Germans and Churchill had carried out the plan to use gas, he would have been staking everything on one throw of the dice: he would have to defeat the Wehrmacht in a single day. If he failed the Germans would be able to use chemical weapons without fear of retaliation, possibly as a terror weapon against civilians to try and break the country's will to carry on fighting.

For Churchill it was an intolerable situation. As far back as 1938 the Cabinet had asked for a productive capacity of 300 tons of mustard gas per week and a reserve of 2,000 tons. On 13 September 1939 this target has been reaffirmed by the War Cabinet of which he had been a member. Now he was being told that the RAF had stocks for only one or two days' action. The situation, he wrote, caused him 'grave anxiety': 'What is the explanation of the neglect to fulfil these orders, and who is responsible for it?'[15] The Chiefs of Staff blamed the Ministry of Supply, and Churchill promptly ordered an inquiry. 'I feel this is a very great danger ... I am determined to proceed against whoever was responsible for disobeying War Cabinet orders without even reporting what was going on.'[16]

The inquiry was headed by Clement Attlee, leader of the Labour Party and Lord Privy Seal in the coalition government. He traced the fault to Sir William Brown, Permanent Secretary to the Ministry of Supply, but wrote that 'it would not be right to attribute to any one individual the responsibility for failure'. Brown kept his job.[17]

Instead – in a move which showed the importance Churchill attached to a ready supply of poison gas – the Prime Minister ordered weekly reports of gas production to be submitted personally to him. Every Friday the Secretary to the Cabinet brought the Prime Minister a set of typed figures. For more than two years, Churchill anxiously scanned them, generally scrawling a comment on the bottom sheet: 'Press on' (15 November 1940); 'Press on. We must have a great store. They will certainly use it against us.' (20 November); 'Press on' (13 February 1941); 'Those concerned should be beaten up' (5 April).[18] By January 1941 production of mustard was still only running at 130 tons a week, a third of full capacity, and Churchill asked Lord Beaverbrook, the dynamic Minister for Air-craft Production, to ginger things up. Beaverbrook sacked one official and stopped all holidays. In July 1941, after yet another fall in production, Churchill wrote in exasperation:

The absolute maximum effort must be used with super priority to make, store and fill into containers, the largest possible quantities of gas. Let me know exactly who is responsible for this failure. At any moment this peril may be upon us.[19]

By the autumn of 1941, although the threat of invasion had receded, the production of chemical weapons, under Churchill's relentless pressure, began to accelerate. By 31 October, Britain had built up a reserve of 13,000 tons of poison gas. To boost production further, Beaverbrook authorized an additional expenditure on gas installations of £3,500,000.[20] There were soon to be almost 6,000 people employed in researching and manufacturing chemical weapons in Britain.

They worked in four main centres, protected by military guards and armed factory police. The chief mustard gas plant was at Randle, near Runcorn in Cheshire – hundreds of tons of mustard were stored in five-ton steel 'pots' encased in concrete. Phosgene was manufac-tured at the nearby Rocksavage works and stored 'in drums in splinter-proof trenches'. Runcorn and Rocksavage are in well-populated areas, and were vulnerable to air attack. The Government even issued the local inhabitants with special army gas masks. To try and reduce the danger, a third great storage depot was tunnelled into the Welsh hills in the county of Flint: the installation was code-named 'Valley'.

A second Welsh chemical warfare establishment was at Rhydymwyn, near Mold in Clwyd. Here, the Ministry of Supply built a gas factory which was joined, in 1942, by an even more secret installation: an isotope-separation plant, part of the British project to create an atom bomb. The atomic plant employed over one hundred people, supervised by twenty Oxford scientists from the Clarendon Laboratory. Employees from one site were not allowed into the other, but as workers at both had to carry gas masks it was assumed by the local inhabitants that they were all engaged on the same project; this, it was rumoured, was a scheme to manufacture synthetic rubber.

While thousands of munition workers toiled in the factories, Porton Down designed new weapons:

... there was the 'Flying Cow', a gliding bomb which rained gobbets of thickened mustard gas on the ground during its flight (another version with unthickened mustard gas was known as the 'Flying Lavatory'); the 'Frank-furter', an elongated mortar bomb for smoke; the 'Squirt', a portable high pressure projector which threw 2 gallons of liquid hydrogen cyanide in a jet to a range of about 25 yards ... Perhaps the most ingenious of all the offensive devices was an anti-tank projectile which first pierced a small hole through armour-plate by means of a hollow charge of explosive and then squirted through the hole into the tank enough liquid hydrogen cyanide to kill all the crew. (No acceptable nickname was ever found for this unsporting weapon).[21]

All the while, Churchill continued to pound the Ministry of Supply with threats, instructions, exhortations and advice, normally in the form of 'Action This Day' memoranda. By the end of 1941 he had transformed the situation. The Chiefs of Staff were told on 28 December that Britain could now take offensive action with mustard gas at five hours' notice.[22] Four Blenheim and three Wellington squadrons were trained in the use of aerial spray. 15 per cent of the British bomber force could be employed in chemical warfare. By the spring of 1942 – thanks chiefly to the extraordinary time and trouble Churchill had gone to – Britain had almost 20,000 tons of poison gas.

1 Casualties of one of the first German chlorine attacks, April 1915. The victim could take anything up to two days to die, coughing up pint after pint of yellow liquid – hence the basin by the patient's side.

2 The first British respirators, May 1915. Each man carried a bottle of soda solution with which he was supposed to moisten the flannel. The masks were little protection: on 24 May, 3,500 men were gassed in a single four-hour attack.

3 & 4 The British chemical weapon which the Germans feared most.
Above, Livens Projectors, fired in batteries of 25 at a time; each sent a
drum of 30 lbs of liquid phosgene hurtling into the enemy's lines. *Below*,
on impact a burster of TNT releases a dense cloud of gas. At the Battle
of Arras in 1917, the British fired over 2,000 Livens bombs
simultaneously in one mass attack.

5 Ambulance men drilling in the standard British gas mask, the 'P Helmet', July 1916. The bag of flannel made the face sweat and the chemical which impregnated it then ran, stinging the eyes and trickling down the neck. In addition to the discomfort, the masks often leaked, the eyepieces cracked, and a lethal amount of carbon dioxide could build up inside the helmet.

6 The Battle of the Somme, July 1916. Machine gunners were frequently issued with oxygen cylinders to enable them to withstand a long gas attack and mow down the first waves of the enemy's assault troops.

7 & 8 The men who pioneered the
Allies' wartime germ weapons
programme. *Above*, a rare photograph
taken near the Scottish isle of Gruinard
in 1942, where the scientists first tested
the anthrax bomb. *L to R*: David
Henderson, Donald Woods, O. G.
Sutton and W. R. Lane. *Right*, Dr Paul
Fildes, leader of the British biological
warfare team.

9 & 10 *Opposite*, in a large shed at
Porton Down in 1942, munitions
workers using specially designed
equipment were to fill five million
small cattle cakes with anthrax –
almost certainly the world's first mass-
manufactured germ weapon. These
photographs are at odds with Britain's
1980 claim never to have possessed
'biological agents . . . in quantities
which could be employed for weapon
purposes'.

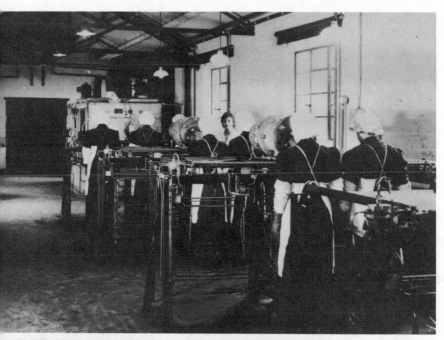

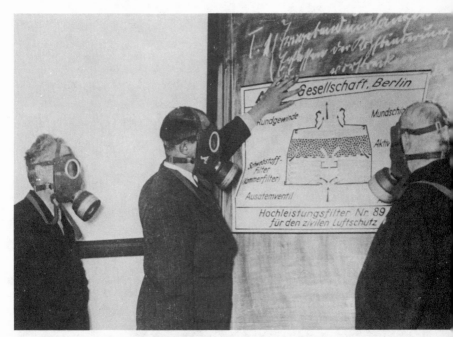

11, 12, 13 & 14 Civilians prepare for gas warfare. *Opposite top*, German High School students are given a lesson in gas precautions. *Opposite bottom*, a dance marathon in a bomb shelter in London's East End provides useful publicity for civil defence. *Above*, Windmill girls rehearse wearing gas masks, April 1941. *Right*, a child's gas mask. The British also developed 'cot respirators' for babies and hood-type gas masks for invalids.

15 & 16 *Right*, the unprimed grenade recovered by the Nazis in May 1942 after the assassination of Reinhard Heydrich. The twin of this specially modified British anti-tank grenade was the weapon which killed Heydrich. Did it contain a filling of lethal germs? *Above*, Heydrich's bomb-damaged Mercedes a few hours after the attack. The Nazi leader suffered relatively minor splinter wounds, but mysteriously died a week later.

17 & 18 The justification for continuing biological and chemical warfare research after the Second World War. *Above*, a Soviet soldier on exercise in anti-gas suit and mask, and *left*, Hungarian troops training against gas. Western intelligence believed the Warsaw Pact was prepared to use gas and germ warfare in any future confrontation.

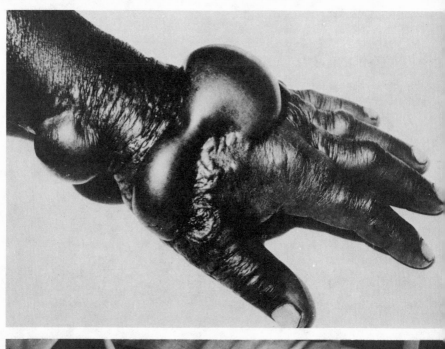

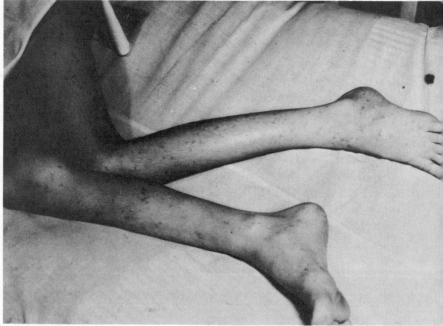

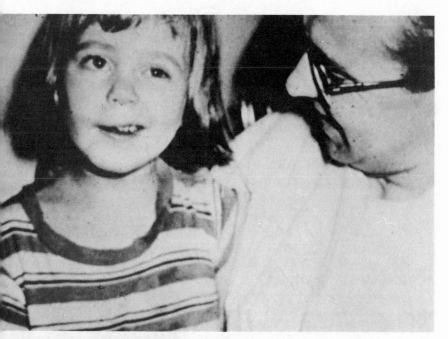

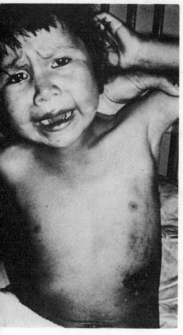

19, 20, 21 & 22 Four of the diseases chosen as weapons. *Opposite top*, the effects of anthrax. Had the Second World War continued into 1946, the Allies expected to be capable of saturation anthrax bombing of six major German cities. *Opposite bottom*, Rocky Mountain Spotted Fever, one of the most severe of infectious diseases, and extensively researched during the 1950s and 1960s. *Above*, facial paralysis caused by encephalomyelitis, several forms of which were refined as 'humane' weapons. *Left*, an early symptom of plague. As the Black Death it had killed nearly one third of the population of Western Europe: during the 1960s it was still being developed as a weapon.

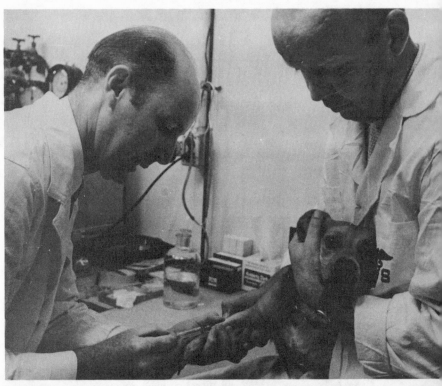

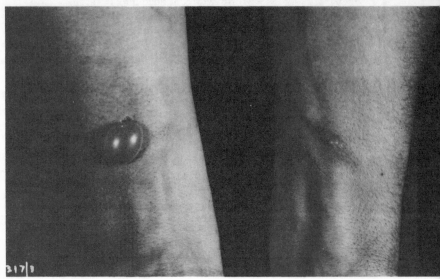

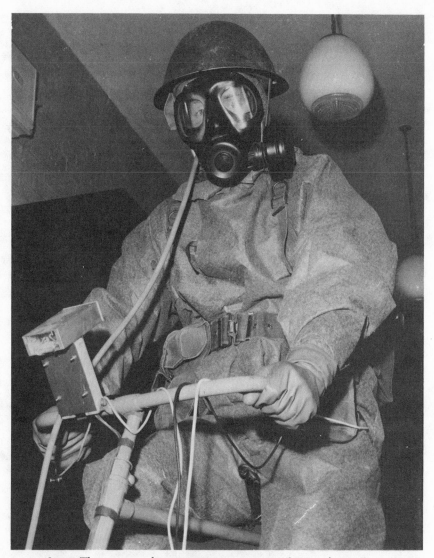

23, 24 & 25 The 1950s and 1960s saw a resurgence of gas and germ research. *Opposite top*, in one of thousands of experiments at Edgewood Arsenal designed to discover a method of waging 'war without death', a dog is injected with an LSD-type chemical. *Opposite bottom*, the effect of only one drop of mustard gas administered to a volunteer at Porton Down. *Above*, a 1960s test of suit and gas mask designed to resist nerve agents. In the UK and USA thousands of servicemen were used to test potential new weapons.

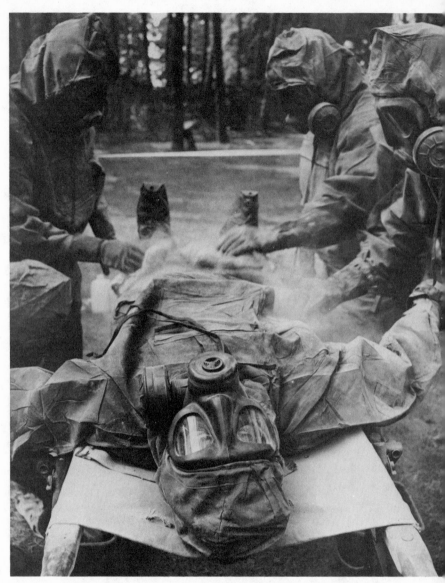

26 Decontaminating a casualty during British exercises in Germany. Nerve agents developed during the 1940s and 1950s are capable of penetrating through the skin itself to attack the nervous system. Casualties – even of bullet wounds – must be 'dusted' all over before being admitted to field hospitals.

27 & 28 Chemical warfare in Vietnam. *Top*, part of *Operation Ranch Hand*, the huge defoliation campaign which was intended to strip the jungle bare. *Bottom*, a 'tunnel rat' emerges from a Viet Cong bunker. US forces used CS gas to flush out the enemy, arguing that, like the defoliation campaign, this was not, despite appearances, chemical warfare.

29 A CIA poison dart gun produced during 1975 Senate hearings into why the agency had disobeyed presidential orders to destroy stocks of biological weapons.

30 British soldiers training against gas attack, 1980. The new gas training range at Porton Down was evidence of mounting alarm at the prospect of chemical warfare in Europe.

Churchill forged the production programme and Churchill re-wrote the country's gas policy. In January 1941, during the 'Victor' anti-invasion exercise, the War Cabinet sanctioned the use of gas.[23] In March 1942, an official minute to the Chiefs of Staff laid down the British position quite clearly: '*It has been accepted* that we should not initiate the use of gas unless it suited our book to do so during the invasion.'[24]

The events of 1940 and 1941 showed that when a country has its back to the wall it is unlikely to put obligations like the Geneva Protocol ahead of military expediency. If a nation's survival is at stake this is perhaps understandable. But as Britain's military position improved, Churchill's willingness to use gas did not diminish. On the contrary – within two years he would actually be pressing for the initiation of gas warfare.

As in every other sphere in the Second World War there was close co-operation between Britain and the United States over chemical warfare. Long before she entered the war, back in the winter of 1940, the Americans secretly began to supply poison gas to the United Kingdom. To preserve her image of neutrality the gas was manufactured in private US plants (which were financed by the British) and then carefully shipped to Europe in foreign-registered vessels; technically the American Government's only official connection was the granting of export licences. At least 200 tons of phosgene a month were being made available to the British using this ruse by the summer of 1941.[25]

It was a remarkable political gamble by the Americans for the deal would have been a propaganda gift to the Germans if they had discovered what was going on. Churchill had opposed the initial approach to the US fearing the repercussions on American public opinion if he should have to use the US gas to repel a German invasion. He was, however, assured that there was strong support in Washington for gassing an invading German army. 'The initial defensive use of gas,' wrote Colonel Barley, the British officer who negotiated the phosgene deal, 'would receive almost universal approbation in America ... The argument that we had signed a convention did not appear to be a good one either to army officers or prominent industrialists.'[26] Barley's report convinced Churchill. Britain took the gas.

The Americans had a different attitude to chemical warfare from the British. Every city in Europe was vulnerable to gas attack, and millions of civilians learned to live with the fear that one day what the enemy's bombers brought might not be high explosive, but mustard gas, phosgene or some new 'super gas'. America was out of range of bomber attack – safe from the fear of airborne chemical retaliation against her cities, the US could contemplate the use of poison gas more dispassionately. Unlike Britain, Germany and Russia there were no legal restraints upon the US to prevent her using gas – the Senate had still not ratified the Geneva Protocol. At the same time the existence of an independent Chemical Warfare Service meant that a powerful pressure group was always around to put its case for an increased Congressional appropriation. In 1940 the US spent $2 million on its Chemical Warfare Service; in 1941 when the chemical rearmament programme was launched, this was increased more than thirty-fold, to over $60 million; in 1942 expenditure reached a staggering $1,000 million. There was a corresponding increase in personnel – from 2,000 to 6,000 to 20,000 in 1942. If the Army, Navy and Air Force were all getting more money, so the argument ran, the CWS should surely get some too. As a result America soon had a poison gas-producing capacity vastly in excess of anything she really needed.

In the three years from 1942 to 1945, the US opened thirteen new chemical warfare plants. The most ambitious was the $60 million Pine Bluff Arsenal in Arkansas. Construction work began on 2 December 1941, five days before Pearl Harbor, on a 15,000 acre site. Within eight months an army of labourers and construction experts had laid miles of road and railway track, built factories, storage depots, laboratories, shops, offices, a hospital, a fire station, a police building, water, gas and electricity supplies and a telephone exchange.

After a time, the statistics of the size and scope of the American poison gas programme begin to glaze the eye.[27] Pine Bluff alone, at its peak, employed 10,000 men and women; it even made use of the labour supplied by a nearby prisoner of war camp. From 31 July 1942 when it first went into production, through to 1945, the Arsenal produced literally millions of grenades, bombs and shells filled with chemical agents, as well as thousands of tons of chlorine, mustard gas and Lewisite. At the end of the war most of it had to be dumped in the sea; its manufacture had cost the American taxpayer $500 million.

The War That Never Was

In 1942 another $60 million installation was opened near Denver in Colorado. The Rocky Mountain Arsenal occupied 20,000 acres, employed 3,000 people and produced 87,000 tons of toxic chemicals by the end of the war. The same year, the Americans opened a test site worthy of their vast investment in chemical warfare – one of the largest gas weapons trial areas in the world, more than a quarter of a million acres on the edge of the Great Salt Lake Desert, in Utah. Known as the Dugway Proving Ground, it was forty times the size of Porton Down and housed test facilities that were a veritable dream for the men of the CWS. Replicas of German and Japanese houses were constructed to examine how well they could withstand chemical attack. Caves were dug into the mountains to see how a well-entrenched enemy might survive a gas shell and bomb barrage. The Americans also acquired from the British an interest in spraying mustard gas from the air; Dugway was so vast there was even room for the USAAF to experiment with high altitude spray. The tests were successful, and the United States, which had entered the war with 1,500 spray tanks, ended it with 113,000.

The Chemical Warfare Service's empire grew huge despite the opposition of the President. Unlike Churchill, Roosevelt had a particular aversion to poison gas, regarding it as barbaric and inhuman. His attitude was well expressed by Admiral Leahy, his senior naval advisor and later President Truman's Chief of Staff. Using gas, said Leahy, would 'violate every Christian ethic I have ever heard of and all of the known laws of war'.[28] Right up until Roosevelt's death, the CWS complained that any proposal they put forward for using poison gas would not be 'seriously considered', but 'immediately rejected due to personal bias' by the President.[29]

Roosevelt was prevailed upon to authorize the giant US programme only because of the widely-held fear that Japan was prepared to initiate gas warfare. Like America, Japan had not ratified the Geneva Protocol, and reports from China continued to suggest that the Japanese were using gas against Chinese soldiers and civilians. One account suggested that 'up to the end of June 1941 the Japanese had used gas 876 times' in their war against Chiang Kai-shek.[30] In October 1941, for example, during a battle in the suburbs of the city of Ichang, Japanese planes were said to have dropped more than 300 gas bombs, many filled with mustard, killing 600 Chinese soldiers and wounding more than 1,000. Photographs of the casualties were published in American newspapers.

Gas atrocity stories make good propaganda, and throughout the war there were regular calls by the US press for America to use gas in revenge. Public opinion polls suggested that as much as 40 per cent of the population favoured the use of gas against Japan, and newspaper headlines screamed their support: 'We Should Gas Japan' (1943); 'You Can Cook 'Em Better With Gas' (1944); 'Should We Gas the Japs?' (1945).[31]

Roosevelt resisted the pressure, although he did issue a series of stern warnings to Japan. 'I desire to make it unmistakably clear,' he stated in June 1942, 'that if Japan persists in this inhuman form of warfare against China or against any other of the United Nations, such action will be regarded by this Government as though taken against the United States, and retaliation in kind and in full measure will be meted out.'[32] The warning was reissued the following year to embrace Germany as well, and expressed in even more sombre language:

I have been loathe to believe that any nation, even our present enemies, could or would be willing to loose upon mankind such terrible and inhumane weapons... We promise to pay any perpetrators of such crimes full and swift retaliation in kind and I feel obliged now to warn the Axis armies and the Axis people in Europe and in Asia that the terrible consequences of any use of these inhumane methods on their part will be brought down swiftly and surely upon their own heads.[33]

It was not to be until the end of the war that the Americans discovered just how exaggerated had been their fears of Japanese gas stocks. Japanese offensive work had actually reached its peak in *1935*. After that it had gone into decline, until by 1941 it had virtually stopped. In 1942 all offensive training at the Narshino Gas School was ended. In 1944 all stocks of gas were recalled by the Japanese High Command. US investigators reported that Japan had developed no gases other than those 'which had been known to the world for 20 years', they had used haphazard research methods, been given no help by the Germans, and that both offensively and defensively the country's supplies were 'inadequate for waging gas warfare on a modern scale'.[34]

At the end of the war, set against just 7,500 tons of Japanese poison gases, the Americans had 135,000 tons: 20,000 tons more than the combined total used by every nation fighting in the First World War.

. . .

Early in November 1943, First Lieutenant Howard D. Beckstrom of the US 701st Chemical Maintenance Company based at Baltimore received orders to prepare to go abroad. He was one of an élite group of chemical warfare experts. Trained at a special centre at Camp Sibert in Alabama, it was one of Beckstrom's jobs to supervise the movement of chemical munitions. His destination on this occasion, he was informed, was the main supply point for the Allied armies in Italy: the Adriatic port of Bari. His cargo was part of the vast American chemical stockpile: 100 tons of mustard gas.

Beckstrom's mission was not uncommon. Throughout the war, the British and Americans moved stocks of poison gas around the world, keeping large dumps close to the various fighting fronts. The Axis powers did the same. Each side shrouded the existence of these stocks in great secrecy for fear that the enemy would discover them and use them as a pretext to initiate chemical warfare. Thus when the British lost Singapore in 1942 the local commander was telegraphed by the War Office in London that it was 'essential no (repeat no) CW artillery ammunition or RAF equipment should fall into Japanese hands'.[35] Supply ships carrying gas bombs at or on their way to Singapore dumped their cargoes in the sea; stocks on land were burnt or thrown into nearby marshes.

Only the senior commander and a handful of his staff ever knew of the existence of gas stocks in his own particular area. It was this policy of strict secrecy which was to lead to the tragedy at Bari.

Beckstrom supervised the loading of the mustard gas at Baltimore onto the SS *John Harvey*, a 10,000 ton merchantman commanded by Captain Elvin Knowles, a veteran of the Murmansk convoys. In all the *John Harvey* carried 2,000 M47A1 100 lb chemical bombs. Just over four feet long and eight inches in diameter, each held 60–70 lb of mustard, enough to contaminate an area of forty square yards. With Beckstrom on the voyage were five other members of the Chemical Warfare Service. They had plenty to occupy them. American mustard gas was notoriously unstable, made by the cheap and speedy Levinstein H process. Each bomb contained 30 per cent impurities – gases which could build up and cause an explosion. The bombs had to be regularly vented, and the casings checked over for evidence of corrosion.

The *John Harvey* arrived at Bari from Sicily on 28 November. Captain Knowles found the harbour choked with Allied shipping.

A *Higher Form of Killing*

Officially even he was not supposed to know the nature of the cargo he was carrying; it was therefore impossible for him to plead with the port authorities to give the unloading of his ship priority. Instead he was ordered to moor at Pier 29 to await his turn.

Four days later, early on the evening of 2 December 1943, the air raid sirens began to wail. That same afternoon, British Air Marshal Sir Arthur Coningham had called a press conference to announce what he considered to be the total Allied air supremacy over southern Italy. 'I would regard it,' he told the reporters, 'as a personal affront and insult if the Luftwaffe was to attempt any significant action in this area.'[36] Now, at 7.30 pm, one hundred Ju 88 German bombers roared in to inflict what proved to be the worst seaport disaster suffered by the Allies since Pearl Harbor.

The attack lasted for twenty minutes. At the end of it, seventeen ships carrying around 90,000 tons of supplies had sunk or were sinking; another eight were seriously damaged. Explosions ripped through the tightly-packed harbour, and shortly after eight o'clock a petrol ship blew up with such force it shattered windows in houses seven miles away. A few minutes later, a second explosion tore through the *John Harvey*. The ship listed and began to sink.

Some of the gas began to burn, some went straight to the bottom of the sea. The rest began to leak out of the ruptured hold and spread through the debris-filled harbour. It mingled with the hundreds of tons of oil floating on the surface to form a deadly mixture. Over the whole scene hung the characteristic odour of garlic – so strong that the men on one ship actually put on their respirators for half an hour. A dense black cloud of smoke mingled with gas began to roll across the harbour and over the town of Bari.

The men who were to be the worst casualties however were not those breathing in the fumes but those floating in the harbour, standing in puddles of oil in life boats, or hanging from life rafts: their entire bodies were being immersed in a lethal solution of mustard gas.

Neither the rescue squads operating at the port and in Bari's hospitals, nor the men themselves had any idea they had been exposed to mustard gas. No one knew what cargo the *John Harvey* had been carrying apart from Beckstrom and his men, and they had been killed along with Captain Knowles in a frantic attempt to scuttle the ship. The hospital was attempting to cope with 800 wounded men (more than 1,000 were already dead) and assumed that most were suffering from nothing more serious than exposure. Still wet, covered in crude oil, they were wrapped in blankets and given warm tea. Most sat quietly in this state for the rest of the night while the mustard gas went silently to work. As a top secret report prepared for the Allied High Command put it two weeks later: 'The opportunity for burn and absorption must have been tremendous. The individuals, to all intents and purposes, were dipped into a solution of mustard-in-oil, and then wrapped in blankets, given warm tea, and allowed a prolonged period for absorption.'[37]

The morning after the disaster, the first of an estimated 630 mustard gas victims began to complain that they were blind. Panic swept through the hospital, and doctors had 'to force them to open their eyes to prove that vision was still possible'. Appalling burns started to develop, variously described as 'bronze, reddish brown or tan' which stripped the body of the top layers of skin. Some men lost 90 per cent of their entire skin covering. According to the report, 'the surface layers came loose in large strips' which 'often took the hair with them'. The burns were 'most severe and distressing in the genital region. The penis in some cases was swollen to three to four times its normal size, and the scrotum was greatly enlarged.' These burns were described as causing 'much mental anguish'. Out at sea, the US destroyer *Bistera*, which had picked up thirty casualties from the harbour at Bari before making her escape, was also in severe difficulties. By dawn the following morning her officers and crew were almost all totally blind, and many were badly burned. It was eighteen hours before they eventually landed in Taranto harbour.

While the *Bistera* was limping into port, the first casualties were beginning to die at the hospital in Bari. Within two weeks, seventy men were dead. Preliminary post mortems showed the classic signs of death from mustard gas: a badly burnt and blistered skin, lungs and respiratory tract stripped of their lining, a windpipe blocked with a solid column of mucous. The only difference was the severity of the symptoms. It was as if, under test conditions, the worst possible mustard gas burns had been deliberately produced. The bodies of forty 'representative' victims – made up of men from 'at least twelve nationalities or races' – were shipped to Porton Down and Edgewood Arsenal 'for microscopic examination and study'.

In the town itself there were similar scenes of misery. More than 1,000 civilians were killed at Bari – many of them as a result of the great cloud of mustard gas which billowed over the town, others after being swamped in the oil-and-mustard tidal wave which engulfed the seafront. For weeks afterwards previously healthy townspeople lingered in their beds. For civilian and soldier alike it was a grim preview of what full-scale chemical warfare might entail.

As the confused details of the disaster reached Allied High Command there were successive waves of panic – first that the Germans themselves had initiated gas warfare, then, when preliminary investigations revealed that the havoc had been wrought by American gas, that the Germans would use it as an excuse to start an all-out chemical war. As the Allied armies were now on the offensive in Italy, and hoped soon to land on the French coast, it was likely that using gas would work greatly to Hitler's advantage. Churchill, informed of the situation by General Alexander, expressed 'his astonishment that a ship with such a cargo should have been sent to Bari'; he would, he said, await the result of an inquiry 'with the greatest interest'.[38]

At first General Eisenhower tried to keep the whole affair secret. The families of the men whose bodies were being dissected in England and America were informed that their son or husband had been killed by 'shock, haemorrhage, etc, due to enemy action'. For all record purposes, Eisenhower proposed to describe 'skin afflictions and burns' and 'injuries to eyes' as simply due to 'enemy action'; 'lung and other complications' were put down to bronchitis. He telegrammed the Combined Chiefs of Staff that he 'considered these terms will adequately support future claims by those injured for disability pensions'.[39] As a further security measure, complete postal censorship was imposed at every British and American military base. The policy of secrecy was approved by Roosevelt and the British War Cabinet.

Nevertheless it was soon apparent that Eisenhower had no chance of keeping what had happened at Bari a secret. Thousands of civilians had fled the town, spreading wild stories of deadly new weapons. Gas casualties had been unloaded at other ports suffering from undiagnosed wounds. By January, Allied hopes of secretly briefing commanders and doctors with details of what had happened had vanished in a welter of rumour and half-truth: 'It is believed that the knowledge is now so dispersed among divergent groups including civilian population in Bari area that no, repeat no, effective briefing can be accomplished'.[40] In February the Chiefs of Staff, after being told that news of the incident was likely to break at any moment, prepared a statement along lines originally suggested by Eisenhower, reiterating that 'Allied policy is not (repeat not) to use gas unless or until the enemy does so first but that we are fully prepared to retaliate and do not deny the accident, which was a calculated risk'.[41]

A few months after the accident, the Allies directed their area commanders to inform their chief medical officers when stores of gas weapons were moved into their localities. In the meantime, the build-up of gas stocks in Italy continued, until there were sufficient chemical weapons stockpiled to enable the Allies to wage full-scale gas warfare in the Mediterranean for forty-five days.

Bari shows very clearly just how sensitive the issue of chemical warfare was among the Allied commanders. Although it rarely features in either official staff histories or personal recollections, thousands of hours were spent by the men who guided the course of the Second World War in discussing gas: when and if it should be used, what new developments there had been, what the other side's policy was, what weapons they had, how best to appear well-prepared for chemical attack without at the same time giving the impression that you were about to launch one. For a war which never was, it occupied much time and deep thought, as well as expertise, money and resources.[42]

This was particularly true in the aftermath of Bari and in the run up to D-Day. The Chief of the United States Chemical Warfare Service writing in 1946 calculated that the use of gas by the Germans against the Normandy beach-heads 'might have delayed our invasion for six months'.[43] That was a situation which the British in particular were anxious to avoid. They were unhappy with Roosevelt's open-ended pledge to embark on full-scale gas warfare if chemicals were used by Japan against China – for the sake of 'one Japanese soldier' using gas, the British Chiefs of Staff feared, the Americans might risk the success of the invasion of Europe. For similar reasons they opposed Eisenhower's ruling as Supreme Commander that white phosphorus could be used by the Allied Air Forces 'wherever it would assist operational plans in support of OVER-LORD'. Normally used to provide a smoke screen, phosphorous could – like napalm – inflect appalling burns if it came into contact with the skin. According to the British this contravened the Geneva Protocol and they asked him to withdraw it from any situation in which it might be used as an anti-personnel weapon. Eisenhower, pointing out that America was not bound by the Protocol, refused, and the British backed down.[44]

Allied anxiety about what the Germans might have waiting for them on the other side of the Channel even ran to the extent of fearing that the Nazis might have some sort of radio-active weapon. This was not as improbable as it might sound. As a by-product of work on the atomic bomb the United States had researched into the feasibility of a 'radioactive gas'. 'Not even the best gas masks,' the Americans informed the British after the war, 'will give protection for long exposure.'[45] Work on radio-active gas was advanced enough for the subject to be brought to the attention of Eisenhower in the run-up to D-Day. General George C. Marshall, the US Chief of Staff, dispatched Major Arthur V. Peterson to SHAEF Headquarters to let Eisenhower into the secret of 'Tube Alloy'. On 11 May 1944 Eisenhower informed Marshall that he took the threat of German use of radio-active material seriously enough to have 'special equipment' . . . earmarked in the United Kingdom for dispatch to the Continent at very short notice.'[46] This mysterious 'special equipment' probably consisted of Geiger counters for measuring the existence of radio-active material. Eisenhower also told Marshall that 'medical channels have been informed as to the symptoms which would occur in these circumstances. This information has been sent out under suitable "cover" . . .'

The 'cover' Eisenhower devised was a circular to the leading medical authorities involved in OVERLORD warning of 'a mild disease of unknown etiology' which had supposedly already been reported. The symptoms the doctors were to look out for were fatigue, nausea, leukopenia (an excess of white cells in the blood) and erythema (reddening of the skin). The 'disease', the doctors were warned, tended to occur in groups: 'sporadic cases are very rare'. Should any cases of this unknown disease be discovered reports were to be forwarded at once to the Chief Surgeon.[47] The 'disease' was, of course, radiation sickness.

Eisenhower told Churchill of the American fear, and Churchill in his turn minuted Ismay: 'I wish Lord Cherwell to explain a certain matter to the Chiefs of Staff at the earliest opportunity, and then for the Chiefs of Staff to let me have their advice thereon. Let this be arranged.'[48]

Cherwell met the Chiefs of Staff on the morning of 19 May, and it was agreed that the possibility of the enemy embarking on this form of warfare in the course of O V E R L O R D need not be taken seriously into account . . . The first twelve instruments [presumably Geiger counters] should be kept in store in Liverpool University . . . No Service personnel should be trained in the use of detectors, but a certain number of civilian physicists should be ear-marked to operate the detectors in case of necessity. There is no need to let these physicists into the secret at present, as instruction in the use of these instruments would be a matter of only one or two days.[49]

There is no further reference to the mysterious 'disease' in the archives. D-Day passed without any use of gas – radio-active or otherwise – by the Germans, and Churchill and the Service Chiefs were quickly forced to turn their attention to more pressing matters.

Six days after the Normandy landings, late on the night of 12 June 1944, a strange stuttering mechanical scream was heard over the southern counties of England; suddenly the noise stopped, and there were a few seconds of silence; then there came a huge sheet of flame and the roar of an explosion. These frightening new weapons were 'C R O S S B O W', the Allied code-name for Hitler's V-weapons. The offensive which had been so long predicted by the secret service had begun, and British civilians were once more back under attack.

Within two weeks the Germans had launched more than 2,000 V-1s against Britain. On 27 June the Home Secretary, Herbert Morrison, reported to the War Cabinet that 1,600 people had been killed and 4,500 seriously wounded; 200,000 homes had been damaged. Morrison warned of a 'serious deterioration' in civilian morale: 'considerable numbers of people were homeless. The attacks had led to serious loss of sleep and the fact that they went on continuously meant that there was no relaxation from the strain'.[50] The Germans were now dropping fifty tons of high explosive on London every day, and nearly 50 per cent of the British air effort was having to be diverted to try to shoot down the flying bombs before they reached the capital.

It was clear to the War Cabinet and the Chiefs of Staff that they had to retaliate – but how? On the night of 21 June Churchill ordered 2,500 bombers to attack Berlin in the heaviest air raid of the war so far. He also suggested that Britain might 'publish a list of, say, 100 smaller towns in Germany, where the defences were likely to be weak, and announce our intention of destroying them one by one by bombing attacks' unless Hitler called off the V-1 offensive. Then, on

4 July 1944, the British turned their attention to poison gas. The Chiefs of Staff called for a report from their think-tank, the Joint Planning Staff, on 'the desirability and practicability of using gas as a retaliation for CROSSBOW attacks. The report should consider the use of gas (a) against the CROSSBOW area alone (i.e. the launching sites), (b) as a general retaliation against Germany.'[51]

The JPS completed their report in twenty-four hours. They turned down the use of gas on purely military grounds:

The use of gas, even employed continuously and in large quantities against these sites all of which have not yet been located, would not be likely to have more than a harassing effect . . .

In our view, it would be impossible to confine the use of gas to attack against CROSSBOW installations and it would be likely that if we initiated it for this purpose, it would bring about the widespread use of gas in Europe.[52]

The JPS picked on three particular arguments against using gas: it would not stop the flying bomb attacks; general gas warfare would be to the disadvantage of the Allies, still precariously lodged in northern France; and the use of chemical weapons would require the prior agreement of the United States, Russia and the Dominion Governments. The Chiefs of Staff accepted the JPS's conclusions, and passed on to Churchill a firm recommendation against using gas.

Churchill, however, was not so easily put off. In May 1942 he had publicly stated that the British were 'firmly resolved not to use this odious weapon unless it is first used by the Germans'.[53] Now his opinion had changed. The flying bomb attacks, indiscriminate in the suffering they bought to London, had enraged him, and fanned his hatred of Germany. The House of Commons might once more have to be evacuated; after months of relative peace, he and his military advisors had been forced back down into their underground bunkers. One bomb had landed in the very heart of the city, blowing up the Guards Chapel at Wellington Barracks in the middle of a Sunday morning service: eighty Guards officers, men and their relatives were killed and another 120 badly injured. Plans were drawn up to evacuate nearly one million people from London as a real sense of fear gripped the capital in a way it never had before, even in the darkest hours of 1940.

To add to the general panic, British Intelligence experts were now (erroneously as it turned out) predicting that the next German secret weapon, the V-2, might carry a warhead of ten tons. The Prime

Minister was haunted not only by his fear of what the Nazi rocket offensive might mean for London, but also by his recurrent nightmare that the Allied invasion of France might end in trench warfare and slaughter on the scale of 1916. On 6 July 1944 Churchill told the Commons that the flying bomb was a weapon 'literally and essentially indiscriminate in its nature, purpose and effect. The introduction by the Germans of such a weapon obviously raises some grave questions upon which I do not propose to trench today.'[54]

Dissatisfied with the first JPS report on gas warfare he set his heart upon another. On 6 July – the same day that he spoke of 'grave questions' in the House of Commons, and the day after the Chiefs of Staff recommended against using gas – he fired off an outspoken memorandum to the service chiefs. It must rank as one of the most extraordinary papers he ever wrote, and is worth quoting in full:

I want you to think very seriously over this question of using poison gas. I would not use it unless it could be shown either that (a) it was life or death for us, or (b) that it would shorten the war by a year.

It is absurd to consider morality on this topic when everybody used it in the last war without a word of complaint from the moralists or the Church. On the other hand, in the last war the bombing of open cities was regarded as forbidden. Now everybody does it as a matter of course. It is simply a question of fashion changing as she does between long and short skirts for women.

I want a cold-blooded calculation made as to how it would pay us to use poison gas, by which I mean principally mustard. We will want to gain more ground in Normandy so as not to be cooped up in a small area. We could probably deliver twenty tons to their one and for the sake of their one they would bring their bomber aircraft into the area against our superiority, thus paying a heavy toll.

Why have the Germans not used it? Not certainly out of moral scruples or affection for us. They have not used it because it does not pay them. The greatest temptation ever offered to them was the beaches of Normandy. This they could have drenched with gas greatly to the hindrance of our troops. That they thought about it is certain and that they prepared against our use of gas is also certain. But the only reason they have not used it against us is that they fear the retaliation. What is to their detriment is to our advantage.

Although one sees how unpleasant it is to receive poison gas attacks, from which nearly everyone recovers, it is useless to protest that an equal amount of HE will not inflict greater cruelties and sufferings on troops or civilians. One really must not be bound within silly conventions of the mind whether they be those that ruled in the last war or those in reverse which rule in this.

If the bombardment of London really became a serious nuisance and great

PRIME MINISTER'S

PERSONAL MINUTE

SERIAL No. D. 217/4

Index..a   87

10, Downing Street,
Whitehall.

<u>GENERAL ISMAY FOR C.O.S. COMMITTEE</u>

1.   I want you to think very seriously over this question of poison gas.   I would not use it unless it could be shown either that (a) it was life or death for us, or (b) that it would shorten the war by a year.

2.   It is absurd to consider morality on this topic when everbody used it in the last war without a word of complaint from the moralists or the Church.   On the other hand, in the last war the bombing of open cities was regarded as forbidden.   Now everybody does it as a matter of course.   It is simply a question of fashion changing as she does between long and short skirts for women.

3.   I want a cold-blooded calculation made as to how it would pay us to use poison gas, by which I mean principally mustard.   We will want to gain more ground in Normandy so as not to be cooped up in a small area. We could probably deliver 20 tons to their 1 and for the

It is a big thing and can ~~~

reason.   I shall of course have to square Uncle Joe and the President; but you need not bring this into your calculations at the present time.   Just try to find out what it is like on its merits.

6.7.44.

rockets with far-reaching and devastating effect fall on many centres of Government and labour, I should be prepared to do *anything* [Churchill's emphasis] that would hit the enemy in a murderous place. I may certainly have to ask you to support me in using poison gas. We could drench the cities of the Ruhr and many other cities in Germany in such a way that most of the population would be requiring constant medical attention. We could stop all work at the flying bomb starting points. I do not see why we should always have all the disadvantages of being the gentleman while they have all the advantages of being the cad. There are times when this may be so but not now.

I quite agree it may be several weeks or even months before I shall ask you to drench Germany with poison gas, and if we do it, let us do it one hundred per cent. In the meanwhile, I want the matter studied in cold blood by sensible people and not by that particular set of psalm-singing uniformed defeatists which one runs across now here now there. Pray address yourself to this. It is a big thing and can only be discarded for a big reason. I shall of course have to square Uncle Joe and the President, but you need not bring this into your calculations at the present time. Just try to find out what it is like on its merits.[55]

Forty-eight hours later, the Chiefs of Staff met to discuss Churchill's dramatic proposal. Sir Charles Portal, Chief of the Air Staff, was sceptical: according to the minutes of the meeting, 'he was not convinced that the use of gas would produce the results suggested in the Prime Minister's minute. It was very difficult to achieve a heavy concentration of gas over a large area.'[56]

There was however one weapon which could possibly overcome this problem: anthrax.

In June 1944 the whole biological warfare programme had come under the control of the Chiefs of Staff. Now, in a minute circulated by the Secretary to the committee, it was pointed out that germ weapons had left the research stage and were in production. After some discussion the Chiefs of Staff

requested the Vice Chiefs of Staff to carry out a comprehensive examination of the points raised in the Prime Minister's minute, and to include in their examination consideration of the possibilities of biological warfare and of the form which enemy reprisals might take.

The Vice Chiefs of Staff passed the matter on to the Joint Planning Staff. The planners' instructions were clear:

The Prime Minister has directed that a comprehensive examination should be undertaken of the military implications of our deciding on an all-out use of gas, principally mustard gas, *or any other method of warfare which we have hitherto refrained from using against the Germans* [authors' italics] in the following circumstances:

(a) As a counter-offensive in the event of the use by the enemy of flying bombs and/or giant rockets developing into a serious threat to our ability to prosecute the war;

or, alternatively,

(b) as a means of shortening the war or of bringing to an end a situation in which there was a danger of stalemate.

The Chiefs of Staff have instructed the Joint Planning Staff to carry out this examination, which should cover the possibilities of the use of biological warfare by us or by the enemy. It should take the form of a thorough and practical examination of the military factors involved and should ignore ethical and political considerations.[57]

These orders were issued on 16 July, ten days after Churchill's initial minute about the use of gas. In the intervening period the Prime Minister had himself apparently broadened the terms of the inquiry to embrace the use of 'any other method of warfare' apart from gas hitherto not used against the Germans. The Chiefs of Staff had independently asked for the inclusion of germ weapons. With the backing of the two most powerful authorities in the country – 10 Downing Street and the Service Chiefs – the stage was now set for a sweeping re-examination of Britain's commitment to the Geneva Protocol. The JPS were specifically asked to consider 'an unrestricted use of chemical and biological weapons'. So secret was their task that they were instructed only to consult *British* military personnel and scientists: the Americans were not to be informed of the policy review.

While the JPS worked on their report, Churchill fumed at the delay. On 25 July he wrote the Chiefs of Staff a curt reminder:

On July 6 I asked for a dispassionate report on the military aspects of threatening to use lethal and corrosive gases on the enemy if they did not stop the use of indiscriminate weapons.

I now request this report within three days.[58]

Late on the evening of the 27th, at a meeting of the War Cabinet, a copy of the long-awaited JPS report[59] was handed to the Prime Minister. Fourteen pages long, it was a complete and chilling review of the precise ways in which using chemical and biological weapons would affect the course of the war.

British and American stocks of gas in the United Kingdom were described as sufficient 'to produce a formidable scale of gas attack on Germany'. Production of gas was sufficient to enable 'a continuous effort by 20 per cent of Bomber Command', but if chemical warfare was initiated, the JPS recommended against a 'continuous effort' and in favour of a massive hammer blow, using the combined strength of the entire British and American bomber force. 25 per cent of the payload would be high explosives, to shatter buildings and spread panic; after that would come the main force, carrying gas bombs.

Phosgene would be dropped 'on the scale of 16 tons per square mile' either against 1,000 tactical targets, or against twenty German cities. The result would be 'heavy casualties amounting to 5–10 per cent deaths of civilians and civil defence personnel'. Mustard gas would be used to attack 1,500 tactical targets, or alternatively sixty cities.

In the large-scale gas attacks on cities, vapour burns would be caused on such a scale as to necessitate wholesale evacuation, thus paving the way to a subsequent incendiary attack. Speedy wholesale evacuation might well be a physical impossibility, in which case large casualties would follow . . .

The initial effect of using chemical warfare against large centres of population in Germany would be to produce great confusion, probably amounting to panic in the areas immediately concerned.

In an appendix, the report's authors included a list of sixty German cities which would be 'favourable targets' in an attack 'calculated to bring about a collapse of German morale'.[60]

The JPS also considered the likely effect of gas warfare on the various theatres of the war. In France:

. . . the first tactical use of gas by us, assuming surprise was obtained, might provide a chance of obtaining decisive local results, thereby enabling us to break through the German defences on a large scale.

On the other hand, if operations in Normandy progress favourably and achieve a degree of fluidity, it would be against the Allied interest to employ gas . . .

Gas on the unprotected populations in the battle area would hamper military operations and unsettle labour. It might seriously impair our relations with the civilian population when it became generally known that chemical warfare was first employed by us.

In the East, in southern France and in the Mediterranean, initiating gas warfare was considered likely to backfire on the Allies by slowing up their advance. In the Balkans 'the use of gas would be likely to deprive us of the active assistance of the Partisans, who are ill prepared for chemical warfare, and of the sympathetic support of civilians whose unhelpful attitude to the enemy at the present time is of value to us.' With regard to Japan there were similar strong military arguments against using gas, particularly as 'during the course of the war against Japan it will probably be necessary to undertake major amphibious assaults of critical importance'. Allied soldiers 'with families at home exposed to gas would be worried and depressed'.

The JPS were in no doubt that 'if the Allies initiated chemical warfare the Germans would immediately retaliate both in the field and against the United Kingdom'. London would be the primary target and could expect to be attacked by flying bombs filled with gas and by up to 120 long range bombers carrying chemical payloads. Repair work to damaged buildings would be slowed up, there would have to be evacuation, and – if phosgene was used – casualties would exceed those inflicted by high explosives 'by a large margin'.

The effect of the use by the enemy of gas on the morale of the British population is difficult to judge. The Ministry of Information reports on morale on the Home Front suggest that when the flying bomb attacks began, some elements of the population were particularly apprehensive lest the bombs should be filled with gas. After nearly five years of war and five weeks' experience of the flying bomb, public morale in the areas affected is less resilient, and might react unfavourably at first if gas were now used, although the shock would diminish as the efficacy of the protective and remedial measures became apparent. The public at large might, however, be resentful of being subjected to gas attack if it felt that this could have been avoided . . .

We believe that the Germans might retaliate on Allied prisoners of war, possibly by forcing them to work in contaminated areas. This would undoubtedly cause great concern to the public at large.

Taking all the factors together, the JPS advised against using chemical weapons. But they put biological warfare in a different category.

For the first and very probably the only time in the war, the use of germ weapons against German cities was contemplated. There is never any mention of the disease under consideration – anthrax – which is referred to throughout the report by its code-name, 'N'.

'N' is the only Allied biological agent which could probably make a material change in the war situation before the end of 1945. There are indications which lack final scientific proof, that the 4-lb bomb charged with 'N' used on a large scale from aircraft might have a major effect on the course of the war.

The 4-lb bombs were loaded, 106 at a time, into 500-lb aircraft cluster bombs. Twenty cluster bombs were regarded as enough to knock out a flying bomb site, 1,000 would contaminate a 'small island', 2,000 a 'large town' of twenty-five square miles. Both the British and the German civilian populations were defenceless against anthrax to which there was 'no known prophylactic measure'.

There seems to be little doubt that the use of Biological warfare would cause heavy casualties, panic and confusion in the areas affected. It might lead to a breakdown in administration with a consequent decisive influence on the outcome of the war.

Whereas chemical warfare was ruled out, JPS did not advance a single military or political argument against dropping anthrax on German cities. The US production programme, however, was stated to be 'behind schedule'. It now seemed unlikely that Britain would have all the quarter of a million anthrax bombs she was expecting by the end of 1944 (the first half of the order Churchill placed with the Americans in the spring: see Chapter Four).

If extreme pressure were applied to the US authorities enough 'N' bombs might be accumulated towards the end of this year for a very few significant token or demonstration attacks to be made on selected objectives, but there is no likelihood of a sustained attack being possible much before the middle of 1945.

The JPS ruled out the use of biological weapons solely on the grounds of time. If the Allied programme had been a year further advanced they might well have come to a different conclusion.

Churchill received a copy of the JPS report on the night of 27 July. On the morning of 28 July the Chiefs of Staff met and approved its contents. They were firmly against the use of poison gas and germ weapons and they added a further significant criticism:

It is true that we could drench the big German cities with an immeasurably greater weight of gas than the Germans could put down on this country. Other things being equal, this would lead to the conclusion that it would be to our advantage to use the gas weapon. But other things are not equal. There is no reason to believe that the German authorities would have any greater difficulty in holding down the cowed German population, if they were subjected to gas attack, than they have had during the past months of intensive high explosive and incendiary bombings.

The same cannot be said for our own people, who are in no such inarticulate condition.[61]

On the 29th, Churchill – who is said also to have received strong representations from Eisenhower against unleashing gas and germ warfare – acknowledged defeat.

I am not at all convinced by this negative report. But clearly I cannot make head against the parsons and the warriors at the same time.

The matter should be kept under review and brought up again when things get worse.[62]

Things did not get worse. The menace of the V-weapons was contained, and the Allied position in Normandy grew stronger; the threat of deadlocked trench warfare, bleeding away millions of lives, which so haunted Churchill, was averted. The Allies were able to finish the war with the promise they made to abide by the Geneva Protocol intact.

It had been a near thing. Although Churchill's idea of using gas seems to have attracted no support whatsoever among the Allied military commanders, the weapon was to hand, and had the war developed differently, the policy might well have changed. Several squadrons of Bomber Command are said to have been given special training in dropping gas bombs in 1944.[63]

And what of biological warfare? None of the arguments which eventually convinced the Chiefs of Staff that gas should not be used applied in the case of anthrax: indeed it was the Service Chiefs, in the knowledge of its destructive power, who had asked for its inclusion in the JPS report in the first place. If its development had been a year further advanced might it not have been used in the summer of 1944? Or, alternatively, could it not have been used at some later date when there were sufficient stocks and if Germany had been able to prolong the war into 1946? At some point presumably the 'ethical and political considerations' deliberately ignored by the JPS and the Chiefs of Staff would have been discussed. When, a year later, a weapon comparable to biological warfare – the atomic bomb – was actually in existence, and offered a chance to shorten the war, the Americans used it. Why, from an ethical or political point of view, should germ warfare have been regarded any differently?

Considering, then, that anthrax might have been used – a weapon of mass destruction with an ability to contaminate terrain almost as great as modern nuclear weapons – the Germans were perhaps fortunate to collapse as quickly as they did. By February 1945, the British were sufficiently convinced that the end of the war was near to wind up all production of poison gas: the Chiefs of Staff asked for permission to discontinue production and discharge the munition workers. It was left to Churchill, the man who had done more than any other to develop the poison gas programme, and who had come close to using it, to issue the necessary order: 'So proceed. The personnel should be thanked. W.S.C. 1.3.45.'[64]

The world missed chemical warfare in the Second World War by inches. It is said, for example, that only the personal intervention of President Roosevelt prevented gas being used against Japan in the closing stages of the war.[65] The so-called 'Lethbridge Report' drawn up for the American High Command recommended soaking the island of Iwo Jima with poison gas in 1944. They concluded that 'the employment of chemical warfare with complete ruthlessness and upon a vast scale' would have a decisive result against the Japanese.[66] The report was approved by the Combined Chiefs of Staff and by Admiral Chester Nimitz, the theatre commander, but when the plan went to the White House it was returned with the comment, 'All prior endorsements denied – Franklin D. Roosevelt, Commander in Chief.' (The Americans went on to suffer 20,000 casualties in their struggle to capture the heavily-defended island.) After Roosevelt's death, the development of the atomic bomb meant that plans to use gas in support of an invasion of the Japanese mainland could be shelved.

From the first year of the war to the last, there was a substantial risk that chemical weapons would be used. The British would certainly have used them against a German invasion. The Russians feared the Nazis would use them on the Eastern Front, and Churchill offered to send Stalin 1,000 tons of mustard gas for retaliation.[67] The German Foreign Minister, Ribbentrop, threatened the Italians with gas attacks if they deserted the Axis cause.[68] According to one report, Göring, under interrogation at Nuremburg, stated that the Nazis did not use nerve gas against the D-Day landings, becaused they feared gas retaliation which would have paralysed the Wehrmacht's transportation system, still heavily dependent on horses.[69] And the British and the Americans both evaluated the benefits of using gas in the closing stages of the war.

At no point was the fact that chemical weapons were banned under international law a major consideration in the decision not to go ahead and use them (except possibly in the personal antipathy of Roosevelt – ironically one of the few countries free from legal obligation not to use gas was led by one of the few world leaders with a moral aversion to the weapon).

Gas was not used because at any given stage in the war there were sufficient military disincentives to stay the hand of the belligerent who reached for the gas weapon. Hitler wanted peace in 1940 more than he wanted to wipe out the men at Dunkirk; by the time he did want to use gas, in 1944, he no longer had the bomber force left to deliver it. The British might have used gas in France in 1940 to halt the *Blitzkrieg* if they had had the stocks; by the time they had the poison gas and the bomber force in 1944 they were on the offensive and would have been slowed down by chemical warfare.

It is impossible to draw any lesson for the future from the non-use of gas in the Second World War – or, indeed, any hope. It was nearly used, but wasn't, because of the precise military circumstances prevailing at the time. These were short-term, and unlikely to be repeated. In 1945 this was appreciated on all sides, and there was no move for chemical disarmament, as there had been after the First World War. The British and the Americans viewed the future of chemical and biological warfare with increasing trepidation. For a new and unknown factor now had to be included in any calculations of military policy in the future: Russia.

SIX

New Enemies

Gas, with the tank and the aeroplane, was one of the most significant developments of the last war, but alone among these three has not been used in this war. The principal reason seems to have been that the power militarily ascendent at various times either had scruples against using gas or believed that his military ends could be best achieved without resort to it . . . We cannot be certain that in a future war an attacking power will be governed by similar scruples or conditions. Indeed, the emphasis on 'Blitzkrieg' (which any aggressor would certainly attempt) would encourage him to employ every means to achieve his end with speed and decision.

Third draft of the Tizard Report, February 1945

At the end of the war British sailors loaded twenty elderly merchant vessels with captured German gas shells, and sailed them into the Baltic. Off the coast of Norway they donned gas masks, placed explosive charges aboard, and then watched as, one by one, the ships exploded, taking tens of thousands of tons of gas to the seabed. From bases in Scotland, one hundred thousand tons of British gas weapons were taken out to sea and sunk. In the Far East American sailors sank captured Japanese weapons in the Pacific. Mustard gas stocks which had fallen to the advancing Russian armies were tossed into the Baltic in wooden crates while machine gunners opened fire and sent them to the bottom of the sea.[1]

But despite these well publicized attempts to renounce gas – a weapon which had, after all not been used during the Second World War – the allies were already beginning to argue among themselves over who should possess the secrets of the Nazi nerve agents. It was inevitable that the advancing allied armies would come across nerve gas arsenals, and, in due course, upon the very factories where the stuff was produced.

The British were in no doubt about what should be done with the stocks of German chemical weapons which fell to their forces. Most would be destroyed, but some supplies of mustard gas and nerve agent would be 'retained for possible use in the Far East'. 'On grounds of security it would have been desirable', a report to the Chiefs of Staff noted drily, 'to prevent such stocks falling into the hands of the Russians *and the French*'² (authors' emphasis). In the event it proved easier to keep the supposedly ideologically reliable French from the nerve gas: over Russian acquisition of nerve agent the British had no control.

Among all the other problems facing Hitler and his General Staff as the noose tightened around Germany was the question of how to dispose of more than 1,200 tons of still secret nerve agent. As early as August 1944 the Nazi chemists had begun destroying the documents which described the research and manufacture of tabun and sarin. By early 1945 the factory at Dyhrenfurth was itself due to be abandoned as part of the general German retreat. On 23 January Wilhelm Kleinhans finally left the factory which had been his home for the previous three and a half years. Inside the buildings a frantic search was continuing for any last evidence of the manufacture of nerve gas. All the bombs and shells had been removed from the underground filling plant, and tons of liquid nerve agent had been poured straight into the River Oder. As the sound of the advancing Russian army grew steadily nearer, demolition experts laid explosive charges beneath all the vital factory buildings. But before they could be detonated, the Russians had surrounded the factory. In a last desperate attempt to prevent the secrets of tabun and sarin falling into Soviet hands, the Luftwaffe was ordered to bomb the place. For reasons still unexplained, the German air force failed. As an American intelligence report put it later: 'It is believed that the full scale GA plant and the pilot scale GB plant at Dyhrenfurth near Breslau fell virtually intact into the hands of the Soviet army, as it swept across Germany.'³ The Russians captured even more than this intelligence assessment suggests: they also took the nearly completed factory at Falkenhagen, where the Nazis had been planning to turn out no less than 500 tons of sarin every month.

There were even more serious implications. In addition to the two factories where the Nazis were producing tabun and sarin, the Russians also discovered the secrets of an even more poisonous nerve agent which the German scientists had refined but not manufactured in quantity. The chemists had first produced the substance they called soman, later known as GD, in the spring of 1944. Tests had shown the new nerve agent to be even more toxic than the two substances the Germans had already adopted for use as weapons.

One can only guess at the reaction of allied scientific intelligence on discovering that the Germans had discovered an even more potent nerve agent. But there was worse to come. During interrogation of one of the German war chemists, Professor Richard Kuhn, in April 1946, British scientific intelligence discovered that all documents relating to work on soman had been taken away on the orders of the German High Command, and buried in a disused mine-shaft ten miles east of Berlin. Professor Kuhn told his questioners that he understood the documents had been removed from the mine-shaft by Professor Colonel Kargin of the Red Army, who had taken them to the Karpov Institute in Moscow.[4]

The British, American and Canadian specialists examining the samples sent back from Germany were, therefore, working under some considerable pressure. While they were still analysing the nerve gases, and attempting to isolate the specific mechanisms within the nervous system which were affected by them, the Russians possessed entire factories which could be rendered operational in a matter of months. While the western scientists worked to discover what, if anything, could be done to counteract the terrifying effects of the nerve agents, the Russians were dismantling the factory taken during the liberation of Poland. Intelligence reports suggested that by 1946 it had been reassembled on the banks of the Volga, and was back in production.

The Western allies were able to take some consolation from the fact that in the over-all balance they had done marginally better than the Russians when it came to personnel: more of the senior German chemists finished the war in British or American zones than in Russian occupied areas. Since the factories already built in Germany represented the 'state of the art' some time previously, in the longer term, with the benefit of the opinions of the German scientists, the west considered itself better placed. But in the short term there was an obvious imbalance. Western discomfort was made more acute when it was announced in June 1947 that a Stalin Prize, First Class, had been awarded to Academician Alexander Arbusov for 'investigations in the sphere of phosphorous – organic combinations', the active ingredients of nerve agents.[5]

Although the sources of information about the Soviet capacity for gas warfare were limited, (in the end one relied upon the evidence of refugees, captured German and Japanese intelligence assessments of the Russian capacity, and scientific deduction), at war's end the Americans concluded that the Soviet Union possessed a wide range of different gases. There were they thought, probably thirteen or fourteen in all, and including First World War gases such as hydrogen cyanide, phosgene and mustard gas, in addition to the nerve agents. The belief that the Russians possessed this large chemical armoury was sufficient to ensure the survival of the wartime chemical defence establishments in the United States, United Kingdom and Canada. But disturbing though the chemical imbalance between west and east might have appeared, Western generals were more immediately concerned about biological weapons.

It might have seemed that the primacy of biological weaponry, with its huge capacity for destruction, had ended when the mushroom cloud rose over Hiroshima on 6 August 1945. Since the western allies now enjoyed immense atomic superiority, there were many who argued that the distasteful business of waging war with disease could be forgotten. Yet the very imbalance caused biological warfare research to receive its greatest impetus: as the Soviet Union at that time had no atomic weapons, it was thought that they might regard biological weapons as a temporary substitute. In the cold war atmosphere of mistrust and suspicion, biological research and propaganda allegations grew steadily.

On Christmas Eve 1949, Moscow Radio announced that twelve Japanese prisoners of war were to be charged with waging biological warfare in China. The Russians claimed that the Japanese had been producing vast quantities of bacteria, and had planned to wage biological warfare against the Allies. The allegations became more specific the next week. Three days later Moscow Radio claimed that Detachment 731 of the Kwantung Army had used prisoners of war for horrific biological warfare experiments, and then, the following day, that one of the prisoners had confessed to his interrogators that the unit had been established on the orders of the Emperor himself. On 29 December *Pravda* came to the point. The United States was protecting other Japanese war criminals, and engaging in biological warfare research herself.

According to an account of the trial published in Moscow the following year, all the Japanese prisoners were sentenced to terms of imprisonment ranging from two to twenty-five years. They were said to have admitted to carrying out gruesome experiments. The evidence of Major Karasaw Tomio was explicit:

Some ten persons were brought to the proving ground, were tied to stakes which had previously been driven into the ground five metres apart, and a fragmentation bomb was exploded by electric current fifty metres away from them. A number of the experimenters were injured by bomb splinters and simultaneously, as I afterwards learned, infected with anthrax since the bomb was charged with these bacteria.[6]

A second Japanese officer was said to have testified that he had watched a fellow officer in Detachment 731 'infecting ten Chinese war prisoners with gas gangrene. The ten Chinese prisoners were tied to stakes from ten to twenty meters apart, and a bomb was then exploded by electricity. All ten were injured by shrapnel contamined with gas gangrene germs, and within a week they all died in severe torment'.[7]

The Khabarovsk War Crimes Trial, as it was known, was more than mere anti-American and anti-Japanese propaganda. New evidence, discussed in Chapter Seven, shows that the United States was indeed shielding Japanese bacteriologists from war crime charges in return for data on human experimentation. But the ringing Soviet denunciations of the barbarity of germ weapons were themselves hollow. Behind the smokescreen of Khabarovsk, the Russians themselves were preparing for biological war.

The Russians were correct to allege that the United States was making plans for biological warfare. But the tone of righteous indignation which accompanied the Soviet pronouncement was, it seems, no more than a smokescreen.

At the end of the Second World War a number of Wehrmacht intelligence files fell into allied hands. Among those of most interest were the documents dealing with what the Germans had believed to be the Soviet capacity for germ warfare. It was clear from these papers that the Russians had begun work on biological defence during the 1930s. According to Russian prisoners and defectors interrogated by the Germans, early research had been conducted by the People's Health Commissariat, and was later transferred to the Red Army Biochemical Institute. Experiments in the production of bacteria had been carried out at a field station on the Volga in the summer of 1935, to be followed up by 'especially dangerous work' in a new field testing station on an island in the Seliger Lake, near the town of Ostashkov, north-east of Moscow.[8] In 1940 a German spy reported the existence of another germ warfare base deep in the southern Soviet Republic of Turkmenistan, some several hundred miles north of the border with Iran.[9] The agent reported that a group of Kulaks who had been banished by Stalin to Vozrozhdeniya Island in the Aral Sea were ordered off at six hours' notice in 1936. The following summer several hundred strangers arrived, and a boat belonging to the Biotechnical Institute appeared on the lake. Unauthorized civilians were instructed to keep at least eighty kilometres away. Little was known of the work carried out on the island, although according to a second source the personnel sent there included physicians, microbiologists, chemists and construction engineers. There were reports of thousands of squirrels being delivered to the island, of a variety whose fleas were capable of transmitting plague. Other experiments were thought to have involved testing tularemia, leprosy, cholera, dysentery, typhoid, paratyphoid and tetanus.

The most sensational allegation to surface in the German reports was the testimony of a Russian deserter by the name of Von Apen.[10] He was an Air Force captain, of part-German extraction, who smuggled his wife aboard his aircraft and landed at a forward German airbase. Von Apen claimed to have been a member of a group specially trained for work in germ warfare. He alleged that the Russians had decided to experiment with germ warfare on the borderland between the Soviet Union and Mongolia. Three diseases were chosen: plague, anthrax, and cholera, under the general codename Golden Triangle. Von Apen claimed to have taken part in experiments in which plague germs had been sprayed from beneath aircraft. In other tests, a specially bred and highly aggressive strain of grey rat had been dropped in parachute cages containing glass phials of bacteria. Upon impact the container would smash, covering the rats, which would then be automatically released from their cages to spread the disease throughout the target area. Other devices he claimed to have seen were glass bombs filled with bacteria broth and artillery shells filled with germs.

Von Apen also alleged that Soviet scientists had carried out human experiments in Mongolia. He claimed that in 1941 experiments had been conducted with plague, anthrax and glanders. The victims had been political prisoners, although Japanese prisoners of war were also thought to have been used. Von Apen described how prisoners in chains would be brought to a tent, on the floor of which were pens filled with plague-infested rats. Prisoners would be made to stay inside the tent with the rats until they had been attacked by the rats' plague-carrying fleas. During the summer of 1941 a prisoner who had been subjected to this grotesque experiment escaped from his captors. A minor plague epidemic began, according to the defector, which the Soviet authorities could check only by calling in the Air Force. Between three and five thousand Mongols died in the attempt to stop the spread of the disease. Their corpses were burned with large quantities of petrol.

In the early days after the Second World War it was extremely difficult for the British or Americans to check many of the astonishing claims they came upon in the captured German files. They concluded, however, that there was more than adequate evidence that the Soviet Union had been, and was still, engaged in some form of biological warfare research. Although little was known of the nature of contemporary work, it was thought that the Russians maintained some six sites for biological warfare research, most of them in the Urals.

The British and Americans recognized that their intelligence was inadequate. But the evidence was judged more than sufficient to justify continuing similar work in the west. When they came to assess the vulnerability of the United Kingdom to a potential germ attack they discovered that London, containing over 12 per cent of the population, was only 500 miles from airbases in Soviet occupied eastern Germany. When the Joint Technical Warfare committee assessed how easy a retaliatory strike with biological weapons might be, they realized that the civilian targets against which bacterial devices would be most effective were dispersed across the huge expanse of the Soviet Union. Even using British Empire airbases in Nicosia (Cyprus) and Peshawar (India), there was only one Soviet city of more than 100,000 population within 500 miles range, and only thirty-five such centres of population within 1,000 miles range.[11] Clearly, at the very least, there should be a major research programme aimed at developing some defence. Intelligence, it was freely admitted, was inadequate. But no such reticence found its ways into the stories which began appearing in the press.

RUSSIA REPORTED PRODUCING 'DISEASE AGENTS' FOR WAR
In eight 'military bacterial stations', one of them on a ghost ship in the Arctic

Ocean, the Soviet Union is mass-producing enormous quantities of 'disease agents' for aggressive use against the soldiers and civilians of the free world. In particular, the Red Army is stockpiling two specific 'biological weapons', with which it expects to strike a strategic blow and win any future war decisively, even before it gets started officially.[12]

This sensational story appeared in the *San Francisco Examiner* from an apparently unimpeachable source, the former deputy chief of US Naval Intelligence.

But despite the tone of certainty which informed this and many other reports, western intelligence on Soviet biological warfare preparations has been woefully inadequate. Much of the information on Soviet plans came from clues picked up in Soviet scientific literature. By watching the award of academic honours, and by noticing obvious gaps in series of published papers, western scientific intelligence could judge what fields of chemical or biological research Soviet Military scientists had entered. The picture was slowly and painstakingly built up to the point where information from defectors or agents could provide the final ray of light. The information was inevitably patchy, sometimes contradictory, and always inadequate. Even after twenty years of intelligence on the subject the most that could be said was that 'the Soviet potential for biological operations is *believed* to be strong, and *could* be developed into a major threat'[13] (authors' emphasis).

There seems little doubt that the Soviet Union did conduct extensive research into germ warfare in the late 1930s and early 1940s. It was felt legitimate to conclude that such research was unlikely to have stopped at some arbitrary point after the Second World War. But firm intelligence to suggest the nature of the work was notably lacking.

For most of the post-war years military microbiologists developed 'retaliatory' germ weapons against threats they did not know to exist, and then attempted to develop defences not against the weapons of a potential future enemy, but against the diseases they themselves had refined.

The Russians have said virtually nothing about their preparations for chemical and biological warfare. Indeed the only official statement that the Soviet Union possessed even chemical weapons was made before the Second World War began, when a Soviet General was quoted as saying:

Ten years or more ago, the Soviet Union signed a convention abolishing the use of poison gas and bacteriological warfare. To that we still adhere, but if our enemies use such methods against us, I can tell you that we are prepared – fully prepared – to use them also, and to use them against aggressors on their own soil.[14]

After this statement, in 1938, the Soviet Union maintained an absolute silence on its capacity for chemical and biological warfare.

To those who doubted whether the Russians were seriously interested in chemical or biological warfare, the specialists would point to the Soviet Army Chemical Troops, established in the 1920s, consolidated in the 1930s, and reorganized during the 1940s.

A former Red Army Colonel who defected to the West claimed that the main reason the Russians had not used gas in the Second World War was that the Soviet High Command had been afraid of German retaliation. He claimed that since the end of the war the importance of chemical warfare training had increased enormously. The Army of Occupation in Germany was equipped with Chemical Units. Training had been intensified. In 1953, for example, the 290th Guards Infantry Regiment was receiving two training sessions of four hours every week. 'Usually', he said, 'one day a week a chemical alarm sounded, and then all instruction – marching, running, driving of motor cars, etc, had to be carried out while wearing a gas mask'.[15] To many western hawks, this was enough. Why should the Soviet Army be training its troops in how to withstand a gas attack, unless the Soviet Army planned such attacks itself?

Certainly during the 1950s, the Russians were expecting chemical and biological weapons to be used against them by the West. In 1956 Marshal Zhukov told the Twentieth Party Congress: 'Future war, if they unleash it, will be characterised by the massive use of air-forces, various rocket weapons, and various means of mass destruction, such as atomic, thermonuclear, chemical and bacteriological weapons.'[16] Zhukov did *not* say that the Soviet Union planned to use these weapons herself. By 1960 the head of US Army Research was telling a Congressional inquiry: 'We know that the Soviets are putting a high priority on the development of lethal and non-lethal weapons, and that this weapons stockpile consists of about one sixth chemical munitions.'[17] If it was true that one sixth of the total amount of weapons available to the Soviet Union was made up of chemical shells and bombs, it represented an alarming threat to the United States and her NATO allies. Some years after this estimate had been acccepted by Congress, however, the American investigative journalist, Seymour Hersh, discovered the basis on which the figure of 'one sixth' had been arrived at.

The American Army had been keen to ship chemical weapons of their own to forward bases in West Germany, said Hersh. They knew the request would be politically sensitive, and so presented evidence to justify its necessity. The proof consisted of analyses made from aerial spy photographs of large storage sheds in the Soviet Union. The sheds looked similar to those at American Army gas weapon bases, and the Chemical Corps then made some calculations. 'The Army computed the roof size of the Russian sheds, figured out how many gallons of nerve gas could be stored in a comparably sized shed in Utah', said Hersh's 'normally reliable' source, 'added a twenty per cent "fudge" factor, and came up with the estimate'.[18]

In the looking glass world of Cold War intelligence gathering, judgements had to be based on whatever information could be gained, from whatever source. If the assessments made from spy photographs were inaccurate, there was more disturbing information from other sources.

On 11 May 1963 a middle-aged Soviet Army officer named Oleg Penkovsky was sentenced to be shot for treason. His trial had been open to observers for only four days, but during that time they had heard a breathtaking catalogue of his alleged crimes. The State Prosecutor told the court that Penkovsky had passed to British and American intelligence some 5,000 separate photographs of secret political, military and economic documents. Even from the few details given, it was clear that Penkovsky was one of the most spectacularly successful agents to have worked for the West.

Although a colonel in military intelligence, Penkovsky had little in common with many of the convinced Party members who made up his colleagues. To begin with, he was the son of an officer in the White Army who had died during the Civil War in 1919 at the hands of the Bolsheviks. Penkovsky had overcome this flaw in his pedigree to rise through the ranks of Military Intelligence, becoming a Colonel by the age of thirty-three. A good looking, open-faced man with a weakness for good food and wine and a solitary cast of mind, Penkovsky looked set to serve out the rest of his military career as a loyal, hardworking officer.

But in 1960 President Khrushchev ordered a review of Soviet military strategy. Penkovsky decided that the Kremlin had concluded that in any future war the Soviet Union would strike first and ask questions afterwards. It was, he felt, a terrifying decision to have reached, and he determined to become a spy.

Penkovsky was instructed to look after a British businessman then in Moscow to arrange for a forthcoming Trade Delegation. The British 'businessman', Greville Wynne, was in fact a spy. He met Penkovsky in his room at the National Hotel, Moscow, where the Russian hinted that he wished to pass on information. When, in April 1961, Penkovsky arrived in London with a Soviet Trade Mission, Wynne arranged a meeting at the Mount Royal Hotel. Here the Soviet officer was introduced to two British intelligence officers who gave the names of Grille and Miles, and two Americans, who called themselves Alexander and Oslap. Penkovsky told the four agents he would continue to work for Soviet Intelligence and to spy for the West at the same time. He had become a double agent. During the next fifteen months he passed on an enormous volume of intelligence material, much of it about plans for chemical warfare.

Penkovsky believed the Soviet Union was prepared to wage both biological and chemical warfare against the West. Exactly what he told his spymasters about Soviet plans for such warfare is not known, even today. During the mid-sixties the CIA sponsored a book entitled *The Penkovsky Papers*, purporting to be made up of extracts from the spy's diary and personal notebooks. According to this account of his intelligence activities, Penkovsky told his MI6 and CIA contacts that there was a 'Special Seventh Directorate of the General Staff which is involved in working out methods of chemical and bacteriological warfare.'[19] He described a testing ground near Moscow where a new type of gas was under development. It was, he said, odourless, colourless, and extremely toxic. The scientists there called it 'American': why, Penkovsky could only guess.

What the 'authorised version' of Penkovsky's intelligence reports did not mention was that the United States, by the time of the book's publication the possessor of the greatest gas arsenal in the world, also intended to ignore the general restriction on 'no first use' of gas. For at the very time that Penkovsky was said to be expressing his horror at Soviet plans which contemplated possible first strikes with chemical or biological weapons, the United States had also taken the decision that she could no longer restrict herself to using the weapons

A *Higher Form of Killing*

in retaliation only. The new United States policy, which will be explored further in Chapter Seven, allowed American forces to attack first, subject only to the approval of the President.

Penkovsky's information was soon pressed into service in the propaganda war. He himself was executed on the afternoon of 16 May 1963. A Soviet general told *Izvestiya*:

When it was announced to him that the Supreme Soviet had rejected his plea for mercy and he was to be executed, there was not a trace of the poseur's manner which he had maintained in court. He met his death like a despicable coward.[20]

Doubtless Penkovsky's information represented only a small part of the over-all volume of intelligence on Soviet plans for chemical and biological war. Its value lay in the fact that it came direct from a Soviet source. Unlike the nuclear armouries of the superpowers, details of which are relatively freely available, the exact size of the chemical or biological arsenals were secret from the moment the Cold War began. In a prevailing atmosphere of secrecy it was inevitable that suspicion should grow.

Many Western authorities believed that the Soviet Union invested heavily in chemical weapons during the 1950s as a cheap alternative to the tactical nuclear weapons which the United States had developed and the Russians could not match. Even by the 1960s there had been little evidence to suggest that the tons of mustard and other gases produced during the Second World War had been destroyed. It was also known that the Russians had the means and the expertise to produce nerve gases: while they began with tabun, soon they were believed to be mass producing soman, or G D, the agent the Nazis had refined but never managed to get into production. Soman is thought to be the favoured Soviet nerve agent, far and away the most powerful of the G-agents, and able to break through the blood/brain barrier with ease. By the late 1960s the Russian array of chemical weapons was thought to range from Lewisite and mustard gas-filled land-mines to shells and bombs charged with blood agents like hydrogen cyanide, and rockets armed with nerve gas warheads.[21]

In response to this perceived threat the West developed a range of weapons which must, to Moscow, have looked equally awesome.

SEVEN

The Search for the Patriotic Germ

Even before the Second World War was over, a small committee in London had begun to plan for future wars. Reporting to the Chiefs of Staff, and through them to the Cabinet, the committee, chaired by Sir Henry Tizard, was charged with preparing a report on 'The Future Potentialities of Weapons of War'. The brief of the committee was so vague that any and every idea seemed worth considering. Could atom bombs be used to cause tidal waves to swamp an enemy? Could chemicals dissolve enemy concrete? Could high voltage be 'thrown', to electrocute an advancing fleet?

Tizard sifted through the various proposals put to him, including a number on the future uses of biological weapons. But his final report[1] concluded that, while atomic weapons would alter the nature of war for ever, biological devices would be of very limited value. He proposed a programme only of defensive research, aimed at inoculating the public against diseases likely to be used by an enemy.

Tizard's report, intended to be a basis of future British defence planning, was presented to the Cabinet in June 1945. In August, an American B29 bomber dropped the first atomic bomb on the city of Hiroshima. The Joint Technical Warfare Committee decided at once that Tizard's report, a cornerstone of future strategic thought, should be rewritten to incorporate the horrific evidence of the effects of atomic weapons. As the committee set about redrafting their proposals they received a series of papers and visits from the men who had led the British Biological Warfare effort during the war, dismayed that their labours and discoveries were being ignored.

At a meeting in November 1945, Dr Paul Fildes dismissed the idea that a country could defend itself against biological attack merely by a programme of research and vaccination: discovering the vaccines could take years, and a mass immunization programme would be so obvious as to invite attack with a different disease. Another submission argued that the use of diseases against crops could not be discounted in future wars. But the most forceful proposal came from Brigadier

Wansbrough-Jones, who suggested that biological warfare research
was younger than atomic weapons research by some twenty years,
having begun only in 1940. 'It seems legitimate to conclude', he wrote,
'that in ten years time, Biological Warfare may be 100 times more
efficient . . . than it is now'.[2] Finally there came the suggestion that germ
weapons might be more suitable for use in wars 'in which it was not
worth using atom bombs, or . . . in which they were barred'.

These forceful arguments from Britain's germ warfare experts
carried the day. The new version of the report on future wars in July
1946 coupled atomic and biological weapons together, even citing a
number of advantages of the latter over the former; for example,
'while it would be difficult rapidly to expand the production of
atomic bombs at short notice, there would be relatively much less
difficulty in the rapid expansion of biological weapons.'[3] This crucial
document, rewritten to include the latest information on the effects
of nuclear war, ended up revising its opinion of, and endorsing,
biological weapons. Copies of the report were made available to the
Pentagon, for it was clear that the pattern which had begun during
the war – of the British initiating research and the United States
producing the weapons – would continue, although now in a far
more pronounced manner. Independently defence scientists in the
United States had reached the same conclusions as their British
counterparts – that in any future war, biological weapons were
almost as likely to be employed as atomic bombs.[4]

In the same way as the Allies had come to believe during the war
that, because they were investigating biological weapons, Hitler was
likely to be doing the same, so now the British and Americans
determined that since they had decided that biological weapons were
likely to be used, even in the terrible new age which had dawned at
Hiroshima, then the Russians must have reached the same conclusion. A limited amount of intelligence, supported by a great deal of
alarmism, appeared to endorse this view. The British and Americans,
when they assessed their vulnerability, reached gloomy conclusions.

The inherent nature of the national economy and pattern of living make the
civilian population of the United States, as well as its domestic animal
population and crops, highly vulnerable to a B W [biological warfare] attack
. . . It must be recognised that defensive measures against a full scale B W
attack would at best be of limited effectiveness[5]

a senior US Chemical Corps officer told the Pentagon.

The Search for the Patriotic Germ

The British wished to concentrate purely on defence against germ attack, but felt it was 'essential to proceed with research into the offensive aspect of biological warfare, as until sufficient research in this sphere had been carried out, the true problems of defensive measures could not be wholly assessed'.[6] It was this attitude which led the British to begin an aggressive recruiting policy which would increase three-fold the small band of microbiologists employed in germ warfare research at the end of the Second World War. It led them to conduct a series of tests with other candidate disease weapons, and in 1947, to establish a separate microbiological research station. The new germ warfare base was to be built next to the chemical warfare station at Porton, and to include what was then the largest brick building in the United Kingdom.

It is some indication of the sensitivity with which British postwar biological warfare work was regarded that almost all of the papers relating to the subject are still not available for public inspection. At a meeting in 1950, the Chiefs of Staff addressed themselves to the problem of unwelcome public attention. The service chiefs were worried by the implication that in justifying the need for biological warfare research, the impression might be created that a germ attack represented a real threat (as they believed it did). In February they agreed a statement to be released 'in the last resort in anticipation of unwelcome publicity':

It is the view of His Majesty's government that the aggressive nature of this form of warfare has been exaggerated. Nevertheless it cannot be discounted and it is their duty to do all in their power to safeguard this country against possible attacks of this nature.[7]

This reassuring statement was a far cry from the Chiefs of Staffs' own assessment of the perils of biological attack.

In the United States, where nearly 4,000 people had been employed at the four top-secret, germ-warfare installations by the end of the war, staff levels were initially reduced. But the man who had led American research into germ weapons during the Second World War, George W. Merck, of the Merck Pharmaceutical Company, recommended that work continue.[8] Camp Detrick, the former National guard airfield an hour's drive from Washington, was chosen for the purpose. The true nature of Camp Detrick's work during the war had been so well concealed that local people knew little or nothing about what went on there. One local rumour was that the place, with its tall chimneys, was being used for the extermination of prisoners.

Over the coming years the scientists at Camp Detrick and Porton Down would investigate almost every known fatal disease. While most would not be tested on humans, the Western researchers were nevertheless able to base much of their work upon a compendium of case studies which supposedly did not exist.

The obsession with germ warfare which developed in the postwar years soon led to disregard for legal scruples. As we have seen, the Soviet authorities did attempt to bring charges against the Japanese officers responsible for the hideous human experiments conducted at field stations in occupied China. It might have been expected that similar charges would be laid against Japanese military biologists captured by the Americans. But in an extraordinary decision which was to remain secret for thirty years, the Americans offered immunity from prosecution if, in exchange, the Japanese would hand over details of their experiments on prisoners of war.

Initially the Americans had been sceptical of reports that the Japanese had tested their biological weapons on human beings. Early reports from Far East Headquarters suggested that they were too unreliable to be taken seriously. When members of MacArthur's staff questioned General Ishii Shiro, the founder of the notorious Unit 731 and the leader of the Japanese germ warfare programme, he produced the standard answer of military biologists the world over: research had indeed been conducted, but purely as a means of defence against possible enemy attack. Since Ishii's staff had destroyed their biological warfare plants and murdered surviving human 'guinea pigs' in the days immediately preceding the Soviet occupation of Manchuria, American investigators could not lay their hands on firm evidence to disprove the claim.

But from the evidence they uncovered during their advance into Manchuria, the Russians concluded that Ishii was lying. They requested permission from the Americans to interview him and other military bacteriologists being held by the United States. Legal advisers in Washington took the view that the Russians had no legal basis for their request, but that it might be considered a friendly gesture to allow them to do so. Beforehand, however, the Japanese were to be interrogated again by American biological warfare specialists. This time the investigation yielded results.

In May 1947 Ishii – frightened by the possibility of being handed over to the Russians – dramatically changed his story and admitted to his interrogators that the Japanese had conducted 'field trials' with anthrax weapons against the Chinese. Nevertheless the majority of the allegations against Ishii and his former colleagues remained no more than hearsay and rumour. In the opinion of several of the legal advisers, they did not constitute the basis for war crime charges. Clearly the question of whether the charges could be made to stand up in court influenced Washington's decision on whether or not to prosecute the Japanese. But by the time this was being considered, the investigation itself was operating in a hazy area in which the demands of justice were being balanced against possible propaganda and intelligence gains. In particular, the Pentagon wished to consider a proposal General Ishii made during interrogation. According to a Top Secret memorandum transmitted to Washington by cable on 6 May 1947, 'Ishii states that if guaranteed immunity from "war crimes" in documentary form for himself, superiors and subordinates, he can describe (the germ warfare) program in detail'.

To assess the value of Ishii's information the Pentagon sent two senior biologists from Camp Detrick to Japan. Dr Edwin V. Hill and Dr Joseph Victor arrived in Tokyo on 28 October, and began their investigations with vigour. On 12 December 1947 they reported that they had interviewed no less than nineteen Japanese biological warfare specialists. They had discovered that the Japanese had investigated an enormous array of diseases, including anthrax, plague, tuberculosis, smallpox, typhoid and cholera. A number of Japanese admitted that they had tested potential germ weapons on human beings.

The American biologists were clearly stunned by the information. The scale of the research far exceeded any tests conducted by the Allies during the war, not only in the range of diseases, but also in the accounts of how particular ailments affected their victims. The Japanese had not only deliberately infected prisoners with disease, but had 'sacrificed' selected cases during their experiments in order to discover the effects of the diseases at different stages.

The experiments were as horrific as any conducted by the Nazis, yet the Camp Detrick specialists dispassionately concluded in their summary of the report of BW Investigations of 12 December 1947 that the potential benefits of the research for the Western biological warfare programme far outweighed the demands of justice. If the

Japanese were to be questioned by the Russians, then they rather than the Americans would obtain the benefits of wartime research. Their concluding recommendation read as follows:

Evidence gathered in this investigation has greatly supplemented and amplified previous aspects of this field. It represents data which have been acquired by Japanese scientists at the expenditure of many millions of dollars and years of work. Information has accrued with respect to human susceptibility to these diseases as indicated by specific infectious doses of bacteria. Such information could not be obtained in our own laboratories because of scruples attached to human experimentation. These data were acquired with a total outlay of $250,000 to date, a mere pittance by comparison with the actual cost of the studies. . . . It is hoped that individuals who voluntarily contributed this information will be spared embarrassment because of it, and that every effort will be made to prevent this information falling into other hands.

This concern to spare the Japanese doctors possible 'embarrassment' found a ready response in Washington where, in order to maintain a lead over Soviet plans for germ warfare, the full extent of American knowledge of Japanese wartime plans was kept secret for thirty years.

The particularly insidious aspect of germ warfare – the opportunity it gives for carrying out an attack without an enemy realizing that he is a victim until it is too late for him to be able to defend himself – particularly appealed to the American Chemical Corps. They began to investigate how easily bacteriological weapons might be used in clandestine guerilla operations against large government buildings housing thousands of vital government workers. They decided to mount a dummy attack on the largest office building in the world, the Pentagon, headquarters of the United States armed forces. Men from the newly established Special Operations Division at Camp Detrick simply walked into the massive building, and dropped a pint and a half of harmless bacteria into the air conditioning system. They reported later that it had been enough to prove that a biological warfare agent could be spread throughout the building. Other possibilities they considered were the contamination of food, paper, or, particularly, water supplies. 'Saboteurs,' they decided, 'equipped with small quantities of botulinus toxin, cholera, dysentery or typhoid organisms could introduce effective quantities into the water system of a city by pumping the agent into a fawcet located near a principal water main'.[9]

But there was the possibility of an even larger attack. Diseases might be sprayed into the air from a ship or aircraft, and allowed to drift across the country. To discover whether such attacks, feasible in theory, were practical propositions, the British, Canadians and Americans collaborated in a succession of experiments. After preliminary meteorological research to discover how clouds of bacteria might behave at altitude, they began a series of mock attacks.

The details of many of the experiments, which effected the lives of millions of people, are still classified. It is known, however, that in 1948 the British War Office conducted an exercise known as Operation Pandora, to determine the vulnerability of the United Kingdom to 'weapons of mass destruction', the now accepted form of words for atomic and biological weapons. In the winter of the same year ships of the Royal Navy carrying British, Canadian and American microbiologists were sent to the Caribbean for Operation Harness. Over thirty years later, the results of Operation Harness are held to contain 'information, the disclosure of which is presumed to cause identifiable damage to national security'.[10] Operation Harness is commonly thought to have been an exercise in which harmless bacteria were released to simulate a germ attack. In fact real germ weapons were used. Nor was Operation Harness unique. There were at least two other exercises in the Caribbean in which real diseases were tested. They were code-named Operations Ozone and Negation and took place in the winters of 1953 and 1954. Several thousand animals were brought from Porton Down and tethered to rafts at sea some miles off the Bahamas, which was then a British colony. The microbiologists watched through binoculars, as from upwind clouds of bacteria were released to drift over the animals. The diseases tested are thought to have included anthrax, brucellosis and tularemia. The corpses of the infected animals were burned at sea.

While these tests showed the relative virulence of the diseases under examination, they did not solve the central problem of how easy it would be to attack a large city or military base. Experiments with harmless bacteria soon after the war had shown how easy it was for germs to penetrate the interior of a sealed ship, but now attacks were needed against civilian targets. Over the next two decades there would be over 200 experiments in the United States alone in which military and civilian targets, including whole cities, would be attacked with imitation biological weapons. The tests were conducted in total secrecy. If inquisitive officials asked questions they were told the army was conducting experiments with smokescreens to protect the city from radar detection. The targets of the attacks ranged from isolated rural communities to entire cities, including New York and San Francisco.

One of the earliest experiments took place in San Francisco in 1950. The Pentagon believed it might be possible for a Soviet submarine to slip into an American harbour, release a cloud of bacteria, and disappear before the victims of the attack had even begun reporting to hospital. San Francisco, the headquarters of the Sixth Army and much of the Pacific fleet, seemed a likely target for such an attack. Between 20 and 26 September 1950, the theory was tested by two US Navy minesweepers steaming up and down outside the Golden Gate Bridge. On board the naval vessels crewmen released clouds of a spray contaminated with *Bacillus globigii* and *Serratia marcescens*, two supposedly harmless bacteria. The *Serratia marcescens* strain, code-named '8 UK' had been developed at Porton Down during the Second World War because when incubated it turned red, making it very easily identifiable when used in biological warfare experiments.

There were six mock attacks on the city. In their report later the scientists concluded that 117 square miles of the San Francisco area had been contaminated, and that almost everyone in the city had inhaled the bacteria. 'In other words', they wrote, 'nearly every one of the 800,000 people in San Francisco exposed to the cloud at normal breathing rate . . . inhaled 5000 or more particles. Any other area having a steady wind and a degree of atmospheric stability comparable to San Francisco is vulnerable to a similar type of attack, and there are many such areas in the US and elsewhere'.[11] The point had been proved.

But the San Francisco test was only one of many. In 1951, American Navy personnel deliberately contaminated ten wooden boxes with *Serratia marcescens*, *Bacillus globigii* and *Aspergillus fumigatus* before they were shipped from a supply depot in Pennsylvania to the navy base in Norfolk, Virginia. The tests were designed to establish how easily disease might be spread among the people employed to handle the boxes at the supply depot. Of the three infectious bacteria, *Aspergillus fumigatis* had been specifically chosen because black workers at the base would be particularly susceptible to it.

In 1953, after further tests spraying supposedly harmless chemicals and bacteria off the United States coast, the Chemical Corps travelled north to spray the Canadian city of Winnipeg. City officials were told that 'an invisible smokescreen' was being laid over the city. (A similar excuse had been used in tests in Minneapolis, where councillors were told that a smokescreen was being laid to protect the city from radar detection.) There were further tests at Stony Mountain, Manitoba, where the experimenters ran into unexpected problems. According to their report, 'cattle in the area levelled many of the sampler stakes, and considerable time was lost in relocating them . . . (and) there was no adequate defence against the hordes of mosquitoes present in this rural area'.[12] How the scientists survived this biological attack is not recorded.

The British contribution to an understanding of how germ attacks might be carried out was considerable, although Porton Down carried out far fewer such tests. Much of the early American work on how clouds might drift over a city was based on the results of experiments conducted by Porton scientists in which they released smoke clouds in built up areas of Salisbury, Wiltshire, just down the road from the Microbiological Research Establishment, and at Southampton in Hampshire.

The extreme secrecy which characterizes British defence matters makes it impossible at this stage to build up a full picture of British tests, since many are still classified. However, it is known that in 1952 ships of the Royal Navy released clouds of bacteria off the west coast of Scotland. A Ministry of Defence press release, issued in 1954 and still representing the most that can be officially stated about the tests, mentions only that 'in recent years trials have been carried out off the coast of Scotland to obtain the technical data on which . . . precautions should be based'.[13] But these tests were not as innocuous as the bland Ministry of Defence statement claimed. During the summer of 1952, and again during 1953, the *Ben Lomond*, a Royal Navy tank transport vessel based in the port of Stornaway on the Isle of Lewis, regularly set off for a point some six miles off the coast.

But unlike the San Francisco experiments in which supposedly harmless bacteria were used, the *Ben Lomond* carried canisters of disease. The pattern of the Scottish tests, code-named Operations Cauldron and Hesperus, was similar to those carried out in the

Bahamas. About ten miles off the Scottish coast rafts were lowered over the side, and cages of animals placed aboard. The *Ben Lomond* then moved upwind of the rafts, and Porton scientists released clouds of germs. Several thousand guinea-pigs, mice, rabbits, and about one hundred monkeys were killed during these tests, which continued for weeks at a time. At the end of the experiments each day the animals would be brought ashore, where their carcasses would be examined before being carted off to an improvised incinerator.[14]

Details of these experiments are still not publicly available, and so nothing is known of the particular diseases under investigation. The reason for the tests being conducted at sea was obvious enough, however, the wartime experience at Gruinard having shown how long-term could be the consequences of contaminating land. Although Porton would have preferred to continue the tests off the Scottish coast, the weather during the summer of 1953, the second year of the experiments, was considered too unpredictable for further work. The following year the scientists returned to the Bahamas for their research. In the warmer conditions of the Caribbean the tests continued for at least two more years.

The experiments off the Scottish coast and in the Bahamas represent the high point of British post-war biological warfare research. In addition to the tests with germ weapons at sea, the British conducted a series of experiments with harmless chemicals over the United Kingdom. Beginning in the spring of 1957 RAF aircraft were regularly dispatched on missions around the British coast. From specially constructed tanks slung belong the planes they poured out zinc cadmium sulphide, a chemical easily detected, even in minute quantities, in the atmosphere. Monitoring stations were established across the British Isles, where Porton scientists assessed the quantity of the chemical in the air. By the autumn of 1959, when the experiments were completed, almost the whole country had been sprayed with the chemical. Further experiments continued sporadically (as, for example in 1961, when imitation disease clouds were discharged from a chimney at Harwell, Britain's atomic energy headquarters), but the zinc cadmium sulphide experiments had proved to Porton Down that Britain was virtually defenceless against a clandestine germ attack.

In the United States similar experiments continued throughout the sixties. Perhaps the most spectacular simulated attack took place in 1966 when the Chemical Corps Special Operations Division decided to mount a biological assault on New York City. The attack was carried out in strictest secrecy, the experimenters carrying false letters certifying that they represented an industrial research organization. The plan was to discover how easy it would be to poison a city by releasing germs into the underground railway tunnels. Army agents positioned themselves on the pavement above the gratings in the roofs of the New York Subway and sprayed 'harmless bacteria' into the stations. Occasionally the clouds would fall onto passengers waiting for trains, but 'when the cloud engulfed people, they brushed their clothing, looked up at the grating, and walked on', one of the agents recalled.[15]

The army agents concentrated on the Seventh Avenue and Eighth Avenue subway lines, while other team members were sent with sampling devices to the extremities of the underground railway network. Within minutes the turbulence caused by the trains would carry the bacteria throughout the tunnel system. Another technique used by the Special Operations men was to travel on subway trains carrying an apparently normal light bulb which was in fact filled with bacteria. When no-one was looking, the light bulb would be dropped onto the tracks in the middle of a darkened tunnel. They reported later that this was 'an easy and effective method for covert contamination of a segment of a subway line'.[16] The research team concluded that if anyone chose to carry out such an attack on New York, or any of the cities of the Soviet Union, Europe or South America with an underground railway network, thousands, possibly millions, would run the risk of infection. Even in an advanced western country like the United States, a serious illness affecting 30 per cent of the population of a major city would swamp the hospitals and bring the health service to a standstill.

By now the biological warfare scientists in all three countries had proved that an attack with disease was possible, indeed, terrifyingly simple. The last tests took place in November 1969. During their entire twenty year duration, little or nothing had been admitted about their true purpose. Apologists for the Chemical Corps in the United States have attempted to justify the experiments by explaining that they began in a period of deep international uncertainty, compounded by 'our fear of world domination by the Communist countries, primarily the Soviet Union'.[17]

Even before many of these tests had taken place the Chemical Corps had concluded that the United States was 'highly vulnerable' to germ warfare attack. They pointed out that since the end of the war very little new work had been done to produce a biological bomb. It would, they believed, take 'approximately one year of intensive effort' before America could wage biological warfare.[18] True, there was no hard evidence that any potential enemy had developed a biological weapon, but could the United States afford to take the risk of not having her own, should one later be developed elsewhere?

The argument was persuasive. In October 1950 the Secretary for Defense accepted a proposal to build a factory to manufacture disease. Congress secretly voted ninety million dollars, to be spent renovating a Second World War Arsenal near the small cotton town of Pine Bluff, in the mid-west state of Arkansas. The new biological warfare plant had ten storeys, three of them built underground. It was equipped with ten fermentors for the mass production of bacteria at short notice, although the plant was never used to capacity. Local people in the town of Pine Bluff had some idea of the purpose of the new army factory being built down the road, but in general there was, as the Pentagon put it later 'a reluctance to publicize the program'.[19]

The first biological weapons were ready the following year, although they were designed to attack not humans but plants. In 1950 Camp Detrick scientists had submitted a Top Secret report to the Joint Chiefs of Staff on work they had carried out on a 'pigeon bomb'. In an attempt to discover a technique of destroying an enemy's food supplies, the scientists had dusted the feathers of homing pigeons with cereal rust spores, a disease which attacks crops. The researchers discovered that even after a one hundred mile flight, enough spores remained on the birds' feathers to infect oats left in their cages. Then they had experimented in dropping pigeons out of aircraft over the Virgin Islands. Finally, they dispensed with live birds altogether and simply filled a 'cluster bomb' with contaminated turkey feathers. In each of these bizarre tests the men from Camp Detrick concluded that enough of the disease survived the journey to infect the target crop. In 1951 the first anti-crop bombs were placed in production for the US Air Force.

The United States had established the first peace-time biological weapon production line.

But the main objective was the development of a weapon to kill people. The ideal biological agent had changed little from the days of Allied research during the Second World War.

It should be a disease against which there is no natural immunity. It should be highly infectious, and yet the enemy should not be able to produce a vaccine against it or be able to cure the disease with the medical facilities available to him. And from a military point of view, it should be a disease which was easy to reproduce, yet hardy enough to survive and reproduce itself outside the laboratory.

Four diseases looked the most suitable as weapons:

Anthrax   The wartime tests carried out by the British and Americans had shown anthrax to be an extremely hardy agent: the island of Gruinard was likely to be contaminated for the rest of the century. Although not necessarily fatal, there was still no effective immunization available. Originally coded 'N'.

Brucellosis   Otherwise known as Undulant Fever, by the end of the war, Brucellosis had been in advanced stages of development. Since it was rarely fatal, it was now considered as a possible 'humane' biological weapon. Originally coded 'US',

Tularemia   Like Brucellosis, which primarily affects cattle, tularemia (also known as 'rabbit fever') is not normally fatal to humans. It was considered, however, that the chills, fever and general weakness the disease produced would disable an enemy for two to three weeks. Originally coded 'UL'.

Psittacosis   Sometimes known as 'parrot fever', this disease was considered the most powerful of the 'incapacitant' weapons, since it would produce a high fever, rather like typhoid fever, which could later develop into pneumonia. Death could be expected in about 20 per cent of those afflicted. Originally coded 'S I'.[20]

Later many other diseases would be developed for use as weapons, including plague, Rocky Mountain spotted fever, Rift Valley fever, Q fever and various forms of encephalomyelitis. But in 1950 these four looked the most promising potential germ weapons. During the next two decades over seven hundred million dollars would be spent on the development of such weapons in the United States, and hundreds of millions more in research and testing projects in America, Britain and Canada.

As to how these diseases were to be used in a future war, the Chemical Corps had a list of targets for the Strategic Air Force. The first priority should be major cities. 'The morale of the people in these targets is an all important factor, and will certainly affect a nation's will to fight. Attack on these targets should be directed toward achieving maximum anti-personnel effect with the least amount of destruction.'[21] The attacks should be carried out on a massive scale, to saturate enemy medical facilities. The element of surprise would be enhanced, the Chemical Corps had decided, by the 'insidious nature of the attack as regards detection, and the period of incubation before symptoms appear'.

These disturbing plans looked as though they might become fact with United States intervention against the communist forces striking down through Korea. There were huge increases in defence spending throughout the American services, and biological warfare was no exception. The Pentagon suspected that the North Korean and Chinese communists under General Lin Piao might unleash bacteriological attacks upon them. The Americans determined to produce a weapon for use in retaliation. Ten million dollars were immediately set aside for new laboratories at Camp Detrick, and research into protection against germ warfare attacks was doubled.

In the event it was not the communists but the Americans who were most successfully accused of using germ weapons. In February 1952 the North Koreans and Chinese claimed that captured American Air Force officers had confessed to dropping 'germ bombs' on North Korea. The Chinese supported their claims by publishing photographs of what they identified as 'American biological bombs'. The United States described the allegations as nonsense; the pilots had, they said, been brainwashed. The Chinese returned to the offensive by setting up an 'International Scientific Commission' including scientists from the Soviet Union, Italy, France, Sweden, Brazil and the United Kingdom. The British representative was Dr Joseph Needham, an expert in Oriental medicine who later became Master of Gonville and Caius College, Cambridge.

The international scientists who investigated the Korean allegations produced a weighty 700 page report in October 1952, which concluded that 'the peoples of Korea and China did actually serve as targets for bacteriological weapons'.[22] It listed the various techniques used, which ranged from fountain pens filled with infected ink, to anthrax-laden feathers, and fleas, lice and mosquitoes carrying plague and yellow fever. In propaganda terms, the 'International Scientific Commission' was a master stroke, although the

United States again denied the allegations. An American request that the United Nations conduct its own investigation was effectively vetoed by the Chinese and Koreans who refused to co-operate.

Dr Needham remains convinced that the United States did indeed wage biological warfare in Korea. 'Mostly it was experimental work, as far as we could see,' he said in Cambridge nearly thirty years later.[23] Needham believed that Korea had been used for experiments with 'vectors', insects like the yellow fever-carrying mosquito, capable of transmitting disease from one body to another. 'The experiments didn't seem to be very successful', he said, 'but we were unanimous in our conclusions'.

Years later the American government admitted that at the time of the Korean War they had had the means to conduct biological attacks, but claimed that their 'bacteriological warfare capability was based upon resources available and retained only within the continental United States'.[24] Whether the allegations had been true or not, their very publication had cost the United States a great deal of good will. In the end there remained only 'an unverifiable report and its unverifiable denial'.[25]

If anything, rather than discouraging the Chemical Corps, the Korean allegations spurred them on faster into a bacteriological arms race. In the autumn of 1953 they established a separate germ warfare division. By spring the following year their production plant was turning out supplies of *Brucella suis*, one of the bacteria causing Brucellosis. A year later the plant at Pine Bluff, Arkansas, was manufacturing Tularemia germs. The supposedly temporary 'Camp' Detrick was renamed Fort Detrick – an indication of its permanent status. There was so much research conducted that, although yet more laboratories were built there, work had to be contracted out to scientists at Ohio State University, who were charged with attempting to produce vaccines against the diseases the Fort Detrick scientists were refining.

As the amounts of money spent on germ warfare spiralled, the Department of Defense began to rethink its policy. In 1943 Roosevelt had stated that the United States would never use these 'outlawed' weapons, 'unless they are first used by our enemies'.[26] This perfectly unambiguous statement of policy placed the United States, which had not ratified the Geneva Protocol, in the same position as many countries which had. But it was now judged inadequate. In 1956, the United States secretly changed her policy.

The following heavily censored transcript of Congressional testimony is the closest to a public admission of the change to be found in the records of the time. A discussion took place between the Commander of the Chemical Corps, Major General William M. Creasy and Representative (later to became President) Gerald Ford.

Creasy: First I will start with the national policy . . . (discussion off the record)
Ford: May I ask how long that policy has been in effect?
Creasy: Since about October 1956, about a year and a half ago. The national policy has been implemented by a Department of Defense directive . . . (discussion off the record).[27]

Since national policy had been publicly expressed by Roosevelt in 1943, the necessity to go 'off the record' was a clear (albeit unwitting) indication of a major change.

In fact the United States had abandoned the principle of using biological and chemical weapons in retaliation only. US Army manuals which had previously stated that 'gas and bacteriological warfare are employed by the United States against enemy personnel only in retaliation'[28] were rewritten. In future they said 'the decision for US forces to use chemical and biological weapons rests with the President of the United States'.[29] In achieving the repudiation of a 'retaliation only' policy, the American military had finally overcome their greatest inhibition.

But while the United States now had a policy which entitled her to use bacteriological and chemical weapons as and when the President saw fit, and the means to produce large quantities of germs, problems still remained. The most pressing difficulty was the question of how to control the spread of a disease.

The secret spraying carried out in the United States, Britain and Canada had provided critical information about how thick a cloud of bacteria needed to be to spread disease successfully. Experiments at Fort Detrick and Porton Down had shown how long microorganisms would live while floating in the air. Tests on animals had provided invaluable information about how large the individual particles needed to be to break through the body's natural defences. Armed with this information, Chemical Corps generals began to imagine astonishing campaigns.

Biological warfare could have an important role as a deterrent to prevent

Communist China from initiating a war. China, as we have seen, is subject to polar outbreaks. From October to March, at frequent intervals, cold air flows from Siberia, down over the populous areas along the coast. Furthermore, from May through August, summer monsoonal air flows in a layer, possibly 10,000 feet deep, from the South China Sea and the Pacific Ocean over coastal regions. Either of these air layers could be seeded with biological agents from the air or from the water. To be effective as deterrents, lethal agents are required. Anthrax or yellow fever might be possible agents for this purpose.[30]

The man who dreamed up this 'deterrent', Brigadier General J. H. Rothschild, had served as head of the Chemical Corps Research and Development Command, and as Chemical Officer of the US Far East Command. His plan was simple enough, indeed the most basic form of modern biological warfare, for it depended only upon the weather. It had the disadvantage, however, of being uncontrollable: strategic decisions about exactly who was killed by anthrax were, literally, thrown to the winds. Rothschild chose to ignore the results of a theoretical exercise conducted by his own army at the very time he was suggesting his attack upon China.

The situation posed was thus. A large Chinese army had penetrated far into Vietnam, and was advancing on the Cambodian capital Phnom Penh. American troops based in Thailand were unable to break through to intercept the Chinese advance. The President ordered a biological strike. At the end of their analysis of this theoretical attack, the Chemical Corps specialists concluded that while some three quarters of the enemy army would have been killed or disabled, so too would six hundred thousand supposedly friendly or neutral civilians.

This problem — how to spread disease in a controlled manner — preoccupied the Americans throughout the fifties and sixties. The fact that at no time did a viable solution seem in prospect was no deterrent to further offensive research. The Chemical Corps went about their work with gusto, regardless of this apparently enormous obstacle.

There was a great deal of interest in 'vectors', or the transmission of disease by insects. Mosquitoes were an attractive proposition, since many species carry disease, and all pass the disease on by injecting their victim. A soldier in a gas mask has no protection. Of particular interest was the species *Aedes aegypti*, known as the 'yellow fever mosquito'. In 1801 it destroyed an entire army sent by

Napoleon to Haiti. In 1878 a small outbreak of the disease in Memphis, Tennessee, drove 25,000 to flee the city, infected another 18,000, and killed 5,000: the city went bankrupt and lost its charter.

If there was a particular irony about the research into yellow fever as a potential weapon it was that for fifty years American physicians had led the campaign to rid North and South America of the disease. Indeed in 1947 the United States had heartily endorsed a new public health initiative to banish yellow fever from the Americas forever, by eradicating the disease-bearing mosquito. Now the military scientists began to consider it a potential weapon.

Fort Detrick scientists discovered a Trinidadian who had been infected with yellow fever in 1954 and had later recovered. They took serum from the Trinidadian and injected it into monkeys. From the monkeys they removed infected plasma, into which they dropped mosquito larvae. The infected mosquitoes were then encouraged to bite laboratory mice and pass on the disease. This ingenious technique of public health research in reverse worked. The mice duly contracted yellow fever.

Laboratories were built at Fort Detrick where colonies of the *Aedes aegypti* mosquitoes were fed on a diet of syrup and blood. They laid their eggs on moist paper towels. The eggs would later turn into larvae, and eventually into a new generation of mosquitoes. The Fort Detrick laboratories could produce half a million mosquitoes a month, and by the late fifties a plan had been drawn up for a plant to produce one hundred and thirty million mosquitoes a month. Once the mosquitoes had been infected with yellow fever, the Chemical Corps planned to fire them at an enemy from 'cluster bombs' dropped from aircraft and from the warhead of the 'Sergeant' missile.

To test the feasibility of this extraordinary weapon, the army needed to know whether the mosquitoes could be relied upon to bite people. During 1956 they carried out a series of tests in which uninfected female mosquitoes were released first into a residential area of Savannah, Georgia, and then dropped from an aircraft over a Florida bombing range. 'Within a day', according to a secret Chemical Corps report, 'the mosquitoes had spread a distance of between one and two miles, and bitten many people'.[31] The effects of releasing *infected* mosquitoes can only be guessed at. Yellow fever, as the Chemical Corps noted, is 'a highly dangerous disease', at the very least causing high temperatures, headache, and vomiting. In about a third of the recorded cases at that time, yellow fever had proved fatal.

Nor were mosquitoes the only insects conscripted into the service of the army. In 1956 the army began investigating the feasibility of breeding fifty million fleas a week, presumably to spread plague.[32] By the end of the fifties the Fort Detrick laboratories were said to contain mosquitoes infected with yellow fever, malaria and dengue (an acute viral disease also known as Breakbone Fever for which there is no cure); fleas infected with plague; ticks contaminated with tularemia; and flies infected with cholera, anthrax and dysentery.

They had tested the diseases on laboratory animals, but soon the scientists needed to discover whether what killed a mouse or a monkey would also kill a human. Many of them believed that the Russians might already be testing *their* biological weapons on people, and the Chemical Corps were keen to do likewise.

During the Vietnam War, the Fort Detrick researchers found a ready source of human subjects for their experiments in Seventh Day Adventists, who, because of their conscientious objections, served in the United States army as non-combatants. In one series of tests Seventh Day Adventist soldiers were exposed to airborne tularemia. According to one report, 'all control subjects developed acute tularemia between two to seven days after exposure', although all were said to have recovered later.[33] This experiment was unusual in that it was written up for public consumption. But the willingness of some at least of the Seventh Day Adventists to take part in such tests was beyond doubt. 'We like to think of ourselves as conscientious co-operators, not conscientious objectors', as one of their ministers explained in 1967.[34] Numerous other experiments took place with volunteers, and although little is known about their nature, it seems fair to assume that many were more concerned with developing effective vaccines than with testing the power of the bacteriological weapons themselves.

Evidence as to the use of human volunteers in experiments at Porton Down is harder to come by. Service volunteers were regularly requested during the fifties and sixties, but they are said to have been used only for the testing of defensive precautions like vaccines.

However, between 1960 and 1966 scientists from the Porton Down Microbiological Research Establishment took part in a series of tests in which terminal cancer patients were treated with two rare viruses, at least one of which was then being considered as a possible biological weapon.

The experiments took place at St Thomas's Hospital, one of London's leading medical schools. According to a report which later appeared in the *British Medical Journal*,[35] terminal cancer patients were infected with Langat Virus and Kyasanur Forest Disease Virus by two doctors from St Thomas's Hospital and two scientists from Porton Down. Their interest appears to have been in developing a potential vaccine against other diseases transmitted by ticks. The scientists reported that all thirty-three patients died, two of them after contracting encephalitis, an infection causing inflammation and swelling of the brain. 'Transient therapeutic benefit was observed in only four patients',[36] they reported.

Most British biological warfare research since the Second World War appears to have concentrated on purely defensive aspects – the production of vaccines and methods of detecting bacteriological attack. Offensive research in Britain and Canada was unnecessary, since neither could compete with the huge American biological weapons programme. Research at Porton was conducted on a smaller, more discriminating scale. Nonetheless, between 1952 and 1970 the Microbiological Research Establishment consumed in experiments over one thousand monkeys, nearly two hundred thousand guinea pigs, and one and three quarter million mice.[37]

The rate at which the germ warfare laboratories consumed animals presented them with one of their greatest public relations problems. The establishments counter-attacked in a number of ways. Fort Detrick, which by 1960 was the biggest user of guinea pigs in the world, sponsored a lavishly equipped boy scout pack, supplied the local paper with a weekly gossip column, and made a succession of speakers available for local discussion groups.[38] The biological warfare base at Porton Down was always more reserved. Occasionally they boasted that the huge facilities for producing micro-organisms had been used for public health purposes. During the Asian 'flu epidemic of 1957, Porton Down produced over 600,000 doses of 'flu vaccine, a socially valuable exercise which the establishment was keen to publicise. Observers pointed out that an establishment which would produce 600,000 doses of vaccine could equally well produce the same number of doses of biological warfare agent.[39]

In fact, by the 1960s, Porton Down was concentrating almost

exclusively on defensive work. There were a few unfortunte accidents, as when in 1962 Geoffrey Bacon, a well liked and normally
efficient Porton microbiologist, became infected with pneumonic
plague and died. Bacon had been searching for a vaccine which could
be used against plague. But largely it was, as they recognized, a futile
quest. Vaccines might be developed, but they could give minimal
protection if anyone should choose to mount a germ warfare attack
on Britain.

The tests with harmless bacteria during the fifties had shown that
if Britain were to be the victim of biological attack, little or nothing
would be done to protect the country. A steady wind would blow the
germs released from a ship off the British coast across the entire
country in ten hours. For even rudimentary protection every member
of the population would need to be issued with a gas mask, something the Home Office had already decided was impractical. Even
if sufficient funds could be made available to issue gas masks to everyone, there remained another, apparently insuperable, problem. Bacteria live longer in the dark, so any biological attack would be likely
to come at night. Even if such an attack could be detected, and even
if everyone had a gas mask, how could you warn fifty million people
at three in the morning?[40]

But in the United States, the biological warfare work continued
unabated. To many military scientists there the very arguments
which made the idea of protecting the population impossible made
bacteria increasingly attractive weapons for use against an enemy.

At the start of the so-called 'Camelot' era of the presidency of John
F. Kennedy, a thorough-going review of 150 areas of American
defence was ordered. Project 112 arrived in the offices of the Joint
Chiefs of Staff in May 1961, requesting an assessment of American
preparations for biological and chemical warfare.[41] The Joint Chiefs
of Staff asked the Chemical Corps, the very people with the strongest
vested interest in ensuring an expansion of the programme, to
conduct the review for them. Not surprisingly their report found that
American preparations were inadequate, but that with the expenditure of four thousand million dollars, they could be improved. The
plea did not fall on deaf ears.

An initial twenty million dollars was immediately set aside for
expanding the biological weapons plant in Arkansas. A new testing
centre was established.[42] Money was spent developing new weapons

to attack plants. And two new debilitating diseases, Q-fever and tularemia, entered the inventory of American biological weapons. By the time that these weapons were in full production, the United States was treading further and further into the quagmire of Vietnam.

The Vietnam War might have represented the perfect field laboratory for men like General Rothschild to test their theories about seeding clouds with anthrax. But there was by now sufficient evidence of the way in which American and South Vietnamese troops would also be affected to rule it out. Instead the germ warfare laboratories concentrated their efforts on the development of incapacitating diseases which would bring an enemy down with sickness for days or weeks. For some years the Fort Detrick laboratories had been working on enterotoxins causing food poisoning, on the military theory, as one proponent put it, that 'a guy shitting away his stomach can't aim a rifle at you'.[43] By 1964, they believed a weapon based on the theory was feasible. But by now, another disabling disease looked a better candidate.

Venezuelan equine encephalomyelitis is a highly infectious disease producing nausea, vomiting, chills, headaches, and muscle and bone pains which may last up to eight days. Clearly an enemy crippled by a disease of this kind would be unable to fight. Arguments were made that this was a 'humane' weapon: in taking away the Viet Cong's will to fight it would actually prevent battles, and so save lives. Hypothetical exercises were carried out in Vietnam with this and similar diseases, but still there was the familiar problem. There was no way of ensuring that only the enemy caught the disease. Reluctantly the idea was put to one side.

And yet the research continued. It seems highly paradoxical that germ weapons projects should have survived the realization that there was little hope of restricting their effects to an enemy army. There could obviously be no excuse of 'defensive' research. But the army biologists lived in hope of discovering a disease which would attack only enemy forces, and leave allied soldiers unharmed: it was during the Vietnam war that the concept of an 'ethnic weapon' was first mooted. It must have seemed a vain hope, yet, the germ warfare protagonists argued, without biological weapons themselves, the Americans were powerless to deter the use of such devices by an enemy.

The results of the continuing research could be seen in the maps of

Dugway Proving Ground in Utah, part of which were marked 'permanent bio-contaminated area', after anthrax experiments in the mid-sixties. In the Pacific more tests were carried out with 'hot' agents – the jargon for real biological weapons – on a number of deserted islands. The results of the tests are still classified on the grounds that they reveal weaknesses in American defences. By March 1967 Fort Detrick had developed a bacteriological warhead for the Sergeant missile, capable of delivering disease up to 100 miles behind enemy lines.

The Defense Department had justified the accelerating rush into biological weapons in the early sixties by saying that there was no prospect of any treaty being arrived at which would be acceptable to the United States.[44] Since any argument to ban biological weapons was unlikely, they argued, the United States was bound to continue her research work.

They were wrong. In 1968 the subject of chemical and biological warfare came up for discussion at the standing Eighteen Nation Disarmament Committee in Geneva. Previous attempts to get agreement on an international treaty to ban the weapons had foundered because of an insistence that both chemical and biological weapons be included in the same treaty. Since gas weapons had already been used in war, been proved effective, and were stockpiled on a large scale, they would be much more difficult to outlaw than germ weapons, which as far as could be satisfactorily proved had never been used in war. The British proposed that the two subjects be separated, and introduced a draft Biological Weapons Convention which would commit all signatory states to renouncing the weapons for all time.

There was heavy initial opposition from the Russians and their eastern European allies, and little overt enthusiasm from Washington. The British and Canadians, who had shared their germ warfare expertise with the Americans, nevertheless argued to President Nixon that an international treaty was now a real possibility. What was needed, they said, was a gesture of goodwill.

Nixon was already under pressure on the subject of chemical and biological weapons, and facing mounting domestic opposition (see Chapter 10). On 25 November 1969 he issued a statement. 'Mankind', he said, 'already carries in its own hands too many of the seeds of its own destruction.' The United States was taking a step in the cause of world peace. 'The United States', he went on, 'shall renounce the use of lethal biological agents and weapons, and all other methods of biological warfare.'[45] It was a brave gesture, which proved the spur for which the British had been hoping.

The laborious negotiations in the Palais des Nations, Geneva, received a considerable boost with Nixon's announcement. Within two years the Soviet Union had abandoned its opposition to a germ warfare convention. On 4 April 1972 representatives of the two countries signed an undertaking that they would 'never in any circumstances develop, produce, stockpile, or otherwise acquire or retain' any biological weapons. Over eighty other countries followed suit. The Biological Weapons Convention was a triumph, because unlike many other arms control agreements which merely restricted the development and deployment of new weapons, it removed one category of armaments from the world arsenals altogether.

By the time agreement was finally signed, the research which had begun with a small group of biologists pondering their contribution to the war against Hitler had produced a host of diseases capable of spreading sickness throughout the world. In addition to infections which would destroy wheat and rice, anthrax, yellow fever, tularemia, brucellosis, Q fever and Venezuelan equine encephalomyelitis had all been 'standardized' for use against man.[46] Plans had been laid for their use behind enemy lines in the event of another war in Europe.

At Pine Bluff Arsenal in Arkansas the machinery which for twenty years had been mass-producing disease was used to turn the germs into a harmless sludge, which was spread upon the ground as an army public relations officer explained what a good fertilizer it would make. And, on a small, bleak island off the Scottish coast the warning signs were due to be repainted.

EIGHT

The Rise and Rise of Chemical Weapons

President Nixon's statement ended the biological arms race. But in the field of chemical warfare it was designed to do no more than mark time. Many of the scientists employed at the chemical weapons bases viewed Nixon's decision, that the United States would manufacture no new gas devices for the time being, as merely another temporary hiatus of the kind to which they had by now become accustomed.

The very buildings housing the Chemical Warfare Laboratories in Britain and the United States bear testimony to the alternating enthusiasm and coldness of post-war governments. Many of them might have been pulled down years ago. Instead they have been given a new lease of life by the addition of yet another coat of paint or varnish.

Despite the potentially catastrophic failure of Porton Down and British intelligence to warn of the existence of the Nazi nerve gases, at the end of the war the chemical warfarers owed their survival to their earlier mistake. For ten years after 1945 the scientists at Porton Down and Edgewood Arsenal, working with their associates at the Suffield research station in Canada, continued to investigate the 'G Agents' brought back from occupied Germany. The sensational effects of the gases gave added force to the conclusion reluctantly reached at the end of the Second World War that 'the absence of any large scale chemical warfare in this war should not cause us to abandon research on the subject. It must continue as an insurance'.[1]

The insurance adopted by the British, American and Canadian governments, who had collaborated in their chemical warfare research during the war, took three forms. All three countries at once began work on new gas masks and detection devices against the Nazi nerve agents. In Britain the army requested new gas masks and protective kit as a matter of urgency. The Home Office ordered the production of millions of new gas masks for the general public.

Scientists in all three countries searched for a drug which would give some protection against nerve agents.

The second form of insurance was the decision to manufacture the G agents themselves, first in allied laboratories, and later in full scale production plants, which turned out the deadly liquid by the ton for loading into bombs and shells. Although Canada never manufactured nerve agents herself, her claim to be uninvolved in offensive plans for chemical warfare is undermined by the third step taken by the three wartime allies.

For by the end of the war the research programmes of the British, American and Canadian chemical warfare establishments had become so closely co-ordinated as to be virtually indistinguishable. The British scientists still probably possessed the greatest degree of expertise, but the American economy, and therefore the resources available for manufacturing, had been less damaged by the war. The Canadians had willingly provided the thousand ssuare miles of land at Suffield, Alberta, where Allied weapons could be tested. The three countries decided to formalize their collaboration in a series of meetings which took place in 1945 and 1946.

In 1947 the three countries joined together in an understanding known as the Tripartite Agreement. As a former head of the US Chemical Corps put it: 'We told each other everything. Things Porton felt better able to do, they did. Things we could do best, we did them. A country would take a particular area of research, like a nerve agent, work on it, and come back next year and report'.[2] The arrangement was attractive because it meant that each country could have access to a wider body of research, for no extra cost. For a country like Canada the agreement was particularly beneficial, since the Canadian government was given access to a wide range of research, in exchange mainly for the enormous expanse of prairie near Medicine Hat where the British and Americans tested their weapons. Indeed, as an official Canadian history recorded, by 1950 'most of the field trials of chemical warfare agents which were conducted in the free world were done at Suffield'.[3]

Representatives of the three countries would meet together once a year at a conference in which each would report on the research assigned to them ct the previous conference. This interchange of ideas was consolidated by a regular exchange of personnel. Scientists from Edgewood Arsenal and Porton Down would regularly swap posts for a period of a year or more, an arrangement which continued into the 1980s. But while the Tripartite Agreement provided great practical benefits for all three countries, it also had serious political consequences.

The Canadians had no interest in manufacturing nerve agents themselves, and represented their position as one of 'defensive research only'. By the mid 1950s the British had taken a similar decision not to continue with the production of nerve gas. Both countries then claimed to be involved in research only the better to protect their soldiers and people against gas. It was a publicly acceptable posture which was rendered largely meaningless by the terms of the Tripartite Agreement. As we shall see, not only were both Canada and the United Kingdom fully acquainted with the results of American *offensive* research at the annual conferences and in the frequent interchange of information and personnel, but both countries also actively participated in the quest for new chemical weapons.

In July 1965 the common pool of knowledge was extended to include Australia, whose government signed a Technical Co-operation Programme with the other three countries. Little is known about the nature of the Australian contribution to the chemical warfare agreement. There are persistent rumours, strenuously denied by the Australian government, that her main contribution is in the provision of tropical testing grounds for chemical warfare equipment.[4] During the Second World War the British had used Australia to test new gases, but the arrangement ended in 1945. Despite the Australian government's answer to protesters that there is no testing ground for chemical warfare in the country, in 1980 the Director of Porton Down claimed that the main contribution of both Australia and New Zealand to the agreement was for the testing of equipment developed in Great Britain and the United States.[5]

The agreements between the western Allies arrived at after the Second World War have lasted to this day. To those who argued that chemical warfare research should be abandoned, the defence planners replied that having accumulated the expertise, it would be foolhardy to abandon further research at the very moment when 'an iron curtain has descended across the Continent', obscuring what the potential enemy might be up to. This argument, that scientists must continue to research ever more effective methods of killing people since they could not know whether a potential enemy might not be doing the same, had been advanced as a justification for the chemical warfare establishments since the end of the First World War. Throughout the 1940s, 50s and 60s it was held to be equally persuasive.

Perhaps there was another reason too. By the end of the war there were literally thousands of men and women who had dedicated their lives to the concept of wars fought with germs and gases. Their aspirations, their careers, their domestic security were to some extent at least bound up with the future of chemical and biological warfare. They argued that the future was so unpredictable, our information about potential future enemies so inadequate, and the state of the art so poised on the brink of momentous discoveries that it would be lunacy to abandon research. It was an argument which in the uncertainty of the new Cold War appeared to make a good deal of sense, and it was a view which triumphed.

The three German nerve agents, tabun, sarin and soman were coded by the British as GA, GB and GD respectively. Although the Nazis had concentrated upon the manufacture of tabun (GA), tests had shown that sarin (GB) was many times more powerful, and soman more powerful yet. The Russians focused their efforts upon manufacturing soman, but the British decided that the alcohol needed for its production was too difficult to make in quantity. The British began a series of tests to establish the potency and other properties of weapons filled with the medium strength agent, GB.

They began with animals. In 1949 a special farm was built at Porton Down solely to breed the animals needed for research. In the early stages vhey used rats which were gassed with GB on the range at Porton. Later, monkeys were placed in cages in the Porton laboratories, and clouds of nerve gas blown over them.[6] Flight Lieutenant William Cockayne, a young RAF officer notionally stationed at the nearby Boscombe Down airbase, but in fact working at Porton, was later to recall how in 1952 he had watched chimpanzees, goats, dogs and other animals being tethered to stakes on the range at Porton before nerve gas shells brought from Germany were fired at them.

The young RAF officer was sent to collect the corpses after the clouds of nerve gas had supposedly dispersed. Although clad in gas mask and protective suit, Cockayne collapsed. It was the end of his RAF career. While in hospital recovering from the gas's attack on his nervous system he was discharged from the force, and later diagnosed as a psychiatric case. For all his civilian life Cockayne was to suffer from uncontrollable muscle spasms, fits of deep depression and inexplicable confusion and terror. It was fourteen years before the Ministry of Defence would even admit that Cockayne had been employed at Porton. Then, using the by now standard justificction for chemical warfare work, they told his MP that Cockayne had been involved not in research into new nerve gases but in 'experiments to assess the vulnerability of our equipment to nerve gas weapons'.[7] This distinction, critical to the preservation of a 'respectable' image for chemical warfare research, was at the time of Cockayne's accident meaningless, since Porton Down was actively developing new weapons for the British army based on the Nazi nerve gases.

The Weapons Unit at Porton Down was dominated by attempts to develop new methods of delivering GB nerve gas to an enemy. They tested dozens of possible weapons – mortar bombs, artillery shells, aircraft bombs – filled with harmless substitutes. But there were severe restrictions on the sort of experiments which could be conducted in the open air in Britain – the stuff was simply too dangerous to risk a cloud of it blowing off the range and into homes and factories. Fewer restrictions applied, apparently, in Britain's African colonies.

Between the end of 1951 and the early months of 1955, groups of up to twenty experts from Porton travelled regularly to West Africa.[8] Here for periods of three months at a time, they carried out a series of tests which, even thirty years later, are still classified 'secret'. During the Second World War, the British had tested their chemical weapons in Canada, Australia and India, in addition to the allied test sites in the United States. Although the facilities in Canada continued to be available to Porton Down, another site was now needed, where weapons could be tested under tropical conditions, India no longer being a colony. The British selected Obanakoro in Nigeria, because within easy reach they could find both jungle and dry sandy ground.

It is commonly assumed that the British never came near the manufacture of real nerve gas weapons. Yet the devices tested in Nigeria show how far advanced was their development. The weapons included 25-lb artillery shells, $5\frac{1}{2}$-inch naval shells, mortar bombs, and small 'bomblets' for use within a larger aircraft 'cluster bomb'. All were British-made.

Meanwhile at Porton Down, experiments were carried out on human 'guinea pigs' to assess the effects of the nerve gases. By 1953 no less than 1,500 British servicemen had volunteered for the Porton

Down tests. But in May that year one of the experiments went disastrously awry.

Immediately afterwards the Wiltshire Coroner took the unusual step of holding an inquest *in camera*. The only members of the public allowed inside the courtroom were personnel from Porton Down and the elderly parents of Leading Aircraftman Ronald Maddison, a twenty-year-old National Serviceman from Consett, County Durham. No details of the inquest were made public, and Maddison's father was instructed not to discuss his son's death, even with his wife. It proved impossible, however, to suppress the details of the airman's Death Certificate. The document revealed that Maddison had died from blocking of the bronchial tubes, a classic symptom of nerve gas poisoning.

Maddison had been a 'guinea pig' for the nerve gas being refined at Porton Down. It appears that experiments had been conducted in which scientists had placed a drop of GB liquid on a volunteer's arm, to test whether it would evaporate before penetrating the clothing and skin, and attacking the nervous system. Maddison had the misfortune to be chosen for an experiment in which a drop of the liquid was placed on his forearm, and then covered so as to prevent its evaporating. The result was to allow the liquid to penetrate through the skin, and so give him a dose far greater than any previous volunteer had experienced. He died surrounded by some of the most knowledgeable chemical weapons experts in the world, who could do nothing to save him.

Porton Down claimed that Maddison had been 'abnormally sensitive' to nerve gas, but even so, work with human volunteers stopped for six months while a government inquiry scrutinized the way in which young volunteers were being used at Porton. The investigation concluded that Maddison's death had been an unfortunate accident, and that the tests should continue. The inquiry had been impressed to learn that the servicemen who volunteered to test nerve gas received no extra pay or other rewards for standing in the gas chambers.

There was another inquest connected with Porton in 1953. The Director of the Chemical Defence Section committed suicide. No one suggested that the balance of his mind had been affected by his work with nerve gas, but his wife told the Wiltshire Coroner that her husband suffered from terrible depression. Sometimes, she said, he would come home late, explaining that he had stayed out walking around in the evening air 'until he felt civilized again'.[9]

If the British were to begin manufacturing nerve gas, they would need a new factory. The mustard gas plant, at Sutton Oak, Lancashire, was thought to be too near human habitation for it to be used safely for the manufacture of the highly poisonous nerve agents. It was razed to the ground, and later became the site of a gypsy encampment.

For the manufacture of nerve gas, the British chose a remote clifftop on the north Cornish coast, where the RAF already maintained an airbase. Nancekuke appgared an ideal site, high on a clifftop, well away from human habitation and with any accidentally released clouds of gas likely to blow out to sea. Many of the same considerations also made the area a popular holiday area, but inquisitive tourists were kept away from the place by eight foot tall fences. The Ministry of Defence later described the plant at Nancekuke as a 'design exercise against the event of the UK requiring a retaliatory capability as a deterrent'.[10] By 1953, this 'design exercise' was producing 6 kilograms of GB nerve agent every hour.

But the British never became fully committed to the production of nerve gas, partly because of memories of the horrors of the First World War, and partly because they simply could not afford the expense of producing a new weapon. At one stage, they sent an urgent message to Washington asking the Americans to supply them with nerve gas as soon as possible. The Top Secret memo which gives details of this request to the American Joint Chiefs of Staff makes no mention of the quantities asked for.[11] It was, perhaps, an interim amount to tide them over until Nancekuke became fully productive.

The plant at Nancekuke on the beautiful Cornish coast manufactured 15 tons of GB, all of which was supposedly used for research there and at Porton. The factory had been designed as a 'pilot plant', as Sutton Oak had been a pilot plant for the manufacture of mustard gas. In the event, the British, unlike their American allies, never developed a full scale nerve gas manufacturing plant, a decision often represented as one akin to unilateral disarmament. In truth there was no need to expand facilities because the British had proved to their satisfaction that the system worked. In times of crisis it would be necessary only to use the experience of Nancekuke to build a larger plant to produce the nerve gas necessary for future weapons.

But although Nancekuke produced only 15 tons of nerve gas, by wartime standards a tiny amount, its gas nevertheless claimed victims. The Nancekuke area, in the midst of the Cornish country-side, is one in which men find it hard to get jobs with any prospect of security. Among those attracted to the new factory being put up by the Ministry of Defence, with its guarantee of employment for the foreseeable future, was a young ex-R A F man, Tom Griffiths. He was lucky: they hired him as a fitter.

On 31 March 1958, Griffiths and a colleague were instructed to repair a sagging pipe.[12] Although the pipe in question formed part of the complicated latticework which made up the nerve gas produc-tionline, they had been assured that the area was 'clean', and they entered the room without either gas mask or protective clothing. Griffiths placed a ladder against the wall, and climbed up to examine the pipe. He was astonished to see a drip of clear liquid hanging from one of the pipe flanges. It could only be GB. Griffiths shouted a warning to his colleague, and jumped from the ladder. The two men made for the door, their breath coming in short gasps, their vision blurred.

Outside in the fresh air, as their breathing returned to normal and objects stopped swimming before them, with the happy-go-lucky fatalism born of working at Nancekuke, the two men congratulated each other on an extremely narrow escape. Griffiths was an intensely patriotic and normally honest man. And yet that evening, when he returned home, he lied to his wife, telling her he was suffering from a migraine attack. Although violently sick during the night, he forbade her to call the doctor, handing her a card with the name and telephone number of the Nancekuke Medical Officer. If anyone was to be summoned, he said, it could only be him. As he explained later, he had signed the Official Secrets Act, which instructed him not to discuss his work with strangers, an injunction he took to include his wife.

Over the coming months, although his condition improved, Tom Griffiths never fully recovered. His workmate was killed in a road accident, and Griffiths himself grew progressively more withdrawn, prone to fits of depression and loneliness when he would sit for hours staring into the fireplace of their small grey council house. He forgot things, became irritable. Sometimes he would be overcome with dizziness, and couldn't breathe properly. Finally, he was unable to work any longer: unfit for further employment at the age of thirty-nine.

It was ten years before Nancekuke's real function was revealed, and Griffiths finally admitted to his wife what he believed to be the cause of his condition. By then the Ministry of Defence had refused any compensation, while it would take another ten years before he was able to win a disability pension.

Nor was this the only accident at Nancekuke. Sixteen years after the end of the war the trophies captured by the Allies from the Germans were still stored there. In 1961 another fitter was told to begin dismantling a huge condenser which had been removed from a German nerve gas factory. The fitter, Trevor Martin, remembers the condenser was about five feet long and two feet in diameter, and 'as rusty as an old anchor'.[13] There was a label attached with the words 'believed clean', and so he wore no gas mask. He removed the end flanges of the container, and found a form of asbestos compound between the joints. There was a great deal of rust and dust.

But by now it was the end of the day. Martin stripped off his overalls and went home to tea. Afterwards he went out to work on his car – there were adjustments to be made underneath the chassis. When he stood up again, he felt dizzy, flushed and breathless. His speech became, he says, 'incoherent'. He felt better later that evening and for the following five days went to work as normal. But on the sixth day his right leg began to twitch uncontrollably. Ths right side of his face was paralysed. He managed to work the three months necessary to claim a weekly £4 pension, but in the summer of 1962, at the age of thirty-seven he was rendered unemployable.

Since then his life has been spent in and out of hospitals, consulting rooms and surgeries. He has been told that he suffers from an inoperable brain tumour, inflammation of the brain, psycho-neurosis, fibrositis and epilepsy. Nineteen years after the accident which he claims caused his condition, Trevor Martin is still pursuing his lonely campaign to prove that he is indeed a victim of nerve gas poisoning. He still suffers from a permanent headache, muscle cramps, acute fatigue, twitches in his right arm, blurred vision, and a breathlessness so acute that he can walk no more than a few hundred yards. Perhaps most distressing of all are his psychological symptoms: what he describes as 'confusion', depression, and a tendency to sit and, for no apparent reason, to weep uncontrollably.

While the British continued their research and evaluation, the

Americans decided to go into production with GB shells and bombs as soon as possible.

The initial experimental work had been carried out at Edgewood Arsenal in Maryland, but soon it was clear that the Chemical Corps needed far more space. They settled on Dugway Proving Ground, a run-down Second World War base in a remote corner of the Utah Canyons near the Skull Valley Indian reservation. It was here that American munitions specialists had built entire Japanese and German villages to test new Allied bombs, but after the war the base had been designated 'inactive'. Now, in 1950, the place was reopened, building contractors moved in, and yet more land was bought or borrowed, until the Dugway Proving Ground covered an area the size of Hampshire. A new administrative area and housing scheme was built to accommodate the thousands of scientists and soldiers expected at the base. And other research stations were opened, in the Panama Canal Zone to experiment with nerve gas in tropical conditions, and in Alaska and Greenland, for Arctic tests.[14]

There was a problem when it came to trying to produce the GB liquid itself. The chemical necessary for production of sarin, Dichlor, was, the Chemical Corps felt, beyond the capability of the civilian chemical industry. They solved the problem by building their own factory to manufacture Dichlor on forty-five acres of land acquired from the Tennessee Valley Authority in Alabama.[15] By 1953 the factory was producing Dichlor in abundance, which the Chemical Corps then carried overland to Rocky Mountain Arsenal, an innocuous looking huddle of buildings ten miles north-east of Denver, Colorado. Here the chemical process was completed, and finished nerve agent produced. It cost, all told, only three dollars a kilogramme to manufacture, and during the cold war years of the mid-1950s the factory turned out between fifteen and twenty thousand tons.[16]

It did not take long to load the sarin into weapons. By the mid-1960s the American armed forces were equipped with an enormous range of weapons filled with nerve gas: artillery shells, rocket warheads, missile warheads, and a range of bombs from small 'bomblets' to 500-lb 'Weteye' bombs.[17]

While the United States in her role as Defender of the Free World continued to develop new gas weapons, Britain, beset by economic problems, reassessed her interest in chemical warfare. A number of considerations bore down on the British Ministry of Defence, most notably the need to save large amounts of money. Gas had not, after all, been used in the Second World War. The German nerve agents had been thoroughly analysed at Porton Down, and the British had developed their own shells and bombs. There was a pilot nerve gas plant operating in Cornwall. And the United States was producing nerve gas weapons which she was prepared to make available to the British.[18] In 1956 The Ministry of Defence came to a decision that after forty years of developing new weapons, Britain would get out of gas.

This decision to renounce chemical weapons, although largely based upon economic considerations, came to be seen as a moral gesture. This decision, in later years vaunted as an example of the moral courage of the nation, was, at best, a half truth. True, the remaining stocks of British phosgene and mustard gas from the Second World War, together with thousands of tons of captured German nerve gas weapons, were loaded aboard ship and taken to a point off the Inner Hebrides above the thousand fathom line. Here, as the gas weapons were sent to the bottom of the sea, the British renounced their capacity to wage chemical warfare. Research on new nerve gas weapons was cancelled.[19] From henceforth Britain would be concerned only with devising new methods of protecting her soldiers against attack.

During the 1930s Porton Down had evaded the restrictions on developing new chemical weapons by conducting research 'under the rose'.[20] Now faced with a government decision to halt the further development of new gas weapons, Porton Down had a different cover in the Tripartite Agreement.

In September 1958, two years after the British government ruling, representatives of Porton Down met their American and Canadian counterparts at the Thirteenth Tripartite Conference on Toxicological Warfare, held in Canada. It can be assumed that all three countries, although two were now committed to purely defensive research, pooled their information. But the summary of the conference also records that:

The three nations agreed on several major points, including the following: (a) research should be continued on organophosphorous compounds [nerve agents] specifically in areas where there is a possibility of marked enhancement in speed of action and resistance to treatment; (b) all three countries should concentrate on the search for incapacitating and new lethal agents.[21]

In other words, Britain and Canada, although both officially concerned purely with defensive research, agreed to continue research into new weapons. Porton Down would justify such research by arguing, as was argued during the 1930s, that research must be conducted into new 'Weapons against which defence is required'. But the history of chemical warfare since the Second World War is a succession of British discoveries which were later turned into weapons by her partner in the Tripartite Agreement.

In 1952 chemists at the Plant Protection Laboratories of the giant Imperial Chemical Industries were attempting to develop a new pesticide. One of the I C I chemists, Dr Ranajit Ghosh, discovered a substance which appeared to be so toxic that not only would it destroy insects, but it might also kill humans. He sent a sample, together with the chemical formula, to Porton Down.[22]

Dr Ghosh's new liquid was heavier and more viscous than the German G agents, closer to the consistency of engine oil than anything else. At one stage in its manufacture it had the appearance of frozen milk, but it had little or no smell. The Porton scientists discovered that although it was different in appearance, it worked in the same way as the German nerve agents, by interfering with a vital enzyme needed to control muscle movements. It seemed a potent weapon.

In 1952, the British had not yet decided whether to mass produce weapons filled with the German G agents. Under the terms of the Tripartite Agreement they were bound to pass the information on this new nerve agent to the United States and Canada. The Canadians had no interest in developing a new weapon, but to the American Chemical Corps the liquid was attractive. It would penetrate through the skin itself, but was many times more powerful than sarin (a few milligrammes of the new substance would kill), and whereas the G agents tended to evaporate, the heavy, viscous liquid from Porton Down would lie in poisonous puddles for weeks. Whole areas of the battlefield could be turned into virtual no-go areas. Soon chemists at Edgewood Arsenal had refined one variant of the Porton liquid. They named it 'V X'.

The two countries collaborated in a series of tests to establish how V X could be manufactured. It was the British, once again, who were the first to develop a reliable production process at the Nancekuke base in Cornwall. But by the time the process had been perfected it was 1956, and the British government had decided that Britain would renounce chemical weapons. The results of the British process studies were passed to the Americans under the terms of the Tripartite Agreement.

The Americans chose an old heavy water plant in Indiana as the site on which they would begin manufacturing V X. It was situated at Newport, a few miles north of Terre Haute, Indiana, where the Allies had been planning to mass produce the anthrax bombs to be used in the Second World War. From the outside, the new factory at Newport looked unexceptional, its main characteristic being a ten storey tower where the forty miles of pipes involved in the process culminated in the final production of V X. In a lower building the oily liquid was loaded into rockets, shells and bombs.

Each of the three hundred or so workers at the Newport factory was made to undergo a rigorous physical examination before being employed.[23] Inspectors in the production tower were required to don gas masks and heavy protective clothing before sampling the liquid for its fatal purity every ninety minutes. They were expected to undergo blood tests, and to take a shower three times a day.

The Newport factory, built at a cost of eight million dollars, was run for the Pentagon by the Food Machinery and Chemical Corporation of New York. By 1967 it had produced between four and five thousand tons of V X, and a new generation of chemical weapons had entered service with the United States. V X had been loaded into landmines, artillery shells, aircraft spray tanks, even the warheads of battlefield missiles.[24] In less than ten years a potential British pesticide had become the most poisonous weapon in service with the American forces.

In the late 1950s, with two nerve agents being prepared for the battlefield, the US Chemical Corps set out to teach people to 'love that gas'. There was no underestimating the size of the task facing them. In the folk memory of the 1950s gas was still the most feared and horrific of all the non-nuclear weapons. Then, as now, the word 'gas' immediately conjured up photographs of blinded men being led away to lingering deaths in squalid field hospitals.

As the United States Defense Science Board put it, gas was now a weapon capable of inflicting 'devastating casualties on unprotected personnel, both military and civilians'.[25] In light of this view, popular attitudes had to be changed, and the Chemical Corps set out to

A Higher Form of Killing

manipulate public opinion into an acceptance of chemical weapons. The thrust was basic: the Soviet Union had massive stocks of chemical weapons, the West far fewer. The propaganda techniques chosen ranged from private speeches by senior Chemical Corps officers to selected interest groups, to articles by recently retired members of the Chemical Corps, and off-the-record briefings for potentially sympathetic journalists. Senior officers were made available for interviews. Previously classified documents were leaked to chosen newspapers.

A favourite example of the propagandists was the Second World War battle of Iwo Jima, in which 6,000 marines had died and a further 19,000 had been wounded. The Chemical Corps now suggested to the American public that the lives of American servicemen lost at Iwo Jima could have been saved had the decision been taken to use gas.

Some others, on the advice of the public relations consultant hired by the Pentagon, went further. 'Man is now confronted by the possibility that he can eliminate death from war', claimed one of the articles planted in the press.[26] In another press report the former commander of the Chemical Corps announced that 'there is no question in my mind that for the first time in history there is the promise – even the possibility – that war will not necessarily mean death'.[27] These outlandish advertisements for gas multiplied. In magazines and newspapers all over the United States, and later in Britain, articles began appearing which suggested that soon wars would be fought without any bloodletting.

As one government scientist put it; 'Ideally we'd like something we could spray out of a small atomizer that would cause the enemy to come to our lines with his hands behind his back, whistling the Star-spangled Banner. I don't think we'll achieve that effect, but we may come close'.[28]

Whether the Chemical Corps genuinely believed this science fiction is not clear. At any event, the public relations campaign brought results. The latter stages coincided with the decision of the Kennedy administration that the United States could no longer rely upon a doctrine of massive nuclear retaliation to deter her enemies. Between 1961 and 1964, the annual budget for chemical and biological warfare almost trebled. But what were these weapons that had such a selling point in the campaign to present gas as 'humane'?

The Rise and Rise of Chemical Weapons

I was put in bed, and the last thing I remember seeing is the boy who went in the gas chamber with me, the paratrooper. I will never forget what he looked like, in the sense that he couldn't accomplish anything. He could not pick up his sheets, he could not lay down, he could not see. His eyes, like mine, were jerking erratically. He couldn't accomplish anything on his own . . . The last time I saw him, he was sitting in a bathtub in full uniform with boots and everything else, smoking a cigar, taking a bath. And a fellow with him was kind of giggling about it'.[29]

During the late 1950s and early 1960s hundreds of American servicemen and civilians underwent experiments in which they were given so-called 'psychochemicals', drugs which the Army hoped would prove that war without death was indeed possible. In Britain a similar, smaller series of tests involved over 140 experiments in which Porton Down tested LSD, the most potent of the candidate weapons.[30] The search had begun soon after the Second World War.

In April 1943 a research chemist at the Swiss Headquarters of the Sandoz drug company had made an extraordinary discovery. Dr Albert Hoffman was attempting to synthesize a drug from ergot, a fungus which attacks cereals. He began to feel dizzy, tipsy and restless. Hoffmann lay down in the hope that the effects would soon pass off. But they did not. As a succession of colours and patterns drifted across his consciousness, he took the first LSD 'trip'.[31]

Hoffman's discovery of LSD soon began to interest psychiatrists who wondered whether a drug which appeared to open the doors of perception might be valuable in treating mental illness. The results of their experiments were soon known to the chemical warfare scientists in all three members of the Tripartite Agreement, who began to evaluate the drug as a potential weapon.

The early results seemed encouraging.

The British had found LSD had great value in dealing with psychopaths. The Canadian Psychiatric Association Journal reported good results with LSD in reversing frigidity and sexual aberrations. American mental hospitals reported that treatment of schizophrenic children with LSD met with some success when all other known methods had failed,

reported an American assessment.[32] The British followed up these early findings with experiments of their own on volunteers. But their results did not support the enthusiasm the Americans were now showing for LSD as a potential weapon. The British found that:

During acute LSD intoxication the subject is a potential danger to himself and to others; in some instances a delayed and exceptionally severe

187

response may take place and be followed by serious after-effects lasting several days.[33]

This was to remain the British view: psychochemicals like LSD were simply too unpredictable in their effects to be worthwhile as weapons of war. They were bothered too by the cost – at a price of £100 a pound, and a ton thought necessary to cover a square mile. LSD was soon ruled out as too expensive.[34] Research in Britain continued only sporadically. But others were undeterred.

Excitement over the possibilities of LSD even reached China, whose representatives are believed to have negotiated a clandestine deal with a British company for the supply of 400 million dosage units of the drug. The arrangement was made in the early 1960s, with the British firm acting as middle men, buying the drug itself from a Czechoslovak manufacturer.[35]

In the United States the Chemical Corps remained convinced that LSD, or some similar drug, represented a powerful potential weapon. They embarked on a programme of secret tests to determine the effects of the candidate drugs.

Shortly before ten on the morning of 8 January 1953, Harold Blauer, a tennis professional undergoing treatment at the New York State Psychiatric Institute, was given an injection. Six minutes later, according to his medical report, he was 'out of contact with reality', his arms flailing. At one minute past ten the report noted rapid oscillation of the eyeballs. Ten minutes later, Blauer's body was 'rigid all over'. Ten minutes after that he went into a deep coma, from which he never recovered.[36]

Harold Blauer had believed he was undergoing conventional psychiatric treatment in a conventional psychiatric hospital. But in fact he was an unwitting guinea pig in US Army tests to discover a technique for 'war without death'. Blauer had been given a drug about which the doctor in charge knew next to nothing, since it was identified only by its Edgewood Arsenal number, EA 1298. The doctor later told investigators 'we didn't know whether it was dog piss or what it was we were giving him'.[37] EA 1298 was a derivative of mescaline, one of many drugs the Edgewood Arsenal scientists were testing in the lengthy search for ways of making an enemy 'come out singing the Star-spangled Banner'. So little was known about the drug that the huge amount injected into Blauer's body had stimulated him to death. While Harold Blauer is the only person known to have died as a result of the secret army experiments, hundreds of thousands of dollars were spent on supporting research at prestigious universities and hospitals. Between 1953 and 1957 the United States Army gave 140,000 dollars to Blauer's hospital, the New York State Psychiatric Institute, to discover what effect selected drugs would have on patients.

There were other tests, involving nearly six hundred American servicemen and nine hundred civilian volunteers.[38] Some of them were written up, in bemused detail, for the benefit of a wider audience. Among the many effects of three selected drugs on a group of 159 'normal enlisted men' at Edgewood Arsenal were:

a failure to distinguish between objects and persons ... one subject attempted to take a casual bite from the doctor's forearm, while another apologised to the drinking fountain when he bumped against it ... One man tried to write his name on a piece of chicken with a ball point pen, and another tried to leave the room through the medicine cabinet.[39]

Another series of tests was filmed by the Chemical Corps, and later released to army units under the title 'Armor for the Inner Man'. The film shows American servicemen manning an anti-aircraft gun, carrying out surveys, completing assault courses. Each is then given a pill. Later the film shows the soldiers unable to complete any of their assigned tasks. They loaf about and giggle. Po-faced officers ask questions, but the men are unable to answer. They stagger about, unable to stand upright. From these and other tests the army concluded that psychochemicals, in removing the will to fight, were powerful potential weapons.[40]

From the military point of view, psychochemicals appeared immensely attractive. They seemed to offer all the advantages of chemical or radiological weapons, with none of the disadvantages: no damage to property, no dead bodies, and no danger of infection.

The army settled on a substance which they code-named BZ. It possessed some properties similar to LSD, but had the advantage that, unlike many of the drugs they had tested, it could easily be distributed as an airborne cloud. BZ took about half an hour to affect its victim, but its after-effects could last for at least two weeks. During the first four hours the victim would find his mouth and throat parched, his skin hot and flushed. He might vomit, his vision would be disturbed. He would stagger about, speaking with a drunken slur or mumbling nonsense. Later he might lose his memory, and would probably suffer hallucinations.[41]

The American Army commissioned a commercial company to produce B Z in bulk and chose the biological and chemical weapons plant on an old Second World War base in central Arkansas as the site on which the B Z would be loaded into bombs. In 1962 they spent two million dollars on the B Z plant at Pine Bluff Arsenal, and over the next two years one hundred thousand pounds of it was produced. But despite all the years of research and the expense of building special factories, B Z, the 'humane weapon' has probably never been used.[42] The Army continued to experiment with the gas during the '60s, in a series of tests at Dugway Proving Ground in Utah, and, in conditions of extreme secrecy, at a site on Hawaii.[43]

In the end the Army concluded reluctantly that even though B Z had been manufactured and loaded into bombs, it was not a reliable weapon. An enemy general under its dangerous delirium was as likely to push the nuclear button as he was to lie down and sham dead or stand up and sing the Star-spangled Banner.

By 1979 the total British stock of B Z was one gram, 'for reference purposes' in the vaults at Porton Down.[44] The search for the humane gas had come to naught.

In November 1961 three C123 'Provider' transport planes of the United States Airforce took off from their base in the Philippines, bound for South Vietnam. All three were equipped with huge tanks capable of holding 1,000 gallons of liquid. High pressure nozzles were fitted beneath the wings and tailplanes. They were to be the instruments of the biggest use of chemical warfare since the First World War.[45]

The mission of these aircraft, and the many others which later joined them, was named 'Operation Ranch Hand', and was directed not against people, but against the environment of Vietnam. Even so, it is still held responsible for tragic human consequences.

The theory of Operation Ranch Hand was simple enough. The Viet Cong's main advantage in their war against the South Vietnamese and Americans was surprise, the ability to mount an ambush and then slip away into the dense protective cover of the jungle. Operation Ranch Hand aimed to strip the jungle bare.

There was nothing new about the theory behind the American plan. As in so many areas of chemical warfare the initial discoveries which made it possible had been British. In 1940, UK scientists had discovered a number of chemicals which, while apparently closely related to natural plant hormones, were capable of killing crops with surprising efficiency. Although the British felt unable to deploy enough aircraft to mount attacks on the farms producing German food supplies, in the United States research on both biological and chemical agents for attacking plants continued at a great pace. By the end of the war American scientists had investigated over a thousand chemicals for their effects on vegetation, and had developed three main agents.[46] Had the war continued, they would have used chemicals to destroy the Japanese rice crop, and so starve the country into surrender.[47]

Because the Second World War had ended before the plan could be put into effect, it was the British in one of their final colonial wars who first used chemical weapons against plants. In their battle against Chinese guerillas in Malaya during the late 1940s and early 1950s, the British sprayed trichlorophenoxyacetic acid, better known as 245T, one of the chemicals developed as a weapon by the Americans, onto suspected guerilla food plantations in an effort to starve them into surrender. In other attacks they used the herbicide to destroy jungle cover. The effects of the British spraying were made known to the small group of American scientists who continued desultory anti-crop research during the 1950s. But with the beginning of American involvement in their own war against guerillas in South-east Asia, Fort Detrick rapidly accelerated its investigations. In the eight years beginning in 1961 its scientists would investigate no less than 26,000 chemicals for their potential usefulness.

Six were chosen for the job of denuding the jungle, coded as Agents Green, Pink, Purple, White, Blue and Orange, after the colours painted onto the drums in which they were delivered to the airfields of South Vietnam. The men into whose aircraft they were loaded chose as their slogan 'Only we can prevent forests'. They boasted that 'we are the most hated outfit in Vietnam'.[48]*

The lumbering aircraft were an easy target for Viet Cong ground fire, but their spraying was soon judged a success. By 1964 Operation Ranch Hand aircraft were dumping their poisonous rain over the whole of Vietnam, from the Mekong Delta to the Demilitarized Zone, and later over Laos and Cambodia too. Soon the spraying was extended. Operation Ranch Hand planes would set out to destroy

* See Authors' Note on p. 196

food plantations of the Viet Cong. The Americans were initially embarrassed at the idea of attacks on food plantations, and in the early days aircraft on defoliation missions would fly with American Airforce markings, which were replaced by the insignia of the South Vietnamese airforce when they flew on anti-crop assignments.[49] Eventually an area the size of Israel had been sprayed, much of it more than once. A spokesman for the Department of Defense stated unequivocally in 1966 that the chemicals 'are not harmful to people, animals, soil or water'.[50]

Of all the chemicals used to strip the jungle, the one which created the greatest bitterness was Agent Orange, used on particularly dense areas of forest. Agent Orange had a spectacular effect, sending vegetation on a rapid and self-destructive growing binge. Plants would explode, leaving a surrealistic landscape where weeds had grown into bushes and where trees, bowed down by the weight of their fruit, would lie rotting in the foul-smelling jungle. The Vietnamese peasants called the areas affected by Agent Orange 'the land of the dead', but American officers claimed that in some places the ambush rate dropped by 90 per cent after the Operation Ranch Hand planes had passed over.[51] Requests from field commanders were coming in faster than the Air Force could ship the stuff out from the United States.

Agent Orange was a mixture of two chemicals, one of which, 245T, had been the defoliant used by the British in Malaya. 245T contains minute amounts of dioxin, one of the most virulently poisonous substances ever produced, at least as toxic as nerve gas and known from experiments to cause deformities in animal foetuses. The proportion of dioxin in Agent Orange was miniscule; so small, it was said, that it could surely cause no damage to humans.

But the quantities being poured from the sky were enormous. Each C123 could discharge its one thousand gallons in five minutes, and would then return to make another sortie over the jungle. In 1968 the domestic weedkillers using the active ingredients of Agent Orange almost disappeared from the American market, so great was the demand from the army in Vietnam.

Within the massive amounts of weedkiller being showered from American aircraft onto the jungles of Vietnam, the small amounts of dioxin accumulated. By the time the spraying had ended, an estimated 240 lb of the stuff had been dumped on Vietnam.[52] A few ounces in the water supply would have been enough to destroy the population of London or New York.

The evidence soon began to accumulate. In Tay Minh Hospital, in the area most heavily sprayed with Agent Orange, the number of still-born babies doubled during the height of Operation Ranch Hand. During the period of heaviest spraying doctors at Saigon Childrens' Hospital discovered that the number of babies suffering from spina bifida and cleft palates trebled.[53] Nor were the effects of the spraying confined to Vietnamese who had been on the ground as the Operation Ranch Hand aircraft passed over.

One September weekend, five years after the end of the war, Paul Reutershan, an American who had served in Vietnam as an aircraft mechanic, doubled up with what he took to be food poisoning. A series of tests at a local hospital revealed not food poisoning, but abdominal cancer so severe that doctors could not operate. It had been established that 245T would produce cancer in some laboratory animals. Reutershan was convinced that Agent Orange had caused his cancer. He began organizing a national campaign: seven thousand former servicemen came forward believing that their cancers and other illnesses or birth deformities in their children were produced by Agent Orange. Before they could organise very far, Reutershan died.

The Vietnam veterans tell stories of paint being stripped from the Operation Ranch Hand aircraft by Agent Orange, of flying spraying missions in helicopters when the entire crew would be covered in herbicide. On over forty occasions aircraft dumped Agent Orange directly onto American military bases. Both the servicemen and reports from Vietnam speak of a higher than average rate of birth deformities.[54] Five years after the war ended in Vietnam there were still frequent cases of Chloracne, a severe skin eruption which also broke out with the accidental release of dioxin after an explosion at a northern Italian chemical factory at Seveso, in 1976.

The American government maintained that in using chemical weapons to attack the jungle it was breaking no international agreements. The understanding upon which this belief was based dated back to the Second World War, when both British and American chemical warfare advisors had argued that anti-plant weapons were not covered by the 1925 Geneva Protocol. Although the United States had still not signed the Protocol, on the grounds that to do so would deprive her of the 'humane' use of riot agents such as tear gas, it was believed that her stance on chemical weapons was no different to that of countries which had acceded. In Vietnam this understanding was stretched to breaking point.

The Geneva Protocol had laid down firm controls over the use of gas in war. But the use of chemical weapons, like tear gas, by domestic police forces was a matter purely for national governments. Both the United States and Britain had established factories to manufacture CN gas after the First World War, and the British were soon using the gas against rioters in the colonies. The weapon which replaced it, and was used in Vietnam, CS gas,[55] provides a near-perfect example of the way in which British chemical warfare research, despite its commitment to purely defensive uses, came to be applied to war.

The British realized in operations in both Korea and Cyprus during the early fifties that their standard tear gas, CN, 'would not drive back fanatical rioters'.[56] Porton Down began the search for another, more powerful weapon, which would affect other parts of the body, since determined demonstrators could resist CN simply by closing their eyes. The scientists at Porton worked their way through almost a hundred chemical compounds, before eventually choosing CS. The advantage of CS was that it produced a whole range of unpleasant effects. The victim felt his eyes burn and water, his skin itched, his nose ran, he coughed and vomited between gasps for breath. The British tested the new gas when faced by rioters in Cyprus in 1958, and reported the power of CS to their colleagues at the Tripartite Conference that year.

The US Chemical Corps immediately established a crash programme, code-named 'Black Magic', to manufacture CS for use in grenades and from spray-tanks mounted on helicopters and aircraft. But while the British could claim that they had only used the gas in police operations, or when the army was acting 'in support of the civil power' (a justification to be used when CS was first used by the army against rioters in Northern Ireland later in the decade), its use by the American forces in Vietnam was nothing of the kind. In 1965 General Westmoreland, the American commander in Vietnam, decided that CS would be invaluable in driving the Viet Cong from their hidden bunkers. Conscious of the sensitivity of the issue, the troops who took part in the operation on which CS was first used officially were thoroughly rehearsed in speaking not of 'gas' but 'tear gas', believed to be exempt from the general ban on chemical weapons.

Some indication of the 'humanity' of CS gas in Vietnam can be gained from one operation in which it was employed.[57] Viet Cong soldiers were believed to be hidden in bunkers in a narrow stretch of jungle. First, helicopters were sent in, pouring out CS gas from their dispenser tanks. Then came huge B52 bombers which 'carpeted' the area with high-explosive bombs. Finally, American troops in gas masks would be sent in to 'clean up' any survivors. As an American spokesman explained later, 'the purpose of the gas attack was to force the Viet Cong troops to the surface, where they would be more vulnerable to the fragmentation effects of the bomb bursts.'[58]

All told, thousands of tons of CS gas were used by American forces in Vietnam. The worry that Vietnam might develop like the First World War, where use of tear gas had been the precursor to use of ever more sophisticated poisons, had not been justified. But at times Vietnam did look like a First World War battlefield, as clouds of gas drifted about, occasionally obscuring the frogmen-like GIs in their gas masks. One French journalist described an attack which bore a disturbing similarity to some First World War encounters:

The commander called to the medics, 'Keep the wounded covered, get them dressed: the gas will burn them'. In any case the gas was catching bare arms and the exposed neck area, leaving men with the same pain as when burned.[59]

In the eyes of some Vietnam watchers, it did not matter that the United States had stopped short of the use of fatal gases, even at the moment of her final humiliation. It was, in the eyes of critics of American policy, a mistake to have used even riot agents. As the *New York Times* put it: 'In Vietnam, gas was supplied and sanctioned by white men against Asians. This is something that no Asian, Communist or not, will forget'.[60]

While aircraft poured defoliant onto the jungles of Vietnam and soldiers lobbed CS gas grenades at suspected Viet Cong, back in the United States work continued on the lethal nerve gases. By the middle '60s there was hardly one of the more distinguished American universities (and many undistinguished ones too) which was not carrying out research into chemical or biological warfare. At the

University of Pennsylvania, for example, some forty civilian scientists employed by the 'Institute for Co-operative Research' were working exclusively on chemical and biological warfare.[61] Whereas the British were devoting most of their energies to the development of new gas masks and protective suits, in the United States much of the work concentrated on the development of new weapons, particularly on problems of how to spread nerve agent more effectively.[62]

By the late 1960s the United States possessed a fearsome chemical armoury. At Rocky Mountain Arsenal, Colorado, stood row upon row of cluster bombs filled with mustard gas and phosgene. The warehouses were filled with more stocks of nerve gas. At Tooele, an old mining town twenty miles south of Salt Lake City, were millions more pounds of G agent, together with VX bombs and shells, and mustard gas, part filled into weapons, the rest packed into eight rows of silver drums stretching half a mile or more into the desert. There were other dumps too, in Arkansas, Indiana, Alabama, Kentucky, Oregon, Colorado and Maryland. On the island of Okinawa in the Pacific was the Far Eastern forward base, and in West Germany another secret gas dump, in the event of a European war. Altogether, there was said to be enough for a twelve-month campaign.[63]

[AUTHORS' NOTE] In the years following the American collapse in Vietnam, the number of former servicemen apparently damaged by Agent Orange continued to grow. By late 1981 no less than 17,000 American former servicemen, a further 4,000 Australians, and another 1,700 from New Zealand and Korea had gathered together to sue the five chemical companies which had manufactured the defoliant. While the companies fought to delay the action being heard, the ex-servicemen continued to die from ailments believed to be associated with the use of Agent Orange. Even among those who seemed to have survived unscathed it is still claiming victims: of the children fathered by men exposed to the defoliant, no less than 40,000 are said to suffer from serious birth defects.

NINE

The Tools of Spies

On 7 September 1978 an exiled Bulgarian writer drove from his suburban home to the huge central London office block which houses the BBC overseas radio services. Before his defection in 1969, Georgi Markov had been a member of the privileged literary élite of Bulgarian society, a popular writer whose work had won him the friendship and confidence of senior members of the Politburo. Now he regularly broadcast commentaries on Bulgarian life back to his native land from the studios of the BBC and Radio Free Europe.

Parking space was hard to find immediately outside the BBC offices, so Markov left his car alongside the Thames, beneath Waterloo Bridge. Having locked the car, he climbed the flight of stone steps to the road above, and began walking towards the BBC. Suddenly he felt a sharp jab in his thigh. Markov turned around. A man was picking up an umbrella from the pavement, mumbling apologies.

That evening Markov began running a fever. His blood pressure fell and continued to drop for the next two days. The fever intensified. Finally, his heart gave up.

If Markov's death had been intended to resemble an accident, the plan fell apart when he was able to tell his wife, shortly before he died, about the incident with the umbrella. When Scotland Yard forensic scientists examined the body, they discovered a small metal ball beneath the skin on Markov's thigh. No bigger than a pinhead, the tiny pellet had four holes bored through it. The analysts became convinced that the pellet had contained poison. But of what type?

The clue came from Paris, where another Bulgarian exile, Vladimir Kostov, was living. Like Markov, Kostov was a journalist. When he read of his colleague's death in the newspapers, Kostov recalled how he had felt a sharp pain in his back while riding the Paris Métro some ten days earlier. Kostov too had developed a fever, although in his case it had subsided after three or four days. Now Kostov requested a thorough medical examination.

An X-ray of his back revealed another metal pellet, buried beneath the skin. The French doctors who removed the object immediately sent it to Scotland Yard's forensic laboratories, where analysis by microscope showed it to be identical to the ball removed from Markov's thigh. The police scientists called in Porton Down, with its unrivalled expertise in germ warfare. Scientists at Porton found that the pellet taken from Kostov's body still contained traces of poison. Soon they had identified it as Ricin, a highly toxic substance derived from the seeds of the castor oil plant. They checked their suspicion by taking a sample of Ricin from the Porton stores, and injecting it into a pig. The fever and heart attack which the animal developed were identical to the symptoms Markov had displayed as he struggled for life in the Intensive Care Unit. The biologists concluded that Kostov had only survived the attack on the Paris Métro because his assailants had failed to put enough poison into the pellet.

Ricin had been one of a series of poisons which the British had considered for use in assassinations during the Second World War. Indeed, even in the 1960s research was still being conducted into the effects of the poison under a contract with Exeter University. But the public evidence of British interest in Ricin was small in comparison with the work which had been carried out in eastern Europe. Even a superficial scan of the published research papers on Ricin revealed a surprisingly high proportion of the work to have been carried out in Hungary and Czechoslovakia.[1]

By the time that Scotland Yard realized they were handling a murder investigation, the assassin had gone to ground. Suspicion fell immediately upon the KGB – trained Bulgarian secret police, who appeared to be engaged in a campaign to silence dissidents who dared to criticise the government of President Todor Zhivkov. In their techniques of assassination, as in all other areas, the Bulgarian secret police are controlled by the KGB.

Like every section of the Soviet secret services, the activities of the KGB Technical Operations Directorate are shrouded in obsessive secrecy. What little is known about the gases and poisons produced by the KGB scientists there comes mainly from the corpses of their victims. A handful of cases will serve to illustrate the range of poisons and chemicals available to KGB agents.

In February 1954 Captain Nicholai Khokhlov arrived in Frankfurt with orders to assassinate Georgi Sergeivich Okolovich, leader of an exiled dissident group. At the last moment Khokhlov's nerve broke. He broke down and warned his intended victim of the danger he was in, before handing himself over to American intelligence. Khokhlov took American agents to a forest outside Munich. There, hidden deep in the woods, he produced an apparently normal gold cigarette case. It had been modified by KGB scientists into a pistol firing poisoned dum-dum bullets.

Khokhlov became a frequent speaker at anti-Soviet gatherings, where his experience as a KGB agent lent authority to his attacks on the Soviet system. But while at a speaking engagement in Frankfurt in September 1957, Khokhlov became violently ill. His face became covered in black, brown and blue lumps, his eyes oozed a sticky liquid, lumps of hair fell from his head. Two days later his German doctors decided that death was imminent. Khokhlov was transferred to an American military hospital, where six doctors began a desperate battle to save his life. They knew little about what had poisoned Khokhlov, but by constantly changing his blood, and with huge doses of cortisone, steroids, vitamins and experimental drugs, they managed to keep him alive. Gradually, Khokhlov recovered. Only later were American experts able to deduce from analysis of the course of Khokhlov's illness that he had been poisoned by the insertion of highly radio-active metal fragments into his food supply.[2]

Two years later another assassin was despatched from Moscow to murder another dissident, this time with a chemical agent, prussic acid. On 15 October 1959 Stefan Bandera, a prominent Ukrainian exile, arrived at his home in Munich just before 1 pm. As he inserted the key into his front door the KGB agent, Bogdan Stashinsky stepped out of the shadows, and pointed a seven inch tube at his face. As Stashinsky pulled a trigger, prussic acid poured into Bandera's face. The effect of the acid, once inhaled, was to cause the blood vessels in the victim's body to contract suddenly, simulating a heart attack. Within minutes Bandera was dead. When Stashinsky defected to the west two years later, he described a range of chemical and biological devices produced by KGB technicians.

In the first week of September 1964 a German electronics engineer was called to Moscow to 'sweep' the West German Embassy for KGB listening devices. The man, Horst Schwirkmann, was highly proficient at his job, uncovering bugs concealed all over the building, all of which he destroyed. Before returning to Germany at the completion of his task, Schwirkmann travelled to a monastery outside Moscow for a Sunday of sightseeing. As he stood admiring the icons inside Zagorsk Monastery, Schirkmann suddenly felt a searing pain across his buttocks and the back of his thighs. The paralysed technician was carried back to the West German Embassy, and thence to the specialist doctors at the United States compound. They concluded that he had been sprayed with Nitrogen mustard gas, a gas developed and stockpiled during the Second World War. Twenty years later, Schwirkmann had become its first victim.

Not all KGB chemical or biological devices are intended to produce fatalities. Equally important, according to defectors, are the incapacitants, designed to disable a victim temporarily. Most notorious in this group are the drugs said to have been slipped into the drinks of diplomats or civil servants prior to their being found in compromising positions with KGB-run prostitutes. Other chemical or biological devices are designed to produce a temporary illness such as a severe stomach upset, which may render it necessary for victims to take to their beds at moments when Soviet intelligence wished to be certain of their absence.

But the Western intelligence agencies have not been content to rely upon the information produced at a small number of autopsies or from hospital records or the evidence of defectors. Such cases, they believed, represented only the tiniest proportion of the work on gases and poisons carried out by the KGB's Technical Operations Directorate. The same arguments which had been used to justify the development of chemical and biological weapons by the armies of the west were also used to justify research in the laboratories of the secret services.

The British and Americans had first begun collaborating on the use of chemical and biological devices by secret agents during the Second World War. The assassination of General Reinhard Heydrich was undoubtedly the most spectacular example of the use of germ weapons by secret agents during the war (see page 88–94). But there had been numerous other missions on which the British and Americans had planned to use similar weapons.

In the early stages of the war plans for the covert use of gas and germ weapons had been relatively crude. During the Libyan campaign of 1940, the British War Cabinet had pondered various methods of contaminating German water supplies with easily available substances such as acid, salt and creosote.[3] By 1942 the British Special Operations Executive had been supplied with a range of gas weapons for use in clandestine warfare. The Chiefs of Staff, meeting in July 1942, recognized the delicacy of issuing British undercover agents with gas weapons, but concluded that the Allies could not wait until gas had been used on a large scale before making the weapons available to undercover organisations like the Special Operations Executive. They ordered that gas weapons were to be shipped to SOE training schools in India, the Middle East, Australia and Canada, and samples were to be demonstrated to the American and Soviet allies.[4]

But the weapons themselves were not impressive. Among them was a tube 4½ inches long, filled with tear gas, which, commented one of the offices present, was 'highly unlikely . . . [to] cause any panic, or hold up work for long, unless the liquid could be brought into contact with the victim's face'.[5] Porton Down had also assisted in developing a tube of 'mustard gas ointment', intended to be squeezed onto objects likely to be touched by a potential victim, which would then cause his skin to erupt into blisters. But even with this device there were problems. Each tube contained only a small amount of ointment, which was anyway likely to lose its effectiveness due to 'weathering'. 'The difficulties connected with the effective use of this store far outweigh its possible advantages', the report concluded.[6]

The problem encountered by the British in attempting to devise reliable methods of carrying chemical and biological agents in sufficient safety and quantity to prove effective on undercover operations was one which bedevilled Porton Down for years. But with the entry of the United States into war in December 1941, the British were soon assisted by a group of American scientists who, in their tireless and fanciful efforts, made the Porton Down men seem pedestrian indeed.

The United States had no tradition of secret agents. When Roosevelt finally decided to create the organisation which became known as the Office of Strategic Services (OSS), the forerunner of the CIA, he made an inspired choice for its Commander in General William 'Wild Bill' Donovan. Donovan, who was then fifty-seven, recruited some 12,000 men to form what eventually became the largest intelligence organisation in the Western world. Among those he approached was Stanley P. Lovell, a Boston scientist and business-man. Lovell was summoned to a meeting one evening in an office at the corner of 25th and E streets in Washington.

Donovan began, in a voice Lovell later recalled as soft and

beautifully modulated, by saying 'I need every subtle device and underhand trick to use against the Germans and Japanese – by our own people – but especially by the underground resistance groups in all occupied countries. You will have to invent all of them, Lovell, because you're going to be my man'.[7] Lovell set about recruiting scientists to join him in developing 'underhand tricks'. The technique he used was to approach candidate scientists and say 'Throw all your normal law-abiding concepts out of the window. Here's a chance to raise merry hell. Come, help me raise it.'[8]

The hell-raisers Lovell gathered around him were soon at work on some of the most daring and ludicrous schemes of the war. As the OSS itself was almost entirely the creation of British intelligence, and largely trained by British agents, so Lovell's scientists worked under the initial guidance of, and later in collaboration with, the British specialists. When Lovell came to write his memoirs some twenty years later he sent a copy of the published volume to Lord Stamp, the British Biological Warfare Liaison Officer, inscribed with the words: 'My deep respect to the little band to which you contributed so much during your Washington days. You were glorious pioneers in an uncharted field of warfare.'[9]

In the early stages much of the American research into clandestine methods of chemical and biological warfare was carried out in collaboration with or at the request of the British. Soon, however, the large resources of the OSS were being devoted entirely to projects of their own devising. Over the next thirty years the OSS and CIA were to produce some of the most imaginative and devastating chemical and biological weapons ever manufactured.

Lovell and two colleagues developed a simulated goat dung, to be dropped from allied aircraft onto German-occupied Morocco during the North African campaign in 1942. Lovell had heard that there were more goats than people in Spanish Morocco, and goat dung was likely to be everywhere. The simulant the American scientists developed contained a chemical so attractive to flies that it could, they believed, wake them even from hibernation. They envisaged millions of flies gathering on the goat dung, which would have been previously contaminated with bacteria causing tularemia ('rabbit fever') and psittacosis ('parrot fever'). Both diseases, likely to cause debilitating illnesses lasting from days to weeks, would be spread to the German troops by the infected flies. Lovell did worry about how Moroccan peasants could be persuaded to accept the presence of goat droppings on their roofs after Allied aircraft had passed overhead scattering the stuff, but in the event the problem did not arise, since intelligence reports indicated that the German troops were being withdrawn, and the operation was rendered unnecessary.

There was no limit to the inventiveness of Lovell's small group of hell-raisers. Many of their ideas seem in retrospect so preposterous that one wonders how anyone could have taken them seriously. OSS anthropologists were asked to report on the area of social behaviour most sensitive to Japanese. They concluded that nothing embarrassed a Japanese more than the smell of his own excrement. OSS chemists made up a compound which perfectly reproduced the smell of diarrhoea. This revolting liquid was then packed into collapsible tubes, which were smuggled into Chinese cities occupied by the Japanese army. When a Japanese officer walked along the street, the OSS reasoned, a small Chinese child would steal up behind him, and squirt the liquid at the seat of his trousers. They christened the device the 'Who? Me?' bomb.

Another experiment centred on the well known aversion of cats for water. Cats, it was suggested to the OSS, always land on their feet, and will go to any lengths to avoid water. Why not wire a cat up to a bomb, and sling both cat and attached high explosive below a bomber? When flying over enemy ships, the explosive cat would be released. The cat would be so concerned to avoid landing in the water that it could, it was argued, be virtually certain of guiding the bomb onto the deck of enemy warships. Experiments with flying cats soon proved to the supporters of the project that even unattached to high explosive, the cat was likely to become unconscious long before Nazi decks seemed an attractive landing place.

No idea was too far out for the American specialists. In their very receptiveness to new and seemingly ridiculous plans, they pushed the frontiers of chemical and biological warfare into the realms hardly dreamed of by the British. At one stage they shipped botulinus toxin pills out to prostitutes in occupied China in the hope that they would be able to poison Japanese army officer clients. On another occasion 'Professor Moriarty', as General Donovan called Stanley Lovell, dreamed up a plan to infiltrate a secret agent into a room on the Brenner Pass where Hitler and Mussolini were to meet. The man was to crush a capsule of nitrogen mustard gas into the water holding a bunch of flowers in the room. As the liquid began to vaporize anyone in the room would be permanently blinded by the gas. Lovell proposed that the Pope be then prevailed upon to issue a statement that the two fascists had been blinded in divine retribution for their contravention of the Sixth Commandment that Thou Shalt Not Kill.

Lovell's own favourite scheme was a plan to attack Hitler with female sex hormones, which would be supplied to an anti-Nazi working in the vegetable garden of the Eagle's Nest. The gardener was to inject the hormones into the Führer's food, with the intention that 'his moustache would fall off and his voice become soprano'.[10] Like most of the other more bizarre plans for secret chemical and biological attacks, this scheme, too, failed. But some twenty years later, the successors to the Second World War 'Hell Raisers' were still toying with the idea of clandestinely tampering with a victim's sexual identity.

With the end of the World War and the first stirrings of the new Cold War which was to dominate international life over the coming thirty years, there were new tasks for the intelligence organisations, and their biological and chemical warfare specialists. As the Office of Strategic Services, hastily formed during the war, was replaced by the highly structured Central Intelligence Agency, so the nature of chemical and biological warfare research changed from a search to discover agents suitable for particular missions, to a long-term plan to isolate drugs and poisons available for use as and when the need arose. In particular the 1950s were dominated by what has come to be known as 'The Search for the Manchurian Candidate'.[11]

Two days before Christmas 1948 squads of Hungarian secret police had surrounded the Archiepiscopal Palace of Cardinal Josef Mindszenty, the Primate of Hungary. Ever since the occupation of his country at the end of the war by the Soviet army, Mindszenty had been an outspoken critic of the new socialist regime, ceaselessly campaigning for freedom to practise his religion, and attacking the government for failing to hold elections.[12]

On 3 February 1949 he was taken from the secret police headquarters to a court-room on Marko Street in Budapest, to face charges of subversion, espionage, and illegal use of foreign currency. As the Cardinal stood in the dock wearing a black suit run up by the police tailor, it was clear that the Hungarian authorities were hoping for a trial which would set an example to their people, a display of contrition in which the eminent churchman would recant his anti-government activities and so help to silence further opposition.

But whatever effect the trial might have had in Hungary was easily outweighed by the response of the West. Cardinal Mindszenty seemed a wreck of a man. His eyes, it was said, were the eyes of a man whose brain was no longer his own. As he stood in the dock confessing to the catalogue of crimes, Western intelligence began to wonder what had happened to him during his time in secret police cells. They concluded that he had either been drugged or subjected to extreme hypnosis.

Senior CIA men believed that the Russians had developed a method of making a man completely subservient to their will. There were reports of Soviet agents arrested in Germany equipped with syringes said to contain a liquid making any victim amenable to the will of his captor. Later, when American servicemen taken prisoner during the Korean War began to make confessions of their 'crimes' and to sign petitions calling for an end to United States involvement in Asia, the intelligence experts became convinced. They believed the Russians had developed a drug which, when administered to a victim, turned him into a robot, responsive only to their orders, and unaware even that he was being manipulated. By the time a high level military study group had concluded that no such drug existed, the CIA had already begun its own search for a reliable method of controlling human behaviour.[13]

It had started in 1950 with 'Project Bluebird', a study to examine the effects of hypnosis and electric shocks on defectors and would-be agents. By the following year the CIA wanted to broaden the investigation into the possible uses of drugs. (There was a scheme to find ways of inducing amnesia in 'blown' agents and defectors with the use of drugs, as an alternative to long periods in CIA custody.)[14] The British and Canadian representatives who took part in the discussions remained sceptical about the chances of discovering a drug which would turn a man into an unwitting agent, but the CIA pressed ahead regardless. The quest continued for almost twenty years.

In April 1953 the CIA's Deputy Director of Plans, Richard Helms, proposed that the agency establish a 'program for the covert use of biological and chemical materials'[15] for the manipulation of behaviour. The project was, Helms believed, 'ultra sensitive', and he therefore argued that it be exempt from all the normal accounting channels, its very existence hidden from all but the most senior officers of the CIA. The Director of the CIA, Allen Dulles, approved the proposal, and the project began, under the codename MKULTRA.

The CIA made an agreement with a centre for the treatment of drug addicts in Lexington, Kentucky, run by a Dr Harris Isbell. Dr Isbell would receive consignments of drugs selected by CIA scientists as likely to be of use in MKULTRA, and would experiment with them upon the addicts in his care. Often addicts would be offered a 'fix' of the drug of their dependency in exchange for the opportunity to give them a drug of the CIA's choice.

The CIA tested large numbers of drugs, including many, like cocaine, which later became part of the drug culture of the sixties and seventies. But, like the Army Chemical Corps, their main interest was in the then little known drug LSD. Dr Isbell's letters back to the CIA note that a number of the addicts to whom he was giving the drug began to show signs of fear of the doctors at the centre. But his curiosity and enthusiasm drove him on nonetheless. After one experiment with LSD in 1953, Dr Isbell reported that:

The mental effects included anxiety, a feeling of unreality, noises were difficult to distinguish, the patients' hands and feet appeared to grow ... patients reported seeing visions consisting of rapidly changing fantastic scenes which resembled Walt Disney movies.[16]

Most of the 'patients' appear to have been 'negro males', and most of the experiments to have involved the unwitting receipt of LSD. In one experiment Dr Isbell kept seven men on LSD for seventy-seven days, a feat which would have terrified even the most hardened 'acid head' of the drug culture.

But to appreciate the effects of LSD on normal people in a normal environment, the CIA could not rely exclusively upon the experiments with drug addicts or volunteers. To gain a full understanding of the effects of LSD, they needed to administer the drug to unsuspecting victims.

Twice a year the scientists from the Special Operations division at Fort Detrick would gather at an old log cabin in the Appalachian mountains to spend a few quiet days discussing their work, and sketching out new areas of research. On 18 November 1953 they were joined by a group from the CIA working on the effects of LSD. On the evening of their second day in the mountains, the men sat around sharing a bottle of Cointreau. Twenty minutes later the senior CIA man present, Sid Gottlieb, told his colleagues that he had spiked their drinks with LSD. The conversation soon disintegrated into confusion and laughter, and few of them managed any sleep that night. The following day all set off to drive home.

Frank Olson, one of the civilian chemists from Fort Detrick, arrived home extremely depressed. Years of experience in Top Secret work had conditioned him to say little about his activities in the laboratories, and when his wife asked him what was wrong he replied only that he had made a mistake and felt that he should leave his job. 'He was an entirely different person', his wife recalled later, 'I didn't know what had happened, I just knew that something was terribly wrong'.[17] Olson remained in this disturbed condition throughout the weekend and while at work at Fort Detrick on Monday. By Tuesday his colleagues had decided he needed specialist psychiatric advice.

One of Olson's colleagues at Fort Detrick, Colonel Vincent Ruwet, offered to accompany Olson to New York to see a recommended psychiatrist. They were joined on the journey by a civilian, Robert Lashbrook, who worked for the CIA. To pass the evening in Manhattan the three men went to see a musical, but Olson became so upset that Colonel Ruwet had to walk him back to their hotel during the intermission. Later, while Ruwet was asleep, Olson went out wandering the streets. At one point he apparently became convinced that Ruwet had ordered him to destroy all his paper money, and tore it up and threw away his wallet.

The New York psychiatrist, who had been chosen because his previous work for the army had given him a top security clearance, diagnosed Olson as suffering from 'psychosis and delusions', and recommended that he enter hospital. Although Olson has planned to return home for the Thanksgiving weekend celebrations before any further treatment, he apparently felt too ashamed to make the journey. While Colonel Ruwet travelled down to explain to Alice Olson why her husband would not be home for the family celebrations, Olson and Lashbrook went back to see the psychiatrist. He recommended again that Olson be admitted to hospital, but the earliest that arrangements could be made was the following day. That evening the two men checked into Room 1018A at the Statler Hotel in midtown Manhattan.

At 3.20 in the morning the CIA man was awoken by the sound of breaking glass. Ten floors below, the body of Frank Olson lay shattered on Seventh Avenue.

Immediately a cover-up began. The police were given the impression that Olson had simply been suffering from a great deal of stress. Alice Olson was told first that her husband had died as a result of an accident at work, and then that he had fallen from a hotel window. No one mentioned the LSD tests. It was only twenty-two years later, when a report into the activities of the CIA mentioned how an unnamed army employee had jumped from a hotel window after being given LSD, that his family were able to establish how Frank Olson had died.

Frank Olson was by no means the only unwitting victim of CIA attempts to discover the effects of LSD and other 'mind bending' drugs. As noted earlier, a decision had been taken soon after the start of MKULTRA that to determine the effects of drugs on intended victims, realistic tests had to be conducted upon unsuspecting 'clients'. In May 1953 the CIA hired one of their more colourful operators to arrange the testing for them.

George White had begun his working life in the classic fashion, as a cub reporter on the San Francisco *Herald Examiner*. But the job failed to offer the excitement he sought, and in 1934 he joined the Bureau of Narcotics, committed to stamping out the illegal use of drugs. In the course of his career with the Bureau he claimed to have shot and killed a suspected Japanese spy, to have been put on trial in Calcutta after a gunfight, shot his way out of a bar in Marseilles, and to have infiltrated a Chinese drug-smuggling brotherhood.[18] With the formation of the OSS during the Second World War, White was a natural recruit. Here he turned his experience with the Narcotics Bureau to advantage, volunteering to test new 'truth drugs' himself.

In May 1953 White became Subproject Three of MKULTRA, his job to provide the environment in which the CIA could test drugs on unsuspecting victims. Under an assumed name he rented an apartment in Greenwich Village, New York City, which the CIA then fitted out with microphones and two-way mirrors. White then engaged prostitutes to lure men back to the apartment, where their drinks would be doctored with drugs like cannabis concentrate and LSD. Then in early 1955 the Narcotics Bureau, who were still his notional employers, transferred White to San Francisco.

In the apartment George White took in San Francisco, the CIA moved in so much electronic surveillance equipment that one former agent was later to remark 'if you spilled a glass of water, you'd probably electrocute yourself'.[19] White brought his own peculiar flair to the place, furnishing it like a caricature brothel – red curtains,

Toulouse-Lautrec posters and pictures of manacled women. It was appropriate enough, for the place was to be used as a government-sponsored bordello. White would watch from behind a two-way mirror sipping chilled Martinis as prostitutes stripped off and had sex with their clients.[20] Initially the project officers were interested to learn how much information a man might be prepared to give at various stages of the sexual encounter. Then the interest turned to drugs. The prostitutes would offer their clients apparently normal cocktails which had previously been spiked with LSD, and the CIA observers would monitor their behaviour.

In another LSD experiment in San Francisco in 1959, CIA agents were told to meet a random selection of people in bars, and to invite them back to a hired house for a party. When the room was crowded, they were to spray LSD from an aerosol into the air. Unfortunately for the experiment, it was an exceptionally warm day, and with the room full of people the windows had to be kept open, creating such a strong draught that it would have been impossible to ensure a reasonable concentration of LSD in the atmosphere. The test was abandoned, and the agents consoled themselves with unlaced drinks.[21]

Years later George White would write to Sid Gottlieb, the head of CIA drug and germ research programme:

I toiled wholeheartedly in the vineyards because it was fun, fun, fun. Where else could a red-blooded American lie, kill, cheat, steal, rape and pillage with the sanction and blessing of the All-Highest?[22]

Where indeed?

And yet, if the CIA were to continue their research into chemical and biological warfare, then they had, they felt, to test the substances on unwitting people. By definition this ruled out volunteers. In a memo classified 'eyes only' on the subject written by Richard Helms in December 1963 it was explained that other approaches had been considered. The CIA had thought of asking local police departments to give the drugs to prisoners, but that would have involved informing local politicians. 'Several times in the past ten years' the Agency had attempted to set up testing programmes abroad, but each time too many foreigners had known for the scheme to be secure. In the end they concluded that the only solution was to continue the arrangement with the Narcotics Bureau – the efforts of George White and others – because it 'affords us more security'.[23]

But if White's activities were the most colourful, they were only a tiny part of MKULTRA. In August 1977 the CIA admitted that there had been no less than 149 subprojects, including experiments to determine the effects of different drugs on human behaviour, work on lie-detectors, hypnosis and electric shock, and 'the surreptitious delivery of drug-related materials'.[24] Forty-four colleges and universities had been involved, fifteen research foundations, twelve hospitals or clinics and three penal institutions. Front organisations had been established to channel funds to institutions which the CIA believed would carry out work for them. Typical was the Society for the Investigation of Human Ecology, which in two years gave money to academic foundations in Britain, Canada, Finland, Hong Kong, Burma, Israel, Holland and Switzerland, as well as to numerous institutions within the United States.[25] Not all these foundations were necessarily conducting work for the CIA's mind control and chemical warfare programmes.

In June 1964 MKULTRA was renamed MKSEARCH. Eleven years after the attempt to develop means of waging clandestine chemical and biological warfare had begun, it was still felt that this was such a sensitive area that the project should continue to be exempt from all normal administrative and accounting controls. By the early 1970s LSD had been abandoned, but other drugs were under investigation. A tantalizing glimpse of the work being conducted is afforded by the report in 1973 on Project OFTEN. The heavily censored two-page report states the CIA belief that the 'Soviets are known to be actively working in the glycolate area', and records that Edgewood Arsenal had already earmarked an unnamed drug – presumably a similar compound – as a potential incapacitant. Twenty volunteers, five prisoners, and fifteen servicemen had been given the drug, and produced symptoms lasting up to six weeks.[26]

Of the final phase of the CIA's involvement in covert chemical and biological warfare, MKDELTA, the 'use of biochemicals in clandestine operations', very little is known. In one form or another, however, the research project had continued for twenty years, until, shortly before he left office, the man who had originated the research ordered that all records be destroyed. What little is now known is a tribute to the inefficiency with which the task was carried out, and the conscientiousness of CIA employees in answering Freedom of Information Act requests.

William Colby, the slim, well-dressed Director of the CIA, remembers 16 September 1975 as a 'ghastly day'.[27] Beneath the assembled television cameras in a Committee Room on Capitol Hill he began to read from a hastily prepared statement.

There had been some confusion over whether Nixon's announcement of November 1969 – that the United States was to destroy all her biological weapons – was an instruction which also applied to toxin devices. Toxins are poisons which, although originally derived from living organisms, are not capable of reproducing themselves and, unlike disease bacteria, cannot be transmitted from one person to another. Three months after his policy statement renouncing biological weapons, Nixon announced that toxins too were to be included in the ban. In a statement issued from Key Biscayne, Florida, and known as the Valentine's Day Declaration, since it was issued on 14 February 1970, Nixon announced that all stocks of toxin weapons were also to be destroyed.

Colby felt uncomfortable as he sat facing the Senate Intelligence Committee in Committee Room 318 of the Russell Senate Office Building on Capitol Hill five years later. As the Committee chairman, Senator Frank Church put it, 'direct orders of the President of the United States were evidently disobeyed by employees of the CIA'.[28] Colby began to explain how it was that the CIA came to have eleven grammes of a substance clearly labelled 'Shellfish Toxin', and a further eight grammes of Cobra venom, five years after the President had ordered their destruction.

During the Second World War American secret agents had been issued with 'L pills', filled with cyanide. The suicide pills, designed to be taken as an alternative to interrogation and torture after capture, had one great disadvantage. Cyanide causes an agonizing death, and may take several minutes to act. The CIA, Colby said, had determined to find a faster and less painful poison.

Colby revealed that on his ill-fated espionage flight over the Soviet Union in May 1960, the U-2 spy plane pilot Gary Powers had carried a supply of the new shellfish poison which had been refined at Fort Detrick on the instructions of the CIA. The poison was hidden in the grooves of a 'drill bit', which was in turn hidden inside a silver dollar he carried everywhere. When Powers's aircraft was shot down by Soviet missiles, he evidently decided to risk interrogation, and did not swallow the poison. Curious KGB counter intelligence officers who examined the silver dollar are said to have given the poison to a dog. It was dead within ten seconds. But there were, Colby explained, other uses for the shellfish poison too.

Beneath the bright lights and whirring cameras, Colby suddenly produced what he described, in masterly bureaucratese, as a 'nondiscernible microbioinoculator'. It looked like a normal .45 pistol. But Colby told the senators it was powered by electricity. A small battery in the handle produced enough power to fire a small poisoned dart one hundred yards. The 'nondiscernible' element of Colby's description now became apparent: tests had shown the weapon to be so effective that a poisoned dart could be fired into a victim without his even noticing that he had been hit.

Though the production of the poisoned dart gun created a sensation, other witnesses were to follow Colby who would describe many other devices. There were, it appeared, weapons which could be used to contaminate roads or railway tracks with biological agents, pens which would fire poison darts or spray gas into a room, umbrellas and walking sticks which would do the same. In fact the shellfish toxin represented only a tiny part of the arsenal which had been developed to wage clandestine chemical and biological warfare.

Colby explained that the toxins which should have been destroyed had been retained 'in an excess of zeal', since they had been enormously expensive to extract, and represented about one third of the world's total supply. The few grammes of shellfish toxin represented enough to give a fatal dose to thousands of people. Colby was asked whether there were any records which would tell the story of the CIA's involvement in chemical and biological warfare. No, he said, they had all been destroyed in 1972.

Such records as remain indicate that CIA interest in chemical and biological warfare dates back at least to 1952, when the Agency approached the Special Operations Division at Fort Detrick. Only a handful of CIA personnel knew of the arrangement between the two organisations, and on visits to the biological warfare base they were known simply as the 'Staff Support Group'. The fact that the CIA was paying for research at Fort Detrick was hidden behind the funding code 'P600'.[29]

According to one of the participants it was 'a kind of Never-Never land'.[30] Among the ideas tossed about were questions such as: could a material be developed to dissolve the Berlin Wall? Could a drug be produced to knock out everyone in a building? Could water divining be used to detect enemy submarines?

While these extraordinary theories were being discussed, other researchers were being sent on expeditions to far flung corners of the globe to gather plant or animal samples which might be used in the manufacture of new weapons.

In 1953 a researcher was despatched to the mountains of central Mexico in search of the fabled Magic Mushroom used by Indians during religious ceremonies and said to 'open the doors of perception'. Nine years later an unidentified CIA officer wrote to his Division Chief about the problems faced on another expedition. The plan had been to develop a poison based upon the gall bladder of the Tanganyika crocodile. The CIA man had decided there were two options:

The first is to have one of our (deleted) buddies in Tanganyika find, capture and eviscerate a native crocodile on the spot and then try to ship its gall bladder, and/or poisonous viscera to the United States ... The second alternative would be to acquire a crocodile ... through a licensed collector, and ship the animal live to the United States.

Undaunted by the complex logistical problems presented in sending the unfortunate crocodile to CIA laboratories, the enthusiastic young agent concluded his report by mentioning that sources in Tanganyika could 'provide us with details concerning methods and techniques employed by the witch doctors in preparing the poison'.[31]

While the CIA scoured the world in search of little-known poisons, its British and Canadian counterparts appear to have devoted their energies to refining poisons already discovered. Little is known of the exact nature of allied research in this field, although a report to the American House of Representatives did reveal that scientists at Fort Detrick had collaborated with Canadian counterparts in the early 1950s in attempts to isolate the 'paralytic poisoning in man often caused by eating toxic clams and mussels'.[32] By 1954, the two groups of scientists had extracted the poison in a 'relatively pure form'.

In fact throughout the post-war years the British and Canadian have collaborated closely with their American counterparts, at least in the initial areas of research. In 1975 a veteran Fort Detrick scientist described the co-operation as 'close co-ordination'.[33] Indeed, the shellfish toxin which the CIA had retained five years after it should have been destroyed had first been properly understood by a British scientist, Dr Martin Evans, employed by the Institute of

Animal Physiology at Babraham on the outskirts of Cambridge.[34] Records from Fort Detrick also show that stocks of shellfish poison were shipped to the microbiological establishment at Porton Down, and to its Australian counterpart, the Defence Standards Laboratories at Ascot Vale, Victoria. During the time of the Senate hearings into the supplies of shellfish poison, one of the Fort Detrick specialists in clandestine biological warfare revealed that in 1975 he had been 'on temporary duty' in Britain where he had been working 'on a collaborative effort' in 'Biological Protection'.[35]

Details of which drugs and poisons the British finally settled upon for their secret services are likely to stay shrouded in secrecy for years to come. It would be astonishing if, unlike the United States and the Soviet Union, the British had not developed such weapons for clandestine use. Perhaps it is some indication of the relative significance of chemical warfare for the undercover services that among the commemorative plaques on the wall behind the desk of the Director of Porton Down is only one from an army regiment. It is that of the Special Air Service, or SAS, the hand-picked special operations unit trained to operate behind enemy lines, and charged with carrying out the 'dirty jobs' of the intelligence services.

In the United States some evidence at least is available to suggest the sort of uses to which clandestine chemical or biological weapons might be put. There were numerous planned attempts on the life of Fidel Castro using chemical or biological devices.[36] Botulinal toxin pills were prepared, to be slipped into Castro's food, cigars were contaminated with the same poison, plans were laid to contaminate his rubber diving suit with spores causing a chronic skin disease. There were even plans to dust his shoes with a chemical which would cause his beard to fall out, so, it was speculated, ruining his revolutionary appeal. None of these schemes came to anything, although in 1960 another poisoning operation came closest to success, when the CIA went after Patrice Lumumba, the radical prime minister of the Congo (now Zaire). Six months after independence Sid Gottlieb, the man who had slipped LSD into Frank Olson's after-dinner drink, was sent to Kinshasa with a supply of poison. Much to his frustration, Gottlieb was unable to find a way of getting the poison into Lumumba's body, and the plan was abandoned.[37]

By the late 1960s the descendants of Sidney Lovell's 'hell raisers' had developed a gamut of chemical and biological devices suitable for every purpose from disguised assassination to minor harassment. Some were described by former CIA agent Philip Agee in 1975:

Horrible smelling liquids in small glass vials can be hurled into meeting halls. A fine clear powder can be sprinkled in a meeting place, becoming invisible after settling, but having the effect of tear-gas when stirred up by the later movement of people. An incendiary powder can be moulded around prepared tablets and when ignited the combination produces ample quantities of smoke that attacks the eyes and the respiratory system more strongly than ordinary tear-gas. A tasteless substance can be introduced to food that causes exaggerated body-colour. And a few small drops of a clear liquid stimulate the target to relaxed, uninhibited talk. Invisible itching powder can be placed on steering wheels or toilet seats, and a slight smear of invisible ointment causes a serious burn to skin on contact. Chemically processed tobacco can be added to cigarettes and cigars to produce respiratory ailments.[38]

There were many other devices which Agee did not choose to mention; three different forms of toxin, all of them fatal, other agents to cause diseases like anthrax and tuberculosis, chemicals to induce anything from hallucinations to heart failure.[39]

When asked why the CIA had developed such a range of clandestine weapons, the architect of much of the programme, Richard Helms, cited the well-worn argument used by the chemical and biological warfare establishment since chemical warfare began. 'A good intelligence organisation would be expected to know what his adversaries were doing and be in a position to protect himself against the offensive acts of his adversaries', adding, unnecessarily, 'if the worst came to the worst, and we were ever asked by the proper authority to do something in this field, we would be prepared to do so.'[40]

In the years which followed Nixon's decision to stop the chemical arms race in 1970, it was an argument which would be heard with increasing frequency.

TEN

From Disarmament to Rearmament

Nixon's decision to call a halt to the chemical and biological arms race had been prompted by a number of motives. The British and Canadian governments were arguing that an international agreement to ban biological weapons looked feasible, providing Nixon would make a gesture of good faith. There was widespread opposition to the use in Vietnam of weapons which, whatever the State Department might claim, certainly *looked* like gas. And there were a number of highly embarassing accidents.

In March 1968 the US Army carried out a series of tests using live nerve agents at Dugway Proving Ground, Utah. Shortly before six on the evening of 13 March an F4 Phantom jet screamed over the base, pouring VX liquid from tanks slung below the aircraft onto a marked-out target area. But there was a fault with one of the tanks being tested, and, while most was released from the expected altitude, some 20 lb remained inside the tank. As the jet climbed out of its bombing run, VX leaked from the container. At the higher altitude, the wind was gusting at up to 35 mph. The nerve agent hung in the air, before finally drifting down to the ground at Skull Valley, some twenty miles north of the test site. A massive flock of sheep grazing in the valley began to fall sick within hours. Local photographers and television crews arrived on the scene in time to see the carcasses of six thousand sheep being slung into hastily dug trench graves. The attendant national and international publicity, in the words of an army public relations officer, 'delivered a crippling blow to the nation's chemical-biological warfare programme.'[1]

The following spring it became known that the United States army planned to ship thousands of tons of obsolete chemical weapons across the country from their mid-west bases to the Atlantic seaboard where they were to be loaded into elderly merchant ships which would then be scuttled offshore. Local residents, the memory of the Dugway accident still fresh in their minds, quickly dubbed the cargo 'the ultimate hazardous freight', and were less than happy at the prospect of the weapons being dumped off their summer beaches.

The problem of what to do with elderly and unstable chemical weapons and the poisonous waste created in their manufacture had been getting the US Chemical Corps a bad press for several years. At Rocky Mountain Arsenal, the main centre for manufacture of GB nerve gas, scientists decided in 1960 to dispose of toxic waste by boring a 12,000 foot tunnel into the earth, to connect with a vast underground reservoir. A month after they began pouring the waste chemicals into the ground, Denver was rocked by its first earthquake for eighty years.

As the Arsenal continued to pour 165 million gallons of waste into the underground cavern over the next five years, the area suffered no less than 1,500 earth tremors. When, in 1966, the dumping was called to a halt, the army announced it would investigate whether the stuff could be pumped out again. Their conclusion, that the liquid wastes could only be removed at a rate of 300 gallons a day, indicated that it would take over a thousand years to empty the well. Although the earth tremors stopped after only part of the waste had been removed, the incident did little for the popularity of chemical weapons.

In the summer of 1969 came more bad news. VX nerve agent was leaking from a container at the American base on the Japanese island of Okinawa and twenty-three servicemen had been taken to hospital suffering from its effects. This was doubly serious, for not only did it further erode what little confidence remained in the adequacy of safety measures at chemical weapons bases, but the Japanese government had not even been aware that gas was based on its soil. The previous summer one hundred children playing on a nearby beach had collapsed with an unknown illness. The Pentagon immediately ordered the weapons to be removed from the island.

This combination of incompetence and accidents led to increasing public hostility towards chemical weapons. After all, it was argued, if a few pounds of nerve agent was sufficient to kill six thousand sheep, what would be the consequence of a full-scale accident?

Nixon's statement of November 1969 was nevertheless a gesture of some courage, representing as it did a decision to disarm unilaterally in the field of biological weapons, and to make no new chemical weaponry for the foreseeable future. The Geneva negotiations which led up to the Biological Weapons Convention owed a good deal to the Nixon decision. But it was inevitable that during the discussions the original British proposals for a Biological Warfare

Convention should be whittled down. While the essence of the British proposals remained unchanged – a complete ban on the manufacture and possession of germ weapons – the critical provisions dealing with the mechanisms whereby one country might check that another was complying with the treaty were made far less effective. In view of allegations which were to surface later in the 1970s this watering-down of the verification provisions was a critical weakness of the treaty.

Despite the fact that such major powers as France and China have still (by early 1982) not signed it, largely because they consider the verification procedures to be inadequate, the 1972 Biological Weapons Convention was a major achievement. One of the provisions of the treaty committed the eighty-seven signatory countries to 'continue negotiations on good faith' with a view to obtaining a similar agreement to ban chemical weapons. The United Nations General Assembly optimistically dubbed the 1970s 'The Disarmament Decade'. In the field of chemical warfare it might more properly have been named 'The Distrust Decade'.

Matters had not been helped by the attitude of the Russians. When the tortuous negotiations to produce a treaty banning biological weapons finally produced an agreement,[2] signatory states included the United States, Great Britain and Canada, who had led Western germ warfare research, the governments of Japan and West Germany, and the entire Warsaw Pact. All undertook 'never in any circumstances to develop, produce, stockpile or otherwise acquire or retain' biological weapons. Any existing stocks were to be destroyed.

The Americans made great play of the destruction of their germ weapons. Photographers were invited to watch as containers of tularemia, anthrax, Q fever and Venezuelan equine encephalomyelitis were mixed with caustic soda or heated to hundreds of degrees Fahrenheit to destroy the virulence for which they had been selected as weapons. Equipment from the Pine Bluff manufacturing plant was similarly treated and melted down to harmless scrap. Guided tours were arranged through the abandoned factory.

As the deadline for the destruction of biological weapons approached, attention turned to the Soviet Union. Would a similar display take place there? The Russians merely issued a statement announcing that the Soviet Union 'does not possess' any bacteriological weapons. Ignoring the question of whether they had ever developed any biological device in the thirty years before the treaty was signed in April 1972 did not help to build confidence between the Superpowers.

In addition, the agreement to ban biological weapons contained one serious flaw. There was no provision for one side to inspect the other's facilities to determine whether or not the treaty was being adhered to. The growing distrust led to a campaign in the Western press the like of which had not been seen since the scare stories of Russian 'disease factories' in the early fifties. Within months of the Biological Weapons Convention coming into effect, suggestions were appearing that the Russians were already breaking its terms.

'There is evidence', said an article in a Boston newspaper, 'that within recent months the Soviet Union has been constructing or expanding facilities which appear to be biological arms production plants, having very high incinerator stacks and large cold storage bunkers that could be used for stockpiling the weapons'.[3] Three months later came another claim, this time from the syndicated columnist Jack Anderson. Anderson told his readers that the chief Soviet medical attaché in Washington had been caught trying to 'weasel suspicious information' from American scientists over dinner at a genetic engineering conference in California. 'His efforts to elicit information that could help the Soviets advance their germ warfare research were obvious', said Anderson.[4]

The claims continued. In January 1978, a correspondent with Reuters news agency reported from NATO headquarters that 'scientific experts' had informed him that the Russians were developing 'three horrific new diseases for warfare . . . Lassa fever, which, according to the sources, kills 35 out of every 100 people it strikes, Ebola fever, which kills 70 out of every 100, and the deadly Marburg fever (Green Monkey Disease).'[5]

Not surprisingly, the effect of these allegations was to throw serious doubt on the value of attempting to negotiate a second treaty with the Soviet Union to ban gas warfare. Indeed, in the summer of 1978 a story appeared suggesting that Nixon's original decision to stop developing new chemical and biological weapons had been the result of work by Soviet spies. 'According to US intelligence officials', said the *New York Times,* 'the Soviet Union attempted to influence then-President Richard Nixon in 1969 to halt chemical and biological weapons development by transmitting information through double agents working for the Federal Bureau of Investigation'.[6] The paper maintained that the director of the FBI, J. Edgar Hoover, had conveyed the information to Nixon personally. While none of Nixon's White House staff was able to recall having been given any information about chemical or biological weapons by FBI agents, the *New York Times* report was sufficient nonetheless to add to the growing disquiet over what the Russians might be up to.

Soon there was a positive cascade of stories about Soviet preparations for germ warfare. A Polish army officer claimed to have been told that KGB specialists in biological warfare had been posted to Cuba.[7] Then in October 1979 came perhaps the most sensational allegation of all.

The fledgeling British news magazine *Now!* splashed across its front cover the headline 'Exclusive. Russia's secret germ warfare disaster'. It reported that 'Hundreds of people are reported to have died, and thousands to have suffered serious injury as a result of an accident which took place this summer in a factory involved in the production of bacteriological weapons in the Siberian city of Novosibirsk'.[8] The Soviet authorities had attempted to hush-up the accident, said the magazine, but information had been obtained from a 'traveller who was in the city at the time'. This 'traveller' claimed that bodies of the dead were delivered to their relatives in sealed coffins. Those few who had managed to glimpse the bodies had described them as being 'covered in brown patches'.

This macabre account, 'exclusive' to *Now!,* bore a remarkable resemblance to an article which had appeared three weeks earlier in an obscure Frankfurt based magazine named *Possev* published by a group of Russian emigrés.[9] In January 1980 *Possev* returned to the story, claiming that, contrary to their earlier report, the accident had occurred not at Novosibirsk, but a thousand miles or so away, in the city of Sverdlovsk. The dissident magazine alleged there had been an outbreak of anthrax in April 1979 caused by an explosion at a military settlement south-west of the city. A north wind, the dissidents said, had carried a cloud of anthrax bacteria over a nearby village, and people had begun to die, at the rate of thirty or forty a month.

By the following month Robert Moss, a columnist with the London *Daily Telegraph,* had picked up the story.[10] Moss, a right-wing journalist with impeccable intelligence contacts, reported that a thousand people had died after an explosion at 'military village 19', where army biologists had been experimenting with an agent known as 'V21'. Two days later, *Bild Zeitung,* a downmarket Hamburg tabloid, published a despatch from Moscow, (where it did not maintain a full-time correspondent) describing in graphic detail the effects of the anthrax incident.[11] Patients had choked to death within four hours. Bodies had been burned. Bulldozers had been brought in to strip away the contaminated topsoil.

On 18 March, one month later, the press corps assembled as usual at the State Department in Washington for the daily briefing on world events and American diplomacy. It was 'a quiet news day', and so one of the press agency correspondents asked the question he'd previously been tipped off about by a State Department source: what was the American attitude to the Soviet germ warfare allegations? The spokesman had his answer well rehearsed: 'an outbreak of disease' in Sverdlovsk, he said, raised questions of whether the Soviet Union had violated the 1972 Biological Warfare Convention. The US Ambassador in Moscow had been instructed to request an explanation. By the following morning the American press was quoting 'intelligence sources' as saying that two or three hundred people had died in an outbreak of anthrax, an outbreak which indicated that the Russians were developing biological weapons.[12] The Kremlin reacted with predictable outrage.

In a rare concession, the Soviet news agency, *Tass,* admitted that there had indeed been outbreaks of anthrax in Sverdlovsk, caused by what it called poor standards of personal hygiene in handling contaminated food. The explanation did sound plausible, since it was well known that anthrax had not been eradicated from large areas of the Soviet Union, and that at the time of the Sverdlovsk incident articles had appeared in the local press advising people on how to treat 'Siberian Sore', as the disease was locally known. What little information had reached the west about Sverdlovsk tended to support this explanation.[13]

But the intelligence experts disagreed. In July the American Congressional Committee on Intelligence issued its report on the Sverdlovsk incident. The outbreak of anthrax, they claimed, could not have been caused naturally. They had been told by 'a Soviet emigré', and had seen from classified intelligence files, that the anthrax deaths were the result of an explosion at a biological weapons factory.[14]

Nothing is likely to be proved about what did or did not happen at Sverdlovsk or in many of the other incidents. Some appear to be pure propaganda, others may be based on fact. They were, perhaps, an inevitable result of an agreement on bacteriological warfare which left many deeply dissatisfied at the absence of any method of ensuring that the other side was complying with the terms of the treaty. In the growing diplomatic frostiness of the late seventies and early eighties it was predictable that the allegations would surface with increasing frequency.

The reports were also more than sufficient to justify the existence in both Britain and the United States of groups of men who continued to work on defence against biological attack. With the decision to renounce germ warfare 'for all time', Fort Detrick had been handed over to the civilian National Cancer Institute. But part of the camp remained secret. Here the Pentagon established the Army Medical Research Institute of Infectious Diseases, where a small group of biologists would continue to work on 'those diseases which plague mankind', in the words of a Pentagon spokesman.[15] Within two years of its foundation, the Institute's staff and budget had trebled. The Pentagon maintains that the Fort Detrick scientists' work is purely defensive – the development of vaccines for example. Yet the 'diseases which plague mankind' are precisely the diseases investigated during the offensive biological weapons programme. The work, says the army, is essential 'just in case'.

A similar pattern was followed in Britain. At Porton Down the Microbiological Research Establishment, where post-war germ warfare work had been conducted, was handed over to the Department of Health, where the laboratories were to be used, among other things, for genetic research. But within the Chemical Defence Establishment at Porton Down, which is still a Ministry of Defence installation, a small, little known biological unit exists. Despite having signed a treaty which notionally banned biological weapons for all time, in 1979 the Ministry of Defence recruited a dozen specialists to 'take care of critical Defence problems in microbiology'.[16] In 1980 one of the laboratories which had been transferred to the Department of Health after signature of the treaty was handed back to Porton Down, for use by the defence microbiologists.[17] The exact nature of the work carried out in the biological laboratories is, of course, unknown. In the words of the present director of Porton Down, the establishments in Britain and the United States are designed to give a 'watchtower capability' for assessing possible new germ warfare threats.[18]

The Biological Weapons Convention did not attempt to restrict or ban germ warfare research, merely the development, production and stockpiling of biological weapons. In maintaining biological warfare research stations, albeit on a reduced scale, neither Britain nor America is breaking the terms of the Convention. But the fact that both countries have considered it impossible to abandon research is eloquent testimony to the fact that, international treaty or not, scientific warfare, once begun, has a life of its own. The 1972 Biological Weapons Convention, major achievement though it was, did not remove the suspicions which created the arms race.

Professor Adolf-Henning Frucht sat in the corner of the Berlin to Prague express, his mind skipping over why he might have been asked to represent his East German medical institute at a conference on scientific planning. He had been surprised by the invitation, since it was a subject in which he took little interest. Just inside the border between East Germany and Czechoslovakia the train stopped to admit the inevitable stream of eastern European officials. One of the uniformed bureaucrats told Frucht his papers were not in order. They led him from the train, across the now deserted platform and into an office. Two officials from the State Security Service were waiting inside. They took him away for interrogation.

Over the next eight months this frail grey-haired professor would endure no less than eighty-seven interrogation sessions with the East German secret police. Who was he working for? How had he become a spy? How did he pass on the information? Transcripts of the questioning sessions piled up on the floor of his interrogators' office. Finally, in January 1968, Frucht was taken for trial at a military court. Within three days the trial was over. Frucht was sentenced to life imprisonment.

For five years the former professor of medicine spent most of his waking hours putting nuts onto screws. Held in solitary confinement for much of the time, his only contact with humanity was the warder who delivered three meals a day to his primitive cell. Frucht kept himself sane by reading the books of the prison library and by rigorous mental and physical self-discipline. After nine and a half years he was collected from prison and delivered to the West German border. Here, as one component in a complicated spy exchange in June 1977, he limped the few yards into the west.

Like a number of other western secret agents, Frucht had become a spy because he was convinced that the Warsaw Pact planned to initiate World War Three. In the early sixties he had been approached by a colleague at the Institute for Industrial Physiology to work on new methods of detecting poisons in the atmosphere. Frucht devised a system of using fireflies, rather on the principle by which miners had taken canaries in cages with them to the coalface to detect the presence of gas. With fireflies, the amount of light emitted would be noticeably affected by the presence of gas in the air.

Professor Frucht soon received a visit from General Hans Rudolf Gestewitz, the senior medical officer of the East German army. The two men began to enjoy relaxed theoretical scientific discussions over dinner. They talked of possibilities for future wars – how, for example, an entire army might be hidden underwater to protect it from nuclear attack.

But from these fanciful, rambling chats came a remark which made Frucht determine that it was his 'darned duty', as he later put it, to become a spy. General Gestewitz mentioned that the Warsaw Pact had developed a chemical agent which would resist the extreme cold and bright sunlight of the Arctic. Frucht had never heard of such a weapon – normally nerve agent would evaporate in the sun, or freeze in extreme cold. The conversation continued in its theoretical way until suddenly the professor realised that they were no longer talking about abstract speculations, but about plans for a real military operation. The scheme, he was told, was for Warsaw Pact forces to attack American Ballistic Missile Early Warning bases in Alaska with chemical weapons.

The attraction of such an attack was obvious enough. If the staff of the early warning stations could be disabled, the United States would be defenceless. General Gestewitz told Frucht that the Warsaw Pact had developed a chemical agent which would remain liquid and effective even at forty degrees below zero. It would knock the technicians at the bases out for twelve hours.

Frucht considered this such a threat to world peace that he resolved to pass the information on to the West. After a series of meetings with agents of MI6 and the CIA arranged at great personal risk, he managed to establish a system for mailing information to dead letterboxes in West Germany.

During the coming months, as different chemical agents were brought to Frucht for analysis at his Institute, he would compile two reports. One would be the official assessment to be sent back to the East German army. A second report he would send to the CIA in West Germany.

In this manner Professor Frucht passed to Western intelligence details of almost the entire Warsaw Pact chemical armoury; details of agents, code-names and protective measures. Among the information he sent to the West was the chemical formula for what he believed to be a new agent, unknown in the West, a variant of the V agents developed in Britain and the United States.[19]

It is hard to assess the effect which Frucht's information may have had upon NATO war planners at Supreme Headquarters. Certainly, however disturbed they may have been by news that the Soviet forces had a new chemical weapon, the intelligence did not affect Nixon, who the following year announced the ban on new American chemical weapons. But, restless at what they saw as giving a dangerous hostage to fortune, the advocates of chemical weapons within NATO had soon begun on a campaign to appeal to the public direct. The year after Nixon's decision, reports began to appear in the western military press of a new Soviet nerve agent. Identified as 'VR 55', the new weapon was said to be similar to VX, but even more potent.[20] Whether this was the gas which Frucht had discovered, or a second new weapon is not known.

In the latter half of the 1970s there emerged a group of military theorists who believed the threat of Russian chemical warfare to be one of the great unrecognised dangers facing the West. In increasingly strident tones they began to argue in favour of chemical rearmament within NATO. One of the more restrained analyses of the Soviet threat was made by Professor John Erickson, an acknowledged authority on the Soviet Army.

Erickson estimated that there were eighty thousand specialist troops in the Red Army, commanded by Lieutenent General V. K. Pikalov, whose battlefield job it was to decontaminate men, machines and weaponry of chemicals. There were a thousand ranges where Soviet troops trained to fight on a contaminated battlefield. Soviet tanks and armoured cars were equipped with elaborate seals and pressurization systems to keep out gas. Chemical training was taken so seriously that Soviet soldiers, he discovered, had been burned by real gas used in training.

Erickson noted that the Russians 'constantly emphasise the likely use by the enemy – presumably NATO – of chemical weapons', yet NATO, as Erickson remarked, had only a small number of such weapons. Furthermore, Russian training emphasised defence not only against nerve gas, but also against blood and lung agents first developed during the First World War, and now unimportant in the NATO stockpile. Erickson decided that 'the attraction of the chemical weapon would appear to be growing for the Soviet command'.[21]

NATO airfields might be knocked out by Soviet missiles releasing their cargoes of heavy and persistent nerve liquid overhead. Nuclear weapon sites might be immobilized for weeks in the same way. Quickly-evaporating nerve and blood gases might be used in attacks on allied anti-tank posts. The advancing Soviet forces would seal their flanks from attack by spreading persistent nerve agents on the ground and thereby make them impenetrable to counterattack. Indeed, while American forces could only 'go chemical' on the authority of the President, Erickson speculated that in the Soviet army a decision to use gas might be delegated to a divisional commander. It was a frightening picture; and then came the evidence of the Yom Kippur War.

For fifty-three minutes on the afternoon of 6 October 1973 a thousand Egyptian guns punched their shells across the Suez Canal and onto the Bar Lev Line, the fortified wall built by the Israelis after the Six Day War in 1967. Having caught the Israelis unawares, the Egyptians poured a thousand tanks and ten infantry brigades across the canal. For a while it seemed that the redoubtable Israeli army faced defeat. But a combination of massive reinforcement and a brilliant counterattack destroyed the impetus of the Egyptians, and forced them to agree to a ceasefire.

As the two armies disengaged, Israeli intelligence officers began to collect trophies from the destroyed and abandoned Egyptian vehicles in the desert. Among the equipment they collected from immobilized armoured cars were rubber capes, gas masks, alarms to warn of the presence of nerve gas, small tin boxes containing glass phials filled with coloured liquids to identify various gases, and automatic syringes filled with an antidote to soman, the main Soviet nerve agent. All carried instructions in Arabic, but had been manufactured in the Soviet Union.

There was no evidence that the Egyptians had intended to use gas themselves. Probably they carried the equipment because, like the Soviet army, they had been instructed to do so. Israeli intelligence immediately passed the captured equipment to the United States, where examination of the extensive Soviet precautions against gas attack resulted the following year in a Pentagon decision to spend one and three quarter billion dollars on improving the defences of American forces.

Ever since their decision not to proceed with any new weapons of their own, the British, Canadians and Australians had been devoting most of their energies to protection for their troops. In addition to animal experiments at Porton Down, which by the late 1970s were consuming 25,000 animals a year,[22] an average of ten servicemen and women arrived at Porton every month to test new equipment.[23] By concentrating on defensive research, the British developed both new gas masks and, most importantly, a cloth whose baked rayon structure protected the body against nerve liquids which could penetrate through the skin. Unlike the heavy rubber suits worn by Soviet soldiers, which became heavy, sweaty and uncomfortable within minutes, the Porton suits could be worn for days at a time without the danger of the wearer collapsing from exhaustion. Porton Down also produced new alarms and decontamination equipment and a series of pink and white pills which would protect soldiers against three or four times the normal lethal dose of nerve gas. Periodically entire British army units would be required to don 'noddy suits', the soldiers' unaffectionate name for the kit designed to protect them against chemical attack, and perform all their normal tasks while wearing the heavy and uncomfortable equipment.[24]

Even after the Pentagon decision that the American forces too needed to improve drastically their chemical defence research and training, many still believed that they lagged far behind the Soviet army. The Commander of the United States army in Europe was called before a Congressional Committee in 1979 to explain his preparations for decontaminating after a chemical attack. General Frederick Kroesen had the following exchange with Congressman Larry McDonald:

McDonald: Do you have any rapid decontamination washing process, or do you do the decontamination process out in the field?
General Kroesen: The manner we are pursuing it right now in Europe, sir, is to have identified for unit commanders the location of all available washing facilities, such as Schnellwasch stations, automobile drive-in washing facilities.
McDonald: Our military is going to be able to requisition the civilian automobile washing stations; is that what we are planning on using?

General Kroesen: In times of crisis we need to know where those kinds of facilities are.
McDonald: Good God.[25]

The conviction was growing among the 'hawks' in NATO that the decision to stop expanding the chemical arsenal had given a dangerous hostage to fortune. In 1980 the British opened a purpose designed 7,000 acre chemical warfare 'Battle Run' training area in the Wiltshire hills alongside Porton Down. The US Army opened a specialist chemical training school in Alabama. The US Chemical Corps, reduced to 2,000 in the early 1970s, was built up to nearly 6,000 by 1981.[26]

But even with superior 'noddy suits', pressurized battlefield headquarters, and an array of sophisticated alarms, detectors, decontamination equipment, pills and syringes, there was still an apparently insuperable problem. Without a credible threat to use chemical weapons themselves, allied soldiers would have to button themselves into their protective kit not when *they* chose, but when a Soviet attack was conceivably imminent. Inside the masks and rubber gloves the delicate tasks of modern warfare become extraordinarily difficult. Sighting a weapon, twiddling the knobs and flicking the switches on modern artillery become clumsy and cumbersome operations. Suddenly everyone on the battlefield looks identical. Since verbal orders are muffled by gas masks, commanders sometimes have to throw stones at their troops to attract their attention. An enemy who is not obliged to dress his soldiers up like frogmen because only *he* knows when a chemical attack may be launched gains an immediate tactical advantage, it was argued.

Meanwhile, the negotiations to secure a treaty on chemical disarmament dragged on. As a gesture in the right direction the United States finally ratified the Geneva Protocol, fifty years after it had been drawn up. Both the United States and the Soviet Union were committed by the Biological Weapons Convention to negotiate 'in good faith' towards a similar agreement on chemical arms. In July 1974, shortly before resigning in disgrace, Nixon met with Chairman Brezhnev in Moscow. To widespread surprise the communiqué issued at the end of their discussions indicated that the two countries would begin preparing a joint initiative on chemical disarmament. Talks between American and Soviet officials finally started in August 1976.

But what began with high ideals continued in an increasingly bad-tempered series of haggles. The two countries stated early in the discussions that they were seeking a comprehensive treaty which would oblige all countries not only to dispose of their present stocks of chemical weapons, but also not to develop any future gas weapons. After the suspicions which had followed the germ warfare treaty, the Americans were determined to establish an adequate system for 'on site' inspection, to ensure that nerve gas plants were no longer operational. By May 1978, after seven sessions of negotiations, the two sides believed they had at least delineated the sorts of weapons which would be covered by the treaty.[27] But an agreement on how to ensure that the treaty was being observed remained elusive.

The military, meanwhile, were growing restless. The United States had produced no new gas weapons since Nixon's ban in 1969. Now, a succession of military experts stated their belief that the Russians were adding to their gas stocks almost daily. 'The hope that the Soviets would emulate US restraint has proved to be wishful thinking', wrote one senior Chemical Corps officer, in a typical complaint.[28] There is, however, a notable vagueness about the details of these claims. Indeed in 1979 figures produced in support of this argument – that up to one third of Soviet bombs, rockets and shells might be filled with gas – bore a great similarity to the estimates current at the time of Nixon's ban in 1969.[29] By contrast with the figures leaked to the press or bandied about in conversation, official military spokesmen have been notably reluctant to make any estimate of the number of Soviet chemical weapons. In 1975 the chairman of the US Joint Chiefs of Staff could say only that 'it is not possible with any reasonable degree of assurance to predict or estimate the size of the USSR's CW stockpile'.[30] In 1980 a senior official in British scientific intelligence could refer only to the estimates already published in the press, that the proportion of Soviet bombs and artillery shells filled with gas amounted to 'anything between five and thirty per cent – you pay your money and take your choice'.[31]

But this absence of reliable information did nothing to shake the belief that the Russians had indeed acquired an enormous arsenal of gas weapons. Although the size of American stocks is classified information, from comments by the Chemical Corps and Department of Defence civilian observers have been able to estimate the quantity at about 150,000 tons of bombs, shells and landmines, about two thirds of which contain nerve gas, the remainder being mustard gas weapons left from the Second World War.[32] The same authorities believe that the Russians stopped adding to their stocks in 1971, two years after the United States called a halt. If true, then the increasing hysteria built up by the proponents of chemical weapons during the 1970 was based upon a fiction.

Nevertheless, the campaign for rearmament continued. The United States had 'frightened and moralised' herself 'into throwing away a vital deterrent', as one hard line politician had it.[33] 'Simply by negotiating the Soviets appear to have tied US hands on chemical weapons',[34] wrote a Chemical Corps officer in 1979. He went on to predict that not having chemical weapons made nuclear war more likely; 'some day a President of the United States might have to choose between acceptance of defeat or nuclear war'.[35]

Paradoxically, the British had used precisely the reverse argument as a reason for not needing chemical weapons themselves. As the Defence Secretary had explained in 1968:

We have not felt it necessary, nor indeed did the previous government, to develop a retaliatory capability here, because we have nuclear weapons, and we might choose to retaliate in that way if that were the requirement.[36]

Now, the argument was being stood on its head: chemical rearmament now could prevent nuclear war later.

In 1979 NATO commanders played out one of their biennial war games simulating the outbreak of World War Three. Codenamed 'Wintex', the exercise involved only the generals, civil servants and politicians who would make the critical decisions about how the war should be fought. In Operations Rooms in Europe and North America they acted out how they would respond to an escalating international crisis which finally pitted NATO and Warsaw Pact against each other in open war. As hostilities intensified, someone in NATO headquarters fed new information into the war plan being flashed to the decision makers in their concrete bunkers: the Soviet army had launched an attack with chemical weapons. What should be the NATO response? The choice alarmed everyone – both the smaller NATO members who disliked gas but wanted to avoid nuclear war at all costs, and the NATO nuclear powers, where many felt that the appropriate response was an attack with battlefield nuclear weapons, which itself ran the danger of inviting full scale Soviet nuclear counter-strike.[37]

The then N A T O Supreme Commander, General Alexander Haig, soon to become President Reagan's Secretary of State, told reporters in 1978 that N A T O's ability to wage war with chemicals was 'very weak'. 'Sometime in the near future,' he said, 'this will have to be reassessed'.[38] His successor as Supreme Commander went further. 'We ought to be able to respond with chemical weapons', he said, 'and they ought to know we have that capacity to respond'.[39] Ten years after Nixon's decision to suspend the manufacture of chemical weapons, by the end of the so-called Disarmament Decade, the advocates of chemical rearmament included some of the most senior figures in the military establishment.

There was already a weapon developed to make up for the deficiencies the generals saw all around them. The idea was simple, and, by the 1970s some twenty years old.

Shells and bombs loaded with nerve gas were not only dangerous to an enemy, but to anyone who had anything to do with them, including soldiers and civilians who happened to live near one of the bases. An accident or leak of the type which had already occurred enough times to sow public mistrust resulted in pools of nerve agent spreading everywhere, likely to kill any living animal within seconds or minutes. The weapons were so dangerous that they could not be moved, except in heavily guarded, extremely slow moving convoys diverted well away from human habitation. Allied governments were unhappy at the thought of weapons filled with some of the most poisonous substances known being based on their soil, but not under their control. Edgewood Arsenal suggested a solution which would overcome both the environmental and political objections to chemical weapons.

Since nerve gas is made from different chemical compounds, they suggested, why not redesign the bombs and shells so they could be filled with two separate canisters, each containing chemicals harmless in themselves, but which when mixed together would form a nerve agent? One agent would stay inside the shell, the other would be stored and transported separately, and loaded into the shell only on the battlefield. When the shell was fired, the wall separating the two canisters would burst, forming a nerve agent inside the shell. When the shell detonated on impact, the nerve agent would spread and vaporise in the air, like any other poisonous gas. They called the new concept a 'binary weapon'.

The idea had first attracted the US Navy, worried about possible accidents with nerve gas leaking from shells stored in the ammunition holds on warships. By the mid-sixties a binary bomb had been designed, and by the mid-seventies a binary 155 mm shell for army howitzers. As voices were raised to claim that the Russians had a dangerous lead over the West in chemical armaments, a campaign began to 'sell' binary weapons to the public. (Although there were environmental advantages, this was purely relative argument, since the chemical in one of the 'safe' canisters for the binary GB shells, a substance known as 'DF', was as poisonous as strychnine.) The designers of the binary weapons at Edgewood Arsenal drew up a list of other supposed advantages of the binary weapons, which incuded relative ease of handling, and an entry entitled simply 'OCONUS Preposition Acceptable'.[40] This curious jargon translates as 'Outside Continental United States Preposition Acceptable', a reference to the Pentagon belief that those countries which had not been prepared to allow the United States to base chemical weapons on their soil on political, ethical or environmental grounds, *would* be prepared to accept the new binary weapons.

The Pentagon produced a plan. A factory would be built, capable of producing 70,000 binary GB nerve agent artillery shells each month. By 1986 the plant would be producing eight inch shells filled with the chemical precursors of VX nerve agent, and 500 lb 'Bigeye' bombs also filled with VX. A final stage of the plan provided for the mass production of chemical warheads for multiple launch rockets, and 'Lance' battlefield missiles. The total cost was estimated in 1980 at 170 million dollars for the plant, and a further three or four billion dollars for the munitions themselves.[41]

But each time a request for money to begin producing binary weapons was included in the Defence Budget, either Congress or the White House turned it down. Between 1967 and 1980 no less than nineteen separate investigations were carried out into the plans for binary chemical weapons. Often when the money was refused to the Pentagon the argument was used that it would be foolish to do anything in Washington which might prejudice the negotiations towards a chemical disarmament treaty making their painfully slow progress in Geneva.

If one event more than any other finally persuaded the supporters of gas that it was time to rearm, it was the invasion of Afghanistan.

Each of the five Soviet divisions which rolled across the border in December 1979 and January 1980 carried with it portable chambers in which troops could quickly strip off contaminated clothing, and trucks mounted with high pressure hoses capable of cleaning the heaviest nerve agent from tanks or troop carriers within minutes. Eyewitnesses spoke of seeing Russian soldiers carrying gas masks and heavy anti-gas suits.

Within three weeks of the Soviet invasion Afghan refugees streaming across the border into hastily erected camps on the Pakistan border were telling horrific stories of how they had been gassed by the Russians.

It seemed that history might be repeating itself: the Russians appeared to be using the same methods as Foulkes had employed during the British Afghan campaign some sixty years earlier. Tactically, the use of gas against guerillas hidden in the steep mountainsides would made a good deal of sense. But firm proof of the claims remained elusive. During interviews with the authors in late 1980, Afghan guerillas told numerous tales of 'strange coloured clouds' which had caused them to cough, sneeze, and finally to collapse. They spoke of green, yellow, black and orange gases dropped from aircraft or fired from shells, and of a white smoke which made their eyes run and started them coughing. But so many journalists, diplomats and spies passed through the refugee camps in the months immediately following the invasion, each asking about 'nerve gas', that the guerillas speak of the stuff as if it were a weapon as commonplace as their elderly Lee Enfield rifles. Since nerve agents are virtually odourless and colourless, we concluded it was highly unlikely to have been used in any of the battles described to us.

Nevertheless, it was clear that the Russians were using some form of gas. Tear gas could be justified in much the same way as the Americans justified the use of CS in Vietnam. By the summer of 1980 the US State Department had decided it was 'highly likely that the Soviet forces have some form of chemical agent in Afghanistan',[42] but despite producing a long and rambling account of the alleged use of gas both in Afghanistan and South East Asia, it could not be specific.

A year later, on 3 September 1981, the American Secretary of State, Alexander Haig, arrived in Berlin to deliver a speech he and his aides had been preparing for several weeks. Haig was greeted by nearly fifty thousand demonstrators, protesting against the new emphasis the Reagan administration appeared to be placing upon defence, at the expense of social programmes. The protestors were particularly opposed to plans to manufacture the neutron bomb, a nuclear weapon which kills by radiation while leaving buildings and equipment unscathed. They claimed that the weapon was to all intents and purposes a gas, and therefore banned under the Geneva Protocol. Opposition to neutron weapons had been sufficiently vociferous for the Carter administration to shelve plans to manufacture and deploy them in Europe. Haig, convinced of the need not only to produce the weapon, but to stiffen European resolve generally, delivered a speech in which he claimed that the United States now had 'physical evidence' of an entirely new form of CBW being waged by the Russians and their allies.

This astonishing claim was based upon a few fragments of leaf.

American suspicions that the Russians might have developed a new weapon had first begun during the civil war in Yemen in the 1960s. Despite persistent denials, it was abundantly clear from the accounts of war correspondents and Red Cross officials that the Soviet-armed and Egyptian-supported republican forces had been using gas against royalist soldiers and civilians. By January 1967 the then British Prime Minister Harold Wilson had felt sufficiently confident of the claims to inform the House of Commons that he believed chemical weapons had been employed.[43] Eyewitness reports of horrific blistering and blindness seemed to suggest that mustard was one the agents used. Other case studies which did not mention blistering, but which did refer to people vomiting, collapsing and dying, were assumed to indicate that some form of nerve agent had been sprayed. It is widely believed that if chemical weapons had been used they could only have been supplied by the Soviet Union. But with an international treaty to ban gas an apparently imminent possibility, the Yemeni case was soon forgotten.

But in 1975 new allegations were made, this time in South East Asia. Within months of the American withdrawal from Saigon, Hmong tribesmen, who had formed the backbone of the CIA's 'secret army' in Laos during the war, began arriving in Thailand claiming that Vietnamese aircraft had bombed them with gases which caused horrific, and hitherto unknown, symptoms.

One fifty year old tribesman described how two light aircraft had suddenly appeared near his village at Pha Na Khun in the foothills north of Vientiane. As the first plane skimmed over the village at treetop height it belched forth a yellow and green powder. As the powder floated to the ground the villagers began to stagger dizzily about. Many began to vomit and defecate, others collapsed. Suddenly the second aircraft fired a rocket which exploded some sixty feet above the ground, swamping the Hmong in red smoke. They began to gasp and cough. Blood poured from their mouths and noses. Within fifteen minutes, 230 of the villagers were dead. Only twenty survived.[44]

This dramatic account was to be repeated time and again by refugees from the war against Soviet-supported forces in Laos and Kampuchea. The multiplicity of symptoms described in these attacks with what the refugees called 'yellow rain' disturbed the Pentagon. No known chemical weapon could produce the particular combination of symptoms which the victims reported. The powder seemed to have the properties of several of the known chemical agents – burning like mustard, choking like phosgene, and killing as swiftly as nerve agent. But no previously known weapon was capable of producing the massive internal bleeding which the refugees reported.

Army scientists became convinced that the Soviet Union had developed an entirely new weapon. Looking back at the casualty records of the Yemen civil war they discovered that there too there had been reports of acute haemorrhaging, although at the time few had thought the symptom of great significance. Various theories were put forward to account for the properties of the supposed new weapon. Some believed that the Russians had developed what they called a 'double punch' weapon, a cocktail of two different gases. Other research suggested that they were supplying their Vietnamese allies with an entirely new agent, derived from poisonous coral or snake venom.[45]

Until the spring of 1981 the refugees' stories remained the tittle-tattle of war, on the borderline between fact and propaganda. American and United Nations attempts to collect evidence to support or disprove the claims came to naught when research teams were unable to collect sufficient fresh samples of soil water or clothing for any meaningful analysis. But in March 1981, with the aid of local guerillas, the State Department obtained a leaf, a one-inch length of stem, and fragments of other leaves from an area on the Thai/Cambodia border which Vietnamese planes were said to have attacked. Surprisingly, in view of the allegations of 'yellow rain', all were covered in a *white* mould. The State Department rushed the samples back to the United States where they were analysed both by army biologists and by civilian scientists who were unaware from where the samples had come and for whom they were working.[46] The biologists discovered that the leaf was covered in fusaria fungus containing three natural poisons or mycotoxins. The amount of two of the three poisons was found to be 'up to twenty times higher than any recorded natural outbreak', indicating, said the State Department, that the poisons had probably been deposited by man.[47]

In particular the biologists concentrated on one of the poison types, tricothecenes, or T2 toxins. T2 had been known about for years. Indeed, the American suspicions were accentuated when it was realized that much of the research on the toxin had been carried out in the Soviet Union. Russian scientists had begun studying T2 seriously during the 1930s, for by then fungal growths on poorly stored grain had killed thousands of Soviet citizens. So problematical did the poisoning appear to be that much scientific effort had been devoted to manufacturing the toxin in laboratories. Nearly half the openly published articles on T2 dealt with methods of production.[48] Stories of the near epidemics caused when infected food had been eaten described almost identical symptoms to those reported from Laos, Kampuchea and, most recently, Afghanistan. Published Russian accounts spoke of victims suffering from a burning feeling in the mouth and stomach, followed by headaches, dizziness and convulsions before they began to spew blood from every orifice. Given the results of the American laboratory analysis, the apparent similarity of symptoms, and the Soviet ability to produce T2 on the laboratory bench, the State Department concluded that T2 had now probably become the latest Soviet weapon. If so, it was the first new germ weapon in nearly twenty years.

In November 1981, the United States produced more evidence. As one senior State Department official told a Senate inquiry, 'We now have the smoking gun.' Analysis of water from a Kampuchean village and of rock samples from two separate sites in Laos all revealed the prescence of Tricothecene mycotoxins. One sample contained levels of mycotoxin twenty times higher than those recorded in any natural outbreaks. Furthermore, the tricothecene mycotoxins 'do not occur naturally in the combination identified in southeast Asia,' said the spokesman. Having compared the symptoms reported by victims with the known symptoms of T2 poisoning, the State Department concluded that 'the fit was perfect.'

In the view of the United States government, the case was now proven.

In the hope of rebutting Soviet denials, the American government had turned their findings over to a team of experts from the United Nations, who were to mount an independent investigation. But the UN team were denied permission to visit the countries where the attacks were said to have taken place, and were forced, therefore, to rely upon the testimony of refugees: this, they found, was inadequate. As to the items supposedly contaminated with the mycotoxin and supplied to them by the American government, 'since the group cannot ascertain the actual source of these samples it cannot base its final conclusions on the results of such analyses.'

The American government was immensely disappointed with the results of the UN investigation. Privately State Department officials hinted that the inquiry had been deliberately obstructed by officials from the Soviet block. But there remained a number of serious objections to the claim that the Soviet Union had developed a mycotoxin weapon. Not least was the fact the initial allegation had been based upon only one sample. Furthermore there was the question of whether the tricothecene mycotoxins might not be produced naturally on plants in southeast Asia. Finally, why should the Russians have chosen T2 as a weapon when they could probably have achieved the same fatal results with one-fiftieth of the quantity of nerve agent, or one-tenth of the quantity of the amount of mustard gas? In the clamour which followed the American pronouncement, these questions went largely unanswered. To many the claim and counterclaim were eerily reminiscent of the late 1940s and early 1950s, when each superpower had reviled the other, while secretly racing faster into new areas of gas and germ warfare research.

While there appeared little doubt that the Russians and their clients had waged some form of chemical warfare in Afghanistan and South East Asia, the suggestion that the weapon in question was a toxin rather than a gas raised serious questions. Toxin weapons, being of biological origin, were banned under the terms of the 1972 Biological Weapons Convention. The predictable claim from the Soviet news agency Tass that the T2 allegations were a 'big lie' did nothing to allay Western suspicion. Since the Biological Weapons Convention contained no adequate means of ensuring that the

Russians really had abandoned germ warfare, any similar treaty covering chemical weapons looked increasingly unacceptable to the Pentagon.

Increasing cynicism about Soviet intentions had already led in the late 1970s to a more aggressive stance. Remembering the opposition to chemical weapons which had arisen during the late 1960s, and recognizing that any new generation would need to be based in Europe, the Pentagon began discussions with the British. Although initial negotiations with the Callaghan government came to nothing, discussions on the possible basing of chemical weapons in Britain were resumed after the 1979 election brought Margaret Thatcher to power. By the spring of 1980 the British Defence Secretary was publicly ruminating about the size and power of the Soviet chemical arsenal. That summer the British held a series of meetings with their American counterparts which resulted in British support for Pentagon proposals to begin producing a new generation of gas weapons. By December 1980 the British Defence Secretary had been finally converted to the cause of chemical rearmament.[49]

Even before the T2 allegations, the climate had changed so much that in 1980 the Pentagon did not include proposals for a new binary gas weapon plant in its request for funds for the coming year. There was no need. When the budget proposal came before Congress for approval, eager politicians endorsed a suggestion to write into the budget plans to begin work on a new factory capable of turning out 20,000 rounds of 155 mm binary nerve agent shells every month. The entire debate in both houses of Congress took less than three hours.

By the time the T2 allegations surfaced even Richard Nixon, the man who seemed to have halted the chemical arms race in 1969, believed that his efforts had been in vain and that the Russians had rearmed while the United States stood still.[50] In the past governments have justified continuing gas and germ research by pointing to the weapons they believe the enemy to possess. Plans for chemical rearmament in the West are already well advanced. Unless disarmament negotiations suddenly bear fruit, the present climate of suspicion may provide the perfect culture in which to breed a new generation of weapons.

Epilogue

The secret story of chemical and biological warfare demonstrates few things so clearly as the way in which discoveries made in the cause of human welfare can be used to devise ever more sophisticated instruments of death. Discoveries in veterinary science are turned to the development of new biological weapons. A potential pesticide is transformed into a nerve agent. Yet the present generation of weapons is based upon scientific discoveries made up to fifty years ago: until the late 1970s British and American chemists were still attempting to produce an antidote to soman, an agent which had first been developed in the laboratories of Nazi Germany. Horrific though the effects of today's weapons may be, however, they are capable of infinite refinement. The present arsenals are huge: the 'inadequate' stock of nerve gas in the United States is sufficient to kill the entire population of the world four thousand times over.

The reason that this apparently enormous quantity is considered insufficient is that present chemical weapons are extremely inefficient. They do not kill effectively enough. To 'neutralize' a single square kilometre of ground with existing shells and bombs would require enough nerve agent to kill the entire population of China.[1] So the research continues for more 'efficient' gas weapons. Soviet scientists are believed to be refining the rockets and bombs which will be used to spread nerve agent. In the United States experiments have been conducted to discover even more reliable methods of forcing nerve liquid through a victim's skin.

But these areas of research are as nothing when compared with the weapons which would become possible should a chemical and biological arms race begin again. The abuse of modern medicine might make 'war without death', the dream of the 1950s, a feasible proposition once more. Drugs designed to relieve hypertension might be used to induce abnormally low blood pressure, causing a victim to collapse. Other drugs capable of raising body temperature might be used to cause heat stroke, even on a chilly day. The development of 'binary' weapons opens the possibility of employing

239

chemicals previously considered too dangerous to be used in armaments: the poison is produced only as a shell hurtles towards enemy troops.

Man's increasing understanding of the delicate mechanism which make life possible may also solve the problem of how to design a weapon which will kill an enemy, while leaving friendly troops unharmed. In particular military scientists might rekindle their interest in 'ethnic weapons', designed to affect only selected racial groups. An American military manual noted the possibility in 1975:

. . . it is theoretically possible to develop so-called 'ethnic chemical weapons', which would be designed to exploit naturally occurring differences in vulnerability among specific population groups. Thus, such a weapon would be capable of incapacitating or killing a selected enemy population to a significantly greater extent than the population of friendly forces.[2]

Many of these 'naturally occurring differences' are well known: the inability of the digestive systems of particular racial groups to cope with the food of another group, for example. But the differences go further. In the United States, where most of the research has been conducted, it has been established that within the American Indian population 95 per cent of Cherokee Indians have Type O blood, while 85 per cent of Blackfeet Indians have Type A blood. It is reasonable to suppose that other, similar differences occur among less advanced societies. Certainly during the Vietnam war the so called 'Advanced Projects Research Agency', an élite group of scientists working for the Pentagon, was employed to carry out blood tests on selected groups of Asians with a view to 'preparing a map portraying the geographic distribution of human blood groups and other inherited blood characters'.[3] The Pentagon claimed the project was solely to establish the food requirements of American and allied troops.

It is in the field of biological warfare that the most frightening possibilities present themselves. It is now nearly thirty years since Crick and Watson made their momentous discovery of the 'double helix' structure of DNA, the molecule which controls heredity. The discovery has not yet, as far as is known, been applied to the business of war. But in the civilian laboratories of Europe and North America biologists are regularly tampering with the nature of life itself through 'gene splicing' or recombinant DNA. It has been called the most awesome discovery since man split the atom. Should the breakthrough, like atomic physics, come to be applied to warfare the implications scarcely bear thinking about.

As long ago as 1962, forty scientists were employed at the US Army biological warfare laboratories on full-time genetics research. 'Many others', it was said, 'appreciate the implications of genetics for their own work'.[4] The implications were made more specific seven years later, when a Department of Defense spokesman claimed that genetic engineering could solve one of the major disadvantages of biological warfare, that it is limited to diseases which occur naturally somewhere in the world.

Within the next 5 to 10 years, it would probably be possible to make a new infective micro-organism which could differ in certain important respects from any known disease-causing organisms. Most important of these is that it might be refractory to the immunological and therapeutic processes upon which we depend to maintain our relative freedom from infectious disease.[5]

The possibility that such a 'super germ' may have been successfully produced in a laboratory somewhere in the world in the years since that assessment was made is one which should not be too readily cast aside.[6]

Today genetic manipulation is being used to develop new drugs for the treatment of illnesses like cancer. In research laboratories 'gene splicing' is being used artificially to produce Interferon, a substance which occurs naturally in the body and protects against virus diseases. To the mentality which in the past has used advances in health science to develop new weapons, such discoveries must look very inviting. Indeed, the possibility of direct interference with human genes through the use of synthetic viruses opens the possibility not merely of ethnic weapons, but of wars in which the outcome would be determined not on the battlefield but with the birth of a mutant next generation.

If such possibilities now seem in the realm of science fiction, we should do well to remember that in the field of chemical and biological warfare once a thing has been shown to be possible, it has generally been done. Poison gas seemed an equally unlikely weapon before a German professor developed what he chose to call 'A Higher Form of Killing'.

Notes

CHAPTER ONE: 'FRIGHTFULNESS'

1 – Papers of Major General C. H. Foulkes. From a 'Very Secret' report on gas casualties by Lt. Col. Douglas, RAMC.

2 – Public Record Office, London (PRO), WO 32/5183. 'An account of German cloud gas attacks on the British Front in France.'

3 – PRO, WO 142/99. Autopsy report by Lt. McNee, RAMC.

4 – PRO, WO 32/5183. 'An account of German cloud gas attacks on the British Front in France'.

5 – Papers of Joseph Barcroft. Letters to his wife, 8 and 12 May 1915.

6 – Kölnische Zeitung, 26 June 1915. Quoted in Stockholm International Peace Research Institute (SIPRI), The Problems of Chemical and Biological Warfare (Stockholm, 1971), Vol.II, p. 232.

7 – Ibid., 232.

8 – PRO, WO 32/5183. 'Diary of Development of British Respirator.'

9 – PRO, WO 32/5183. 'An account of German cloud gas attacks on the British Front in France.'

10 – C. H. Foulkes, Gas! The Story of the Special Brigade, (London, 1936), p. 17.

11 – Joseph Borkin, The Crime and Punishment of I. G. Farben (London, 1979), p. 5.

12 – Victor Lefebure, The Riddle of the Rhine (London, 1921), p. 31.

13 – Borkin, op. cit., p. 18.

14 – PRO, WO 142/195. 'Early Gas Attacks Against the Russians.' According-ing to W. L. Wicks of the British Embassy in Petrograd, in the course of one attack in May lasting just twenty minutes, 7,800 men wounded by gas were evacuated, and 1,100 left dead on the field.

15 – Robert Graves, Goodbye To All That (London, 1929), Ch. 15.

16 – Foulkes, op. cit., p. 80.

17 – Ibid., p. 72.

18 – Ibid., p. 81.

19 – Ibid., p. 76.

20 – Denis Winter, Death's Men (London, 1978), p. 125.

21 – Foulkes Papers. From Lt. Col. Douglas's secret report on British gas casualties, written in 1919.

22 – H. Allen, *Toward the Flame*; quoted in Winter, *op. cit.*, p. 121.

23 – P R O, W O 142/99. An account of the first German phosgene attack.

24 – *Ibid.*

25 – P R O, W O 142/101. After poisoning by either chlorine or phosgene, patients 'may wake up at night many months later with a terrifying lack of breath'.

26 – Foulkes, *op. cit.*, p, 113.

27 – *Ibid.*, p. 109.

28 – *Ibid.*, p. 127.

29 – *Ibid.*, p. 135.

30 – Julian Perry Robinson, 'The Rise of CB Weapons', SIPRI, *op. cit.*, Vol. I, p. 34.

31 – Foulkes, *op. cit.*, p. 212.

32 – *Ibid.*, p. 200.

33 – P R O, W O 32/5176. 'Gas Shell Bombardment of Ypres, 12–13 July 1917.'

34 – *Ibid.*

35 – P R O, W O 142/99. From a report dated 22 July 1917.

36 – P R O, W O32/5176. Report by Captain Douglas R A M C, Physiological Adviser to the Gas Services, 17 July 1917.

37 – P R O, W O 142/99. Report of a post mortem conducted at No. 47 Field Hospital on 22 July 1917 by Lt. Templeton of the R A M C.

38 – P R O, W O 142/99.

39 – Foulkes Papers. Report on British gas casualties, 1919.

40 – *Ibid.*

41 – General Fries writing in the *Journal of Industrial and Engineering Chemistry*, 1920. Quoted in Lefebure, *op. cit.*, p. 176.

42 – Lord Moran, *Anatomy of Courage* (London, 1966), quoted by Winter, *op. cit.*, p. 126.

43 – P R O, W O 142/225, 'HS manufacture at Avonmouth.' Report by Captain H. M. Roberts, Factory Medical Officer.

44 – Foulkes, *op. cit.*, p. 296.

45 – 'The War Diary of Brigadier Adrian Eliot Hodgkin', an unpublished, handwritten diary. Imperial War Museum, London.

46 – Foulkes Papers. Report on British gas casualties, 1919.

47 – Described in *Mein Kampf*. Hitler is said to have ascribed the recovery of his sight after being blinded by mustard gas to divine intervention – a supernatural sign which made him determined to become a politician.

48 – *New York Times* editorial, 27 January 1920. Quoted by Borkin, *op. cit.*, p. 34.

Haber's laureate did him no good when Hitler came to power. Despite the fact that he had converted to Christianity, Haber's Jewish background led to his being forced to resign his academic posts in Germany when the Nazis came to power. He died – 'a broken man' according to Borkin – in Switzerland in January 1934. 'Germans were not permitted to mourn his passing' (Borkin, *op. cit.*, p. 57).

49 – A. M. Prentiss, *Chemicals in War* (New York, 1937); quoted in SIPRI, *op*, cit., Vol. I, p. 128–9.

50 – SIPRI, *op. cit.*, Vol. I, p. 50.

51 – J. B. S. Haldane, *Callinicus: A Defence of Chemical Warfare* (London, 1925), p. 10.

52 – Lefebure, *op. cit.*, p. 172.

53 – *Ibid.*, p. 174.

54 – Foulkes Papers. Draft report of the Holland Committee on Chemical Warfare Organisation.

55 – Haldane, *op. cit.*, p. 32.

56 – PRO, WO 188/265. 'After-effects of gas poisoning.'

57 – *Ibid.* 'Disability due to gas poisoning', a report dated 16 June 1927 by A. Fairley, Acting Superintendent of the Physiology Department at Porton.

58 – *Ibid.*

59 – Interviewed for BBC Television's *Panorama*, 2 June 1980.

60 – *Health Aspects of Chemical and Biological weapons: Report of a World Health Organisation Group of Consultants* (Geneva, 1970), pp. 33–4.

61 – *Ibid.*, p. 34.

62 – PRO, WO 188/265.

CHAPTER TWO: THE SERPENT AND THE FLOWER

1 – The 'Barcroft Bottle', mentioned in a number of 'Quarterly Reports' submitted by the Commandant of Porton to the War Office – e.g. July–September 1928 (PRO, WO 188/373).

2 – Quoted in Haldane, *op. cit.*, p. 75.

3 – Barcroft's Papers. Letter from Lloyd George, 10 July 1919.

4 – Barcroft's Papers. Letter to his wife describing King George V's visit to Porton, 3 June 1918.

5 – Foulkes, *op. cit.*, pp. 272–3.

6 – *A Brief History of the Chemical Defence Experimental Establishment Porton*, p. 8. (This was a 'restricted' publication, written in March 1961 and declassified in 1981.)

7 – In 1981, reports of experiments at Porton available to historians ran up to 1929. There are 9,000 individual records relating to the First World War alone held at the Public Record Office.

8 – Haldane, *op. cit.*, p. 74.

9 – Sir Austin Anderson, 'Some Recollections of Porton in World War I', *Journal of the Royal Army Medical Corps*, 116(3), pp. 173–7.

10 – *A Brief History of Porton*, p. 7.

11 – Foulkes, *op. cit.*, p. 274.

12 – PRO, WO 188/50. '. . . they consisted of men dying after exposure to HS in liquid vapour form from 24 to 15 days, some with severe intoxication, others with pneumonias at different stages.'

13 – Sir Austin Anderson, *op. cit.*, pp. 173–7

14 – Foulkes Papers. Draft Report of the Holland Committee on Chemical Warfare Organisation, 1919.

15 – PRO, WO 188/50. 'Symptomatology of Action of DA in low concentrations on man.'

16 – PRO, WO 188/374.

17 – Foulkes Papers. Letter to the War Office, 12 August 1919. 'In this country,' the letter continues, 'the heat of the sun distinctly favours its use, as evaporation from the ground will be much more rapid, and more toxic atmospheres will be created. As a consequence inflammations will be more severe and they will appear sooner; while profuse perspiration will encourage blistering, and skin lesions will have a tendency to become septic.'

18 – Foulkes Papers. Letter to the War Office, 5 November 1919. 'Reviewing the whole circumstances there appears to be little or no justification for refusing to employ gas on sentimental grounds: there is little sentiment in war and our men have the first claim on it.'

19 – PRO, WO 188/58. Letter from Salt to Major Wingate in London, 25 February 1920.

20 – For a detailed account of the adoption and signing of the Geneva Protocol, see SIPRI, *op. cit.*, Vol. IV, *CB Disarmament Negotiations 1920–1970*.

21 – Julian Perry Robinson – SIPRI, *op. cit.*, Vol. I, p. 247.

22 – SIPRI, *op cit.*, Vol. I, p. 283.

23 – British Intelligence Objectives Sub-Committee (BIOS) reports on Japanese Chemical Warfare. Vol. II and Vol. V Part A.

24 – *Ibid.*, Vol. VI.

25 – Quoted in SIPRI, *op. cit.*, Vol. I, p. 147.

26 – Quoted in SIPRI, *op. cit.*, Vol. I, p. 144.

27 – From an intelligence summary, 'Notes on CW Preparedness of Enemy and Potential Enemy Countries' (20/32), contained in the papers of Lord Weir, Director General of Explosives (DGX) at the Ministry of Supply, 1939–41. The papers are held at Churchill College, Cambridge.

28 – SIPRI, *op. cit.*, Vol. IV, pp. 180–81.

29 – *Ibid.*, p. 182.

30 – *The Times*, 20 April 1936. Quoted in SIPRI, *op. cit.*, Vol. I, p. 259.

31 – PRO, WO 32/3665.

32 – Weir Papers, 20/32. 'Technical Report on Visit to French Powder and Chemical Warfare Factories' (September 1939).

33 – Weir Papers, 20/32. 'Notes on C W Preparedness of Enemy and Potential Enemy Countries'.

34 – P R O, W O 193/740. 'Anglo-French Conversations on Chemical Warfare.'

35 – *Ibid.*

36 – *Ibid.*

37 – Weir Papers, 20/32. 'Notes on C W Preparedness of Enemy and Potential Enemy Countries'.

CHAPTER THREE: HITLER'S SECRET WEAPON

1 – BIOS Report No. 714. 'The Development of New Insecticides and Chemical Warfare Agents', p. 24.

2 – *Ibid.*, p. 28.

3 – Combined Intelligence Objectives Sub-Committee (CIOS) Report No. 30. 'Chemical Warfare – I.G. Farbenindustrie A.G., Frankfurt/Main'.

4 – *Ibid.* The testimony of Dr Wilhelm Kleinhans.

5 – BIOS Report No. 41. 'Interrogation of German C W Personnel at Heidelburg and Frankfurt.'

6 – CIOS Report No. 30.

7 – CIOS Report No. 31. Chemical Warfare Installations in the Munster-lager Area.'

8 – *Ibid.*

9 – *Ibid.*

10 – *Ibid.*

11 – *Ibid.*

12 – BIOS Report No. 9. 'Interrogation of German Air Ministry Technical Personnel Luftwaffe Lager, near Kiel.'

13 – *Ibid.*

14 – Quoted in the 'Hitler's Deadly Secrets', the *Sunday Times*, 22 February 1981.

15 – CIOS Report No. 31.

16 – *Ibid.*

17 – *Ibid.*

18 – *Ibid.*

19 – *Ibid.*

20 – American evidence presented to the Nuremburg Trials. Document L-103.

21 – BIOS Report No. 782. 'Interrogation of Professor Ferdinand Flury and Dr Wolfgang Wirth on the toxicology of chemical warfare agents.'

22 – Hearings before a US Senate Sub-Committee, 1945. Quoted in Borkin, *op. cit.*, p. 132n.

23 – BIOS Report No. 138. 'Interrogation of German C W Medical Personnel.'

24 – BIOS Report No. 9.

25 – David Irving, *Hitler's War* (London, 1977), p. 633.

26 – See Albert Speer, *Inside the Third Reich* (London, 1970). During his trial at Nuremburg, Speer also claimed that he considered assassinating Hitler in 1945 by introducing nerve gas into the ventilating system of the *Führerbunker*.

27 – BIOS Report No. 542. 'Interrogation of Certain German Personalities connected with Chemical Warfare', p. 25.

28 – According to Winston Churchill in a memorandum to the Chiefs of Staff dated 21 May 1944 (PRO, CAB 122/1323). Churchill suggested that he and President Roosevelt should issue a warning that if the Germans used gas 'we shall immediately use the full delivery power of our Strategic Air Forces to drench the German cities and towns where any war industry exists.' The Chiefs of Staff turned the idea down, on the grounds that giving a warning might help compromise the date for which the Normandy landings were set.

29 – Omar Bradley, *A Soldier's Story* (New York, 1970); quoted in SIPRI, *op. cit.*, Vol. I, p. 297.

30 – Borkin, *op. cit.*, pp. 131–2.

31 – CIOS Report No. 30.

32 – PRO, AVIA 24/18. 'Chemical Warfare – General.'

33 – PRO, WO 193/723. 'Chemical Warfare Intelligence 30 Sept 1939 – 30 June 1944.'

34 – *A Brief History of Porton*, p. 29.

CHAPTER FOUR: A PLAGUE ON YOUR CHILDREN

1 – Interviewed on BBC *Newsnight* programme, 1 May 1981.

2 – Quoted in *The Gathering Storm* (London, 1948), p. 34.

3 – Authors' interview with Dr Rex Watson, Director of Porton Down, 21 July 1981.

4 – Authors' interview, March 1981.

5 – *Sunday Times*, 15 February 1981.

6 – Authors' interview, March 1981.

7 – Interviewed on BBC Television's *Newsnight*, 1 May 1981.

8 – Authors' interview with Dr Rex Watson, 21 July 1981.

9 – Top secret report submitted to the Secretary of Defence's Ad Hoc Committee on CEBAR by Colonel William M. Creasy, 24 February 1950, p. 1.

10 – BIOS Report on Scientific Intelligence Survey in Japan, Vol. V: Biological Warfare (September and October 1945).

11 – *Ibid.*

12 – *Ibid.*

13 – *Ibid.*

14 – *Ibid.*

15 – *Ibid.*

16 – PRO, PREM 3/65. 'Japanese Attempts at Bacteriological Warfare in China'. One of a series of allegations passed on to Winston Churchill by the Chinese Ambassador 'on the instructions of Generalissimo Chiang Kai Shek', July 1942.

17 – *Ibid.*

18 – *Ibid.*

19 – *Ibid.*

20 – PRO, CAB 53/4. Minutes of the COS Committee.

21 – Recollection of Lawrence Burgis, Hankey's private secretary for many years. Quoted in Stephen Roskill *Hankey: Man of Secrets* (London, 1974), Vol. III, p. 22.

22 – Burgis, *op. cit.*

23 – Roskill, *op. cit.*, p. 93.

24 – PRO, CAB 4/26. CID meeting, 17 March 1937.

25 – PRO, CAB 120/782.

26 – PRO, CAB 79/1.

27 – PRO, CAB 120/782. Memo from Lord Hankey to Winston Churchill, 6 December 1941.

28 – Obituary of Sir Paul Fildes in *The Times*, 12 October 1971.

29 – *Ibid.*

30 – Authors' interview, 13 March 1981.

31 – R. V. Jones, *Most Secret War* (London, 1978), pp. 102–3.

32 – Weir Papers, 20/32. 'Notes on CW Preparedness of Enemy and Potential Enemy Countries'.

33 – Roskill, *op. cit.*, p. 471.

34 – Seymour Hersh, *Chemical and Biological Warfare: America's Secret Arsenal* (London, 1968), p. 12.

35 – *Ibid.*

36 – Record of the Nuremburg Trials. Vol. XXI, p. 550.

37 – The records listed in the main index of the Public Record Office in London relating to chemical and biological warfare which are closed to public inspection are: the minutes of the Inter-Service Committee on Chemical Warfare (CAB 81/15, 16, 17 and 18); a file entitled 'The Employment of Chemical Warfare in the War Against Japan' (CAB 81/19); the minutes of the Bacteriological Warfare Committee (CAB 81/53); a file entitled 'Porton Experiments' (CAB 81/54); and the minutes of the Inter-Service Sub-Committee on Chemical Warfare (CAB 81/58).

38 – 'Compliance with obligations concerning the prohibition of bacteriological (biological)weapons', BWC/CONF. 1/4, Ch. 2.

39 – PRO, CAB 120/782.

40 – *Ibid.*

41 – Authors' interview with Dr Rex Watson, 21 July 1981.

42 – *Health Aspects of Chemical and Biological Weapons: Report of a*

World Health Organisation Group of Consultants (Geneva, 1970), p. 41.

43 – Creasy Report, p. 1.

44 – Irving, *Hitler's War, op. cit.*, p. 463.

45 – *Ibid.*

46 – US National Archives, CCS.381. Poland (6630–43) Sec. 1. Report on The Polish Secret Army for the period 1942 to April 1943, submitted to the CCS on 7 September 1943.

According to the minutes: 'SIR JOHN DILL said that he had read the paper with great interest. The British and Polish Governments and General Staffs had been in close touch throughout . . . ADMIRAL LEAHY, on behalf of the Combined Chiefs of Staff, expressed his appreciation for the valuable paper and discussion put forward by the Polish representatives.'

47 – Frantisek Moravec, *Master of Spies* (London, 1981), p. 192.

48 – Jan Wiener, *The Assassination of Heydrich* (New York, 1969), pp. 82–90.

49 – Quoted in Miroslav Ivanov, *The Assassination of Heydrich* (London, 1973), pp. 175–8.

50 – WHO Report, *op. cit.*, pp. 42–3.

51 – Ivanov, *op. cit.*

52 – Anthony Cave Brown, *Bodyguard of Lies* (New York, 1974), p. 226.

53 – Moravec, *op. cit.*, p. 205.

54 – Irving, *op. cit.*, p. 396.

55 – Authors' interview with Dr Rex Watson, 21 July 1981.

56 – Authors' conversation with Dr Alvin Pappenheimer, March 1981.

57 – Quoted in the judgement in the case of Mabel Nevin *et al. versus* The United States of America, 20 May 1981.

58 – PRO AVIA 42/18. Anglo-American exchange of information, 1941.

59 – Julian Perry Robinson, SIPRI, *op. cit.*, Vol. I, p. 121.

60 – *Ibid.*

61 – PRO, DEFE 2/1252. Report to the Chiefs of Staff Joint Technical Warfare Committee, November 1945.

62 – *Ibid.*

63 – PRO, PREM 3/89. 'Crop Destruction': a memo from Sir John Anderson to Winston Churchill, 9 March 1944.

64 – *Ibid.*

65 – PRO, DEFE 2/1252. Report to the Technical Warfare Committee on Crop Destruction.

66 – *Ibid.*

67 – *Ibid.*

68 – PRO, PREM 3/65.

69 – *Ibid.*

70 – PRO, PREM 3/65. 'Most Secret' memo, 8 March 1944.

71 – PRO, PREM 3/65. Memo from Brown to Churchill, 9 May 1944.
72 – *Ibid.*
73 – *Ibid.*
74 – According to Creasy, Vigo could produce 500,000 4-lb anthrax bombs per month; according to Brown's minute of 9 May, capacity was 625,000 bombs per month.
75 – Creasy, *op. cit.*, p. 8.
76 – PRO, DEFE 2/1252. Report to the Joint Technical Warfare Committee on 'Potentialities of Weapons of Biological Warfare During the Next Ten Years', November 1945.
77 – *Ibid.*
78 – PRO, DEFE 2/1252. Paul Fildes in conversation with the members of the Joint Technical Warfare Committee.
79 – PRO, DEFE 2/1252. Report on 'Future Development of Biological Warfare' submitted to the Joint Technical Warfare Committee, 6 December 1945.
80 – PRO, DEFE 2/1252.
81 – Interview on BBC Television's *Newsnight*, 1 May 1981.
82 – WHO Report, *op. cit.*, p. 76.
83 – PRO, DEFE 2/1252.
84 – Press Association report, 1 May 1981.
85 – PRO, DEFE 2/1252.
86 – F. J. Brown, *Chemical Warfare: a study in restraints* (Princeton, 1968).

CHAPTER FIVE: THE WAR THAT NEVER WAS
1 – PRO, PREM 3/89.
2 – Weir Papers, 20/16. 'Memorandum on the Position in the Event of an Early Gas Blitz' (10 February 1941) and extract from the Minutes of the Chemical Warfare Board (28 January 1941).
3 – PRO, CAB 79/7. Minutes of the Chiefs of Staff Meeting, 7 October 1941.
4 – PRO, WO 193/740. 'Scale of Gas Attack to which the Field Force in France may be Subjected.'
5 – Contained in War Office file WO 193/732 at the Public Record Office, London.
6 – *Ibid.*
7 – *Ibid.*
8 – Quoted in Peter Fleming, *Operation Sea Lion* (London, 1975), p. 293.
9 – PRO, WO 193 – 732. Memo dated 30 June 1940.
10 – PRO, WO 193/732. The RAF squadrons armed with chemical weapons were stationed at Grangemouth, Linton (Yorks), Hatfield, West Malling, Old Sarum, Lossiemouth, Walton, Wyton, Horsham St Faith, Oakington, Benbrook and Newton.

11 – PRO, WO 193/732. 'Memorandum on the use of gas in the defence of the United Kingdom.'

12 – *Ibid.*

13 – *Ibid.*

14 – PRO, WO 193/732. Information to sent by Dill to Churchill via Ismay on 2 July.

15 – PRO, PREM 3/88–3.

16 – *Ibid.*

17 – *Ibid.*

18 – *Ibid.*

19 – *Ibid.*

20 – PRO, WO 193/711. Memo from Beaverbrook to Churchill, 20 November 1941.

21 – *A Brief History of Porton Down*, p. 24.

22 – PRO, WO 193 – 711. Meeting of the Chiefs of Staff Committee, 28 December 1941.

23 – PRO, WO 193/732. Memorandum from Sir John Dill, 25 April 1941.

24 – PRO, WO 193/711. File entitled 'Offensive Chemical Warfare Policy'. COS Committee meeting, 19 March 1942.

25 – PRO, WO 193/711. Memorandum by CIGS, October 1941.

26 – Weir Papers, 20/32. Barley's report is quoted by Weir in a memo to the Minister of Supply, 11 October 1940.

27 – These are taken from a recently declassified US Pentagon document giving the history of each main US chemical warfare installation.

28 – Quoted in Julian Perry Robinson, SIPRI *op. cit.*, Vol. I, p. 316.

29 – *Ibid.*

30 – PRO, PREM 3/88–3. 'Japanese Gas Warfare in China.'

31 – Quoted in SIPRI *op. cit.*, Vol. I, p. 321.

32 – Contained in PRO, WO 193/712. Statement made on 6 June 1942.

33 – *Ibid.* Statement of 9 June 1943.

34 – Intelligence Report on Japanese Chemical Warfare. BIOS, Vol. III.

35 – PRO, WO 193/711. Telegram sent to GOC Malaya, 11 February 1942.

36 – Glenn B. Infield, *Disaster At Bari* (New York, 1971), p. 46.

37 – PRO, WO 193/712. Most Secret report: 'Toxic Gas Burns Sustained in the Bari Harbor Catastrophe' by Stewart F. Alexander, Lt. Col., US Medical Corps and Consultant, Chemical Warfare Medicine.

38 – PRO, PREM 3/88–3.

39 – PRO, WO 193/712. 'Most Secret and Most Immediate' telegram, 2 January 1944.

40 – PRO, WO 193/712. 'Important and Most Secret' telegram from General Wilson, 11 January 1944.

41 – PRO, WO 193/712. Telegram from General Eisenhower, 2 January 1944.

42 – An idea of the amount of time Intelligence spent worrying about gas warfare, and revelations of the role of Enigma decrypts in alerting the Allies to German intentions can be found in F. A. Hinsley, *British Intelligence in the Second World War* (London, 1981), Vol. II, pp. 116–22, 674–6.

43 – Quoted in SIPRI, *op. cit.*, Vol. I. p. 297.

44 – PRO, WO 193/713. A brief résumé of the dispute is given in a letter from Sir Archibald Nye to Sir Bernard Paget (C-in-C Middle East) on 15 July 1944. 'We have decided,' he concludes, 'to let sleeping dogs lie.'

45 – PRO, DEFE 2/1252. 'Matters of Fact Relating to Atomic Energy', a report by the Atomic Weapons Sub-Committee to the Joint Technical Warfare Committee, January 1946.

46 – PRO, PREM 3/65.

47 – *Ibid.*

48 – *Ibid.*

49 – *Ibid.* Memo to the Prime Minister from Ismay, 19 May 1944.

50 – Quoted in Roger Parkinson, *A Day's March Nearer Home* (London, 1974), p. 327.

51 – PRO, PREM 3/89.

52 – *Ibid.*

53 – PRO, WO 193/711. Churchill radio broadcast, 10 May 1942. The broadcast was made in response to a pledge Churchill had made to Stalin. The Russians were worried that the Nazis were about to use poison gas on the eastern front. Churchill's 'open-ended' pledge – like that of Roosevelt to the Chinese – appears to have worried the Chiefs of Staff. The relevant section of Churchill's broadcast ran:

> The Soviet Government have expressed to us the view that the Germans in the desperation of their assault may make use of poison gas against the Armies and people of Russia. We are ourselves firmly resolved not to use this odious weapon unless it is first used by the Germans. Knowing our Hun, however, we have not neglected to make preparations on a formidable scale. I wish now to make it plain that we shall treat the unprovoked use of poison gas against our Russian ally exactly as if it were used against ourselves, and if we are satisfied that this new outrage had been committed by Hitler, we will use our great and growing Air superiority in the West to carry gas warfare on the largest possible scale far and wide upon the towns and cities of Germany . . . Of one thing I am sure – that the British people, who have entered into the full comradeship of war with our Russian Ally, will not shrink from any sacrifice or trial which that comradeship may require.

54 – Winston S. Churchill, *Triumph and Tragedy* (London, 1954), p. 39.

55 – PRO, PREM 3/89.

56 – PRO, CAB 79/77. Meeting of the Chiefs of Staff Committee, 8 July 1944.

57 – PRO, CAB 84/64. Instructions to the Joint Planning Staff, 16 July 1944.

58 – PRO, PREM 3/89.

59 – PRO, PREM 3/89. 'Military Considerations Affecting the Initiation of Chemical and Other Special Forms of Warfare'.

60 – The German cities were: Aachen, Bochum, Cologne, Damstadt, Duisburg, Dusseldorf, Essen, Frankfurt, Gelsenkirchen, Hagen, Krefeld, Mainz, Mülheim, München/Gladbach, Münster, Oberhausen, Remscheid, Solingen, Wiesbaden, Wuppertal, Bielefeld, Bremen, Brunswick, Hamburg, Hanover, Kiel, Lübeck, Osnabrück, Rostock/Warnemunde, Wilhelmshaven, Berlin, Chemnitz, Dessau, Dresden, Erfurt, Halle, Kassel, Leipzig, Magdeburg, Plauen, Potsdam, Stettin, Wurzburg, Freiburg, Karlsruhe, Mannheim/Ludwigshafen, Sarbrücken, Stuttgart, Beuthen, Breslau, Danzig, Gleiwitz, Görlitz, Hindenburg, Konigsberg, Augsburg, Munich, Nuremburg.

61 – PRO, PREM 3/89.

62 – *Ibid.*

63 – Max Hastings, *Bomber Command* (London, 1979), pp. 343–4.

64 – PRO, WO 193/712.

65 – SIRI *op. cit.*, Vol. I, p. 298.

66 – PRO, WO 193/712. P 398–A. 19 February 1945.

67 – PRO, PREM 3/88–3. 27 March 1942.

68 – PRO, WO 193/712. Minute from the Secretary of the COS Committee to the Foreign Secretary, 3 September 1943:

At QUADRANT code-name for Allied summit meeting in Quebec in August the Prime Minister asked the Chiefs of Staff to consider a reported threat by Ribbentrop that the Germans would use gas against the Italians, if they turned against the Germans, as an example to the remainder of the satellites. The Chiefs of Staff advised the Prime Minister against making any declaration of our intention to retaliate, because at that time it would have compromised the source of our information (i.e. General Castellano) . . .

69 – Stanley P. Lovell, *Of Spies and Stratagems* (New York, 1963), p. 78.

CHAPTER SIX: NEW ENEMIES

1 – The fullest summary of the disposal of chemical weapons after the Second World War is to be found in 'The Rise of CB Weapons', Julian Perry Robinson, SIPRI, *op. cit.*, pp. 153 n. and 305 n.

2 – PRO, 193/712. 'Disposal of German Chemical Warfare Stocks', report to Chiefs of Staff, 19 June 1945.

3 – *Note by the Secretaries of the Joint Intelligence Committee*, Annex B, 27 January 1949.

4 – 'Interrogation of Certain German Personalities Connected with Chemical Warfare', BIOS Final Report No. 542, Item No. 8.

5 – *Note by the Secretaries of the Joint Intelligence Committee*, Annex B, 27 January 1949.

6 – *Materials on the Trial of Former Servicemen of the Japanese Army Charged with Manufacturing and Employing Bacteriological Weapons* (Moscow, 1950). An account is also given in Hersh, *op. cit.*, pp. 13–18.

7 – *Ibid.*

8 – Undated Pentagon/German intelligence report.

9 – *Note by the Secretaries of the Joint Intelligence Committee*, Annex B, 27 January 1949.

10 – Eight pages of Pentagon document, *op. cit.*

11 – PRO, DEFE 2/1252. Joint Technical Warfare Committee memo, 22 December 1945, TWC (45) 47; Joint Technical Warfare Committee, 5 January 1946, TWC (45) 44 (revised); Joint Technical Warfare Committee, 1 July 1946, TWC (46) 15 (revised).

12 – *San Francisco Examiner*, 2 June 1952.

13 – Testimony to a sub-committee of the Committee on Appropriations, US House of Representatives, March 1962.

14 – *New York Times*, 23 February 1938.

15 – Colonel V. Pozdnyakov, 'The Chemical Arm', in B. H. Liddell Hart (ed.), *The Soviet Army* (London, 1956).

16 – Quoted in R. L. Garthoff. *Soviet Strategy in the Nuclear Age* (London, 1958), p. 104.

17 – Lt. Gen. Arthur G. Trudeau: testimony during Department of Defence Appropriations hearing for 1961, Washington, March 1960.

18 – Seymour Hersh, 'Pentagon Gas Plans Spring a Leak', 15 July 1969. Reprinted in Congressional Record.

19 – *The Penkovsky Papers*, (London, 1965), p. 153.

20 – *Ibid.* Greville Wynne himself believes that Penkovsky was not executed but survived several years in Soviet gaols before finally committing suicide.

21 – Information to the authors from intelligence sources. But for a fuller, sceptical analysis of Soviet weaponry see 'CB Weapons Today', SIPRI, *op. cit.*, Vol. I, pp. 173–84.

CHAPTER SEVEN: THE SEARCH FOR THE PATRIOTIC GERM

1 – PRO, COS (45) 402(o). 'Future Developments in weapons and methods of war'. A report by Sir Henry Tizard's Ad Hoc Committee to the Chiefs of Staff, June 1945.

2 – PRO, TWC (45)–45. Brig. O. H. Wansburgh-Jones, 3 December 1945.

3 – PRO, TWC (46) 15 (Revise). 'Future Developments in weapons and methods of war'. Joint Technical Warfare Committee, July 1946.

4 – The *Merck Report*: a report by George W. Merck, the Director of the War Research Service (1945).
5 Col. William F. Creasy, 'Presentation to Secretary of Defense's Ad Hoc Committee on CEBAR', 24 February 1950, p. 15.
6 – PRO, DEFE 4–3. Sir John Cunningham at Chiefs of Staff meeting, 26 March 1947.
7 – PRO, DEFE 4–24. Chiefs of Staff Committee meeting, 22 February 1950.
8 – *US Army activity in the US Biological Warfare Program*, (24 February 1977), pp. 1–4.
9 – Creasy *op. cit.*, p. 17.
10 – Correspondence with Brigadier-General Niles J. Fulwyler, 9 February 1981. Information on Operation Harness comes from Royal Navy source and Porton Down (authors' interview with Dr Rex Watson, 21 July 1981).
11 – Documents quoted in *Washington Post* 18 September 1979. But, according to the family of one of the 800,000 victims of this attack, the supposedly harmless bacteria used had caused a fatal casualty. Edward Nevin, a retired pipe fitter, had been admitted to hospital suffering from a hernia for what should have been a relatively simple operation. On 1 November 1950 he died of pneumonia. Blood and urine samples showed clear evidence of serrartia. At the time his family accepted his death as the result of an infection striking a vulnerable old man. But the doctors who treated Nevin were puzzled. There had been eleven cases of serratia pneumonia in the weeks following the spraying. It was such a rare outbreak that they wrote an article for the *Archives of Internal Medicine* the following year. When details of the San Francisco tests began to leak out in 1976, the Nevin family suspected that their grandfather's death had been a direct result of the biological warfare tests. An initial judgement by the San Francisco District Court in May 1981 rejected their suit against the US government, but the case seems likely to drag on through the courts for another two or three years.
12 – 'Behaviour of aerosol clouds within cities', *US Army Chemical Corps Joint Quarterly Report*, No. 5, July–September 1953.
13 – Ministry of Defence Press Release issued in 1954, quoted in correspondence December 1979.
14 – Information to the authors from local sources, confirmed by Ministry of Defence and Porton Down.
15 – Documents quoted in *Washington Post*, 23 April 1980.
16 – *Ibid.*
17 – US Army *Information Sheet*, 12 January 1977.
18 – Creasey, *op. cit.*, p. 33.
19 – *US Army Activity* (note 2) pp. 3–1. For some of the details of Pine Bluff Arsenal we are indebted to Seymour Hersh, *op. cit.*, pp. 132–7.

20 – Creasey, *op. cit.*, Table One.

21 – *Ibid.*, pp. 22–3.

22 – *Report of the International Scientific Commission for the Investigation of the Facts concerning Bacterial Warfare in Korea and China* (Peking, 1952).

23 – Authors' interview with Dr Needham, 25 February 1981.

24 – Sworn statement made January 1952, quoted in Hersh, *op. cit.*, p. 20.

25 – SIPRI *The problem of Chemical and Biological Warfare*, Vol. I, p. 230.

26 – See Chapter Five.

27 – Quoted in Walter Schneir, 'The Campaign to Make Chemical Warfare Respectable', *The Reporter* (October 1959), p. 27.

28 – *Law of Land Warfare.* Field Manual 27–10.

29 – *Armed Forces Doctrine for Chemical and Biological Weapons Employment and Defense.* Field Manual 101–40.

30 – J. H. Rothschild *Tomorrow's Weapons*, (New York, 1964), pp. 82–4.

31 – *Summary of Major Events and Problems*, United States Chemical Corps, Fiscal Year 1959 (Army Chemical Center, Maryland, January 1960.)

32 – This was code-named 'Project Screw worm'.

33 – Sawyer, Dengerfield, Hogge and Crozier 'Antibiotic Prophylaxis and Therapy of Airborne Tularemia', *Bacteriological Reviews* (September 1966), pp. 542–8.

34 – Quoted in Hersh, *op. cit.*, p. 124.

35 – Webb, Wetherley-Mein, Gordon Smith and McMahon 'Leukaemia and Neoplastic Process treated with Langat and Kyasanur Forest Disease Viruses: a clinical and laboratory study of 28 patients', *British Medical Journal* (29 January 1966), pp. 258–66.

36 – *Ibid.*

37 – Figures given in parliamentary answer by Geoffrey Johnson Smith MP, 12 July 1971.

38 – Hersh, *op. cit.*, pp. 119–20.

39 – The observation was first made by Robin Clarke and Julian Perry Robinson in 'United Kingdom Research Policy', in Steven Rose (ed.), *Chemical and Biological Warfare*, (London, 1968), p. 109.

40 – This scenario was painted for the authors by Dr Rex Watson, Director of Porton Down, during an interview in November 1980.

41 – *US Army Activity in the US Biological Warfare Programs* (note 6), pp, 5–4–6–3.

42 – Deseret Test Center, Utah.

43 – Comment to the authors by former Chemical Corps officer.

44 – 'No single inspection procedure or combination of procedures were available that would offer a high level of assurance against militarily

significant violation of B W limitation' (*US Army Activity in the US Biological Warfare Programs*, pp. 5–2, 5–3).
45 – Presidential Statement, 25 November 1969.
46 – SIPRI, *op. cit.*, Vol. II, pp. 128–9.

CHAPTER EIGHT: THE RISE AND RISE OF CHEMICAL WEAPONS
1 – PRO, Cos (45) 402 (o). 'Further Developments in Weapons and Methods of War', a report of Sir Henry Tizard's Ad Hoc Committee to Chiefs of Staff, June 1945.
2 – Undated interview with Maj. Gen. Marshall Stubbs by American Citizens for Honesty in Government. Interview notes made available to authors.
3 – D. J. A. Goodspeed, *A History of the Defence Science Board of Canada*, (Ottawa, 1958).
4 – Statement to the Australian Senate by the Minister of Supply, Senator Anderson, 28 November 1968.
5 – Authors' interview with Dr Rex Watson in November 1980. It is also known that Australian scientists carried out experimental research into toxins extracted from jellyfish and sea-wasps in 1968–9.
6 – 'The Lethality to rats of G B and G E from H E/Chemical weapons in the field', Porton Technical Paper No. 239 (1951). And 'The production of casualties in monkeys with G B vapour', Porton Technical Paper No. 424 (1954).
7 – Letter from John Morris MP, Junior Defence Minister to James Dickens M P, 31 July 1968. Our account also draws upon correspondence with Cockayne and examination of medical reports.
8 – The Nigerian tests were confirmed by the present Director and Staff of Porton Down in meetings and correspondence with the authors.
9 – Quoted in *Tribune*, 30 January 1959.
10 – Ministry of Defence press release, 29 October 1970.
11 – Joint Logistics Plans Committee memo, 7 April 1953.
12 – Authors' interview with Tom Griffiths in April 1980. An account of the Griffiths case is also to be found in Elizabeth Sigmund, *Rage Against the Dying*, (London, 1980), pp. 28–42.
13 – Authors' interview with Trevor Martin in February 1981. See also 'Nerve gas man reveals how he was crippled', *Sunday Times*, 7 December 1969.
14 – Fort Clayton, Canal Zone; Fort Greely, Alaska; Camp Tuto, Greenland.
15 – The plant was known as the Muscle Shoals Development works, and was operating by 1953.
16 – There are conflicting accounts of how much was produced. The cost of G B manufacture is given in SIPRI, *op. cit.*, Vol. II, p. 53.

17 – The warheads included Honest John, Little John, and Sergeant missiles.

18 – The American M 34 'cluster bomb' had been fitted with extra handles so that it could be carried by British bombers.

19 – *A Brief History of Porton*, p. 37.

20 – See Chapter Two.

21 – *Summary of Major Events and Problems*, US Army Chemical Corps, Fiscal Year 1959 (January 1960).

22 – Information to the authors.

23 – Part of this description of the Newport Chemical Plant is indebted to Seymour Hersh, *op. cit.*

24 – Missiles included Honest John and Sergeant.

25 – US Army Chemical Corps (January 1960) *Summary of Major Events and Problems*.

26 – *Harpers*, June 1959.

27 – *This Week*, 17 May 1959. Quoted in Walter Scheir 'The Campaign to Make Chemical Warfare Respectable', *The Reporter*, October 1959.

28 – 'U.S. Seeks to develop chemicals that will disable the enemy temporarily', *Wall Street Journal*, 16 August 1963.

29 – Extract from sworn statement given by former US serviceman Dan Bowen to American Citizens for Honesty in Government, 9 July 1979. Bowen had participated in tests at Edgewood Arsenal between 28 February 1961 and 3 April 1961.

30 – Department of Defense statement 26 July 1975, and correspondence with Ministry of Defence 29 April 1980.

31 – A fuller account of the discovery of LSD appears in John Marks, *The Search for the Manchurian Candidate* (New York, 1979).

32 – Inspector-General US Army *Use of Volunteers in Chemical Agent Research*, (March 1976).

33 – *Psychochemical Agents*, Chemical Warfare Laboratories Report No. 2071, 14 September 1956.

34 – Prices given by Dr Neville Gadsby to *Daily Telegraph*, 3 June 1969. According to our information the British continued, however, to investigate other 'humane' drugs, including powerful animal sedatives designed originally to knock out elephants and other large animals.

35 – Information to the authors from Detective-Inspector Richard Lee, who discovered the transaction during investigations for Operation Julie, the world's largest anti-LSD operation. Lee believes the 'China connection' drugs could only have been intended for chemical warfare, but maintains silence on details on the discovery.

36 – Medical report quoted in Bowart, *op. cit.*, p. 90.

37 – Testimony to army investigators, Marks, *op. cit.*, p. 67.

38 – Department of Defence statement, 26 July 1975.

39 – *Pharmacologia*, 1972.

40 – There were numerous other tests, notably to discover the value of LSD in the interrogation of prisoners. In 1960 an interrogation team was sent to Europe to use LSD in the questioning of ten suspects believed to have lied during previous military police investigations. Codenamed Project Third Chance, the interrogation team concluded that LSD was safe, humane, and secure. In 1962, a second team used LSD during interrogations in the Far East, where seven 'foreign nationals' were given the drug. Despite the enthusiasm of its advocates, use of LSD on military prisoners was suspended in 1963.

41 – US Army Bio-engineering R & D Laboratory, *Technical Report 7710*, (Fort Detrick, August 1977); and SIPRI, *op. cit.*, Vol. II, p. 47.

42 – Vietnam might have provided the perfect 'field laboratory' for BZ. There is one account of BZ being used in combat in Vietnam. *L'Express* described an attack by the First Airmobile Division during Operation White Wing in March 1966. The US troops were said to have dropped 3,000 BZ filled grenades on suspected Viet Cong positions. The report was denied by the US government. Some support for their denial can be gleaned from the fact that BZ is said never to have been loaded into grenades. There were at least three other allegations of BZ use in Vietnam, but none was satisfactorily proved.

43 – The Dugway experiment, to 'test the effective dosage of BZ when disseminated in the open', began in late 1964, and was codenamed Project Dork. The Hawaii tests took place in 1966 and 1967.

44 – Ministry of Defence spokesman, 3 August 1979.

45 – The American government maintained at the time that US forces in Vietnam did not use chemical weapons which were subject to international controls. They stated that anti-plant agents and 'harassing agents' did not constitute chemical warfare. Since the end of the Second World War chemical warfare had been alleged in a succession of countries, including China (1946), Vietnam (1947), Egypt (1948), Greece (1949), Korea (1952), Cuba (1957), Algeria (1957), Spanish Sahara (1958), and China (1958). The majority of these charges were dismissed as propaganda. The most authenticated use of gas took place during the Yemen Civil War, between 1963 and 1967. It was claimed that Soviet-manufactured gas, notably mustard, had been employed by Egyptian forces which had intervened on the Republican side. There were also allegations that the Egyptians were using gas, including phosgene, which had been left in the country by British troops during the Second World War. Altogether some 1,400 Royalist tribesmen were said to have been killed, and a further 900 seriously wounded. Independent investigation by the Red Cross confirmed the claim that gas had been used. Although Saudi Arabia attempted to persuade the United Nations to mount an investigation and condemn the use of gas, the UN took no action.

46 – 2, 4 dichlorphenoxyacetic acid, coded LN8; 2, 4, 5 trichlorophenoxy-

acetic acid, coded L N14, and better known as 245T; and iso-Propyl N-phenol carbamate, code L N33. (P R O, D E F E 2/1252 'Crop Destruction', a memorandum for the Joint Technical Warfare Committee (1945), p. 2.)

47 – *Ibid.* p. 1. Strategists calculated that an attack would destroy about 30 per cent of the rice crop.

48 – *Flying*, November 1966.

49 – S I P R I, *op. cit.*, Vol. I, p. 166.

50 – Letter from Dixon Donelly, Assistant Secretary, Department of Defense, September 1966.

51 – S I P R I, *op. cit.*, pp. 178–9.

52 – *Dioxin: a potential chemical warfare agent*, S I P R I *Yearbook* (Stockholm, 1977), p.92.

53 – *Ibid.*, pp. 97–8.

54 – Information to the authors from Vietnam veterans. See also Marta Tarben, *The Agent Orange Time Bomb*, Mike Goldwater and Anthony Barnet, *Wouldn't Hurt a Mouse*, New Statesman.

55 – So called after the two American scientists, Carson and Staughton, who first discovered the compound in 1928.

56 – *Summary of Major Events and Problems*, US Chemical Corps, Fiscal Year 1959 (January 1960), p. 96.

57 – Attack in Bin dinh province, February 1966.

58 – Quoted in Hersh, *op. cit.*, pp. 178–9.

59 – *Le Monde*, 4 January 1966.

60 – Hersh, *op. cit.*, p. 170.

61 – The link was discovered by University of Pennsylvania students in 1965. The I C R had been involved in C B W research since the Korean War. In 1965, its two major projects were Summit and Spicerack. Summit involved research into new chemical weapons for the Chemical Corps. Spicerack was the cover for work for the US Air Force.

62 – Experiments, for example, into weapons combining gas and fuel/air devices, which would detonate and punch a cloud of chemical towards the enemy.

63 – Testimony to Armed Services Committee, US House of Representatives, Hearings on Military Posture, 1970.

CHAPTER NINE: THE TOOLS OF SPIES

1 – Quoted in B B C Television's *Panorama*, 'Who Killed Georgi Markov?', 9 September 1979.

2 – Information on these attacks is drawn from a number of sources. The most readable account of the activities of Khokhlov appears in John Barron, *K G B* (New York, 1974). A fuller version can be found in *Murder International Inc, Murder and Kidnapping as an instrument of Soviet Policy, 1965 Hearings before the subcommittee to investigate the administration of*

the International Security Act and other Internal Security Laws, Judiciary Committee, US Senate, 1965.

3 – PRO, Cabinet Paper 120/783.

4 – PRO, CAB 79/56. Chiefs of Staff Committee, 20 July 1942.

5 – *Ibid.* Comment by ACIGS.

6 – *Ibid.*

7 – Lovell, *op. cit.*, p. 17.

8 – *Ibid.*, p. 22.

9 – *Ibid.* Inscription on fly leaf of copy given by author to Lord Stamp.

10 – *Ibid.*

11 – This was the title of a book by John Marks (*The Search for the Manchurian Candidate, op. cit.*). Although there have been other books published on this subject, Marks' work remains the most reliable, readable and coherent account.

12 – See Josef Mindszenty, *Memoirs* (New York, 1974).

13 – *Use of Volunteers in Chemical Agent Research*, Report of the Inspector-General, Department of the Army, 1975, p. 19.

14 – 'Disposal of Maximum Custody Type Defectors of All Categories'. Memo dated 7 March 1951.

15 – 'Sensitive Research Programs'. Memo for Director of Central Intelligence, June 1964.

16 – *Quarterly Report*, 1 July–30 September 1953. Section on Addicting Drugs, Laboratory of Pharmacology, Addiction Research Center, Lexington, Kentucky.

17 – 'No One Told Them', *Newsweek*, 21 July 1975.

18 – Alan W. Scheflin and Edward M. Opton Jr., *The Mind Manipulators* (London and New York, 1978), pp. 134–5.

19 – 'Senate Panel to Focus on Abuses Linked to CIA Drug Testing', *New York Times*, 20 September 1977.

20 – 'New Details of "House in SF"', *San Francisco Chronicle*, 28 August 1977.

21 – 'CIA Sought to Spray Drug on Partygoers' *New York Times*, 29 September 1977.

22 – Quoted in Marks, *op. cit.*, p. 101.

23 – 'Testing of Psychochemicals and related materials'. Memo from Richard Helms to Deputy Director of Central Intelligence, 17 December 1963.

24 – *Statement to the Senate Select Committee on Intelligence and Senate Committee on Human Resources*, Admiral Stansfield Turner, 13 August 1977.

25 – Annual Reports of Human Ecology Fund, filed with New York State Department of Social Welfare, 1961 and 1962.

26 – *Summary of Project OFTEN*, 29 May 1973.

27 – William Colby and Peter Forbath, *Honorable Men – My Life in the*

CIA, (New York, 1978), p. 442. In an interview with one of the authors in May 1978, Colby claimed that all the allegations of CIA assassination plots 'really involve only one case – Fidel Castro', and there he admitted that the CIA did plan a murder.

28 – 'Unauthorised Storage of Toxic Agents', Hearings before US Senate Intelligence Committee (16, 17, 18 September 1975) p. 10. Chaired by Senator Frank Church, it was known at the Church Committee.

29 – *Ibid.*, p. 161.

30 – *Memorandum for the Record. Discussions with [deleted] on MKNAOMI* (September 1975), pp. 3–4.

31 – Memo from unidentified CIA officer to unidentified Chief of Division, 7 February 1962.

32 – Report to US House of Representatives, quoted in Robin Clarke, *We All Fall Down* (London, 1968).

33 – Dr Edward Schantz, who worked at Fort Detrick for twenty-eight years, in testimony to the Church Committee. Church, *op. cit.*, p. 153.

34 – Although there is nothing necessarily sinister in the connection between an animal health laboratory and a biological warfare establishment, suspicion could only increase when, asked about the nature of the Shellfish Toxin research at Babraham, the Minister responsible would say only that 'the work has been of value in demonstrating the correlation between certain physiological activities' (Neil McFarland, *Hansard*, 14 January 1980).

35 – Charles A. Senseny, testimony to Church Committee. Church, *op. cit.*, p. 162. Senseny had begun work in the Fort Detrick Special Operations Division in 1953, where he had carried out many experiments with Shellfish poison, refined dart guns, and devised methods of forcing biological agents into public water supplies.

36 – According to a report in *Newsday* in January 1977, not all CIA anti-Cuba biological operations failed. The paper quoted an unidentified intelligence source as saying that in early 1971 he had been given a container of virus for shipment to Cuba. Six weeks later the island reported the only outbreak of African Swine Fever in the western hemisphere. Over 500,000 pigs, considered vital to the national economy, were slaughtered. The CIA had no comment to make on the allegation. *Newsday*, 9 January 1977.

37 – 'Alleged Assassination Plots Involving Foreign Leaders', Interim Report of the Church Committee, pp. 20–1. Gottlieb gave evidence under the pseudonym 'Victor Scheider'. Further information from authors' interview with former CIA officer John Stockwell in May 1978.

38 – Philip Agee, *Inside the Company – CIA Diary* (New York, 1975), p. 85.

39 – Information from Fort Detrick employee.

40 – *Unauthorised Storage of Toxic Agents* – Church, *op. cit.*, pp. 103–104.

CHAPTER TEN: FROM DISARMAMENT TO REARMAMENT

1 – Quoted in *First Tuesday*, NBC News, 1 May 1973.

2 – *Convention on the Prohibition of the Development*, Production and Stockpiling of Bacteriological (Biological) and Toxin Weapons and on their Destruction, signed in Washington, London and Moscow, 10 April 1971.

3 – *Boston Globe*, 28 September 1975.

4 – Jack Anderson's syndicated column, 27 December 1975 Nicholas Wade, who investigated these two allegations for *Science*, concluded that there was 'little evidence to suppose that the Soviet Union is in legal violation of the Biological Weapons Convention' (*Science*, 2 April 1976). The slighted Soviet diplomat told *Science* that 'Anderson can say what he likes, this is a free country.'

5 – Reuters dispatch, Brussels, 30 January 1978. *Tass* later described the story as a product of the 'British misinformation department'.

6 – *New York Times*, 5 June 1978.

7 – *San Francisco Examiner*, 22 October 1979. The Polish army captain was said to have told American diplomats that he had heard of the plan while imprisoned in the Gulag Archipelago in 1976. A counter-allegation was made by Fidel Castro in July 1981, when he claimed that an outbreak of dengue which had killed 113 Cubans and infected a further 270,000 was the work of the CIA (speech at Victoria de las Tunas, Cuba, 27 July 1981).

8 – *Now!*, 26 October 1979.

9 – This connection was first noted by Zhores Medvedev in *New Scientist*, 31 July 1980.

10 – Daily Telegraph, 11 February 1980.

11 – *Bild Zeitung*, 13 February 1980.

12 – For example, *Washington Star*, 19 March 1980: 'US Believes Soviet Anthrax Killed 200–300'.

13 – For example, Zhores Medvedev, *New Scientist*, 31 July 1980; Vivian Wyatt, *New Scientist*, 4 September 1980.

14 – Quoted in *New Scientist*, 10 July 1980.

15 – Pentagon spokesman to the authors, December 1980.

16 – Authors' correspondence with Porton Down, March 1981.

17 – The laboratory had been used by the Department of Health for the manufacture of anthrax vaccine.

18 – Authors' interview with Dr Rex Watson, 21 July 1981.

19 – Authors' interview with Professor Adolf Henning Frucht, Berlin, April 1980.

20 – 'Chemische Waffen in Warschauer Pakt', *Soldat und Technik* (1970).

21 – Professor John Erickson, 'Soviet Chemical Warfare Capabilities' (Department of Defence Studies Edinburgh University, 1978), p. 17.

22 – Correspondence from Ministry of Defence to the authors, April 1980.

23 – The service personnel are said to be all volunteers. In the early 1970s they were recruited through approaches from Porton Down to regimental officers, and through advertisements in service magazines. By way of inducement the volunteers were offered extra pay – some opted for the work at Porton to earn money for holidays and Christmas presents. A volunteer in similar experiments at Edgewood Arsenal in 1969 said 'My folks think I'm insane, but they tell us there's no real danger.'

24 – All soldiers are expected to carry an 'autoject' mechanical syringe to inject themselves, should they be exposed to nerve gas. The unpopularity of CBW training can perhaps be guessed at – soldiers are expected to enter a room filled with CS gas, remove their gas mask, and repeat their name, rank and number to the satisfaction of the NCO in command. But full-scale training exercises, among the most thorough in NATO, can be rendered unrealistic by the instruction to return 'noddy' suits in 'good as new' condition: soldiers wishing to eat or relieve themselves must expose themselves to an atmosphere theoretically filled with nerve gas.

25 – Testimony to NATO subcommittee of House Armed Services Committee, 18 and 19 December 1979.

26 – Correspondence from Pentagon to authors, November 1980.

27 – The United States wanted the convention to include 'incapacitants and dangerous irritants, but not safe, irritants or anti-plant chemicals'. For a fuller account of the negotiations see 'Negotiations On Chemical Warfare Control', *Arms Control* Vol. I, No. 1 (May 1980).

28 – Charles H. Bay, 'The Other Gas Crisis – Chemical Weapons', *Parameters, Journal of the Army War College*, September 1979. Colonel Bay was Commander of Dugway Proving Ground, Utah, at the time he wrote the article.

29 – 'Auch Kampstoff – Rustung der Sowjets', *Soldat und Technik* (1968).

30 – *United States Military Posture for FY 1976.*

31 – Conversation with the authors, April 1980.

32 – Matthew Messelson and Julian Perry Robinson, 'Chemical Warfare and Chemical Disarmament', *Scientific American*, April 1980.

33 – Richard H. Ichord, 'The Deadly Threat of Soviet Chemical Warfare', *Readers' Digest*, September, 1979.

34 – Bay, *op. cit.*

35 – Charles H. Bay, 'The Other Gas Crisis, Part Two', *Parameters*, December 1979.

36 – Evidence to House of Commons Select Committee on Science and Technology, 18 July 1968.

37 – Information to the authors.

38 – *Los Angeles Times*, 23 September 1978

39 – General Bernard Rogers in *Now!*, 21 March 1980.

40 – *Binary Munitions Advantages*: Edgewood Arsenal internal briefing document.

41 – *Binary Modernization*, Pentagon Information Paper, 21 May 1980, and 'Old Fears, New Weapons: Brewing a Chemical Arms Race', *The Defence Monitor* (1980) Vol. IX, No. 10, 1980.

42 – *Reports of the Use of Chemical Weapons in Afghanistan*, Laos, Kampuchea, US State Department, released 7 August 1980.

43 – Harold Wilson MP, House of Commons, 31 January 1967

44 – *Final Report of the DASG Investigating Team: Use of Chemical Agents Against the Hmong in Laos*.

45 – See *Deadly Signs of 'Medicine from the Sky'*, Sterling Seagrave, *Washington Star*, 4 May 1980.

46 – One sample was sent to a Philadelphia pharmacologist, who then forwarded it to Professor Chester J. Mirocha at the University of Minnesota. When the *St. Paul Dispatch* revealed the source of the sample in September 1981, the university was still unaware of its origin.

47 – Statement by Walter J. Stroessel Jr, Under Secretary of State for Political Affairs, 14 September 1981.

48 – See Sterling Seagrave *Yellow Rain* (New York, 1981).

49 – Negotiations between British and American officials took place 'at Brigadier level over a period of weeks' according to a Ministry of Defence source. The Defence Secretary comments were made at a meeting of the Royal United Services Institute, 16 December 1980.

50 – 'I never dreamed that I'd be sitting here in 1980 after we started this back in 1969 and we'd have reports of twenty-five Warsaw Pact divisions able to use it. That's what we were trying to stop. Apparently it has not succeeded.' Richard Nixon, BBC *Panorama*, 2 June 1980.

EPILOGUE

1 – Calculations based upon assessment by Julian Perry Robinson, and SIPRI *Yearbook* (1973), p. 271.

2 – US Army Mobility Equipment Research and Development Center, *Decontamination of Water Containing Chemical Warfare Agent*, (Fort Belvoir, Virginia, January 1975).

3 – US Army Spokesman, May 1980.

4 – Testimony before a sub-committee of House Appropriations Committee, Department of Defence Appropriations for 1963, Washington, March 1962.

5 – Testimony before a sub-committee of the House Committee on Appropriations, Department of Defence Appropriations for 1970, Washington, 1969.

6 – This is not an entirely academic speculation. In 1968 Porton Down and Fort Detrick collaborated in the successful transfer of genes between different strains of plague bacillus. The research was done 'for purely defensive purposes'.

The authors would like to thank the following for permission to quote from copyright material: William Blackwood & Sons Ltd (*Gas! The Story of the Special Brigade* by Major-General C. H. Foulkes); Granada Publishing Ltd. and the Macmillan Publishing Co. Inc. (*The Assassination of Heydrich* by Miroslav Ivanov, translated by Patrick O'Brien. Published in the United States as *Target Heydrich*); Dr J. E. Hodgkin and the Imperial War Museum (the Unpublished Diaries of Brigadier A. E. Hodgkin); Routledge & Kegan Paul Ltd (*Callinicus* by J. B. S. Haldane); Weidenfeld & Nicolson and The Macmillan Publishing Co. Inc. (*Inside the Third Reich* by Albert Speer; The Estate of Wilfred Owen, Chatto & Windus Ltd, and New Directions Publishing Corporation ('Dulce et Decorum Est' from *The Collected Poems of Wilfred Owen* edited by C. Day Lewis).

The following have very kindly given permission for the use of illustrations: The Public Records Office (1), Imperial War Museum (2, 3 4, 5 6), General Allan Younger (7), Royal Society (8), Porton Down (9, 10), Keystone Press Agency (11, 12, 13), Porton Down (14), Yivo Institute for Jewish Research (15, 16), Ministry of Defence (17, 18), Wellcome Museum of Medical Science (19), Center for Disease Control, Atlanta (20, 21, 22), US Department of Defense (23), Porton Down (24), Associated Press (25), Ministry of Defence (26), United Press International (27), US Department of Defence (28), United Press International (29), Press Association (30).

INDEX

Index

Index

Index

Index

sians begin manufacture of, 148; Britain, US
and Canada work on, 173–5, 176–85, 216,
239; Soviet agents, 225–6, 229–30; 'binary'
nerves gases, 231–2; 247, 264. *See also*
tabun, sarin, soman, V X
neutron bomb, 234
Nevin, Edward, 255
Newall, Sir Cyril, 83
Newport VX factory, 185
New York, 156, 159
New York State Psychiatric Institute, 189
New Zealand, 175
Nimitz, Admiral Chester, 135
Ningpo, 80
nitric acid, 59
Nixon, Richard M., 171–2, 173, 211, 215,
216, 217, 219–20, 225, 228, 229, 231, 237,
265
NKVD, 89
Northern Ireland, 194
Novosibirsk, 200
Now!, 220
N-Stoff, 58
Nuremberg war crimes trial, 85, 99

Obanakoro (Nigeria), 177
Ochsner, General Hermann, 59
Ohio State University, 163
Okinawa, 196, 217
Okolovich, Segeivich, 198
Olsen, Frank, 207–8
Operation Anthropoid, 89–94
Operation Cauldron, 157
Operation Harness, 155, 255
Operation Hesperus, 157
Operation Negation, 155
Operation Overlord – *see* D-Day
Operation Ozone, 155
Operation Pandora, 155
organo-phosphorous compounds, 53
O S S, 89, 201–4, 208
Owen, Wilfred, 20

Pacific War Council, 81
Pakistan, 233
Panama Canal Zone, 182
Pappenheimer, Professor Alvin, 94
Pearl Harbor, 87, 120
Peck, Air Vice-Marshal, 86
Penkovsky, Oleg, 146–8
Pennsylvania University, 196, 260
Pentagon, 150, 153, 160, 185, 186, 217, 222,
232, 235, 237, 240
Peshawar, 44, 143
PF–3, 66
Pha Na Khun, 234
Phnom Penh, 165
phosgene (CG), 11, 17–20, 23, 28, 33, 35, 44,
50, 51, 52, 59, 112, 113, 115, 131–2, 140,
183, 196
Phytophtera infestans (Mort) de Bary, 99
Picker, Professor, 60
pigeon bomb, 160
Pikalov, V.K., 225
Pine Bluff Arsenal, 116, 160, 163, 172, 190,
218
Pingfan Institute, 76–9
Piricularia oryzae, 99
plague, 74, 76, 77, 78, 79, 80, 81, 82, 85, 97,

142, 143, 153, 161, 162, 167, 169
pneumonic plague, 169
Poland, 44, 89, 139, 249
Portal, Sir Charles, 129
Porton, 37
Porton Down, chemical and biological warfare
establishment: founded in 1916, 21, 37; investigates WW1 gas casualties, 35–6; work
of during WW1, 37–41; established on
peacetime basis, 41–2; work between the
wars, 42–3, 52; continues offensive work
despite Geneva Protocol, 46–7; investigates
German CW after WW2, 57–8, 59, 60;
failure to develop nerve gas during WW2,
66–7; and Gruinard tests, 69–72, 96; and
continuing contamination of Gruinard, 73–
4; establishment of biological warfare
laboratory, 83; manufactures 5 million
anthrax-filled cattle cakes, 86–8, 105; and
assassination of Heydrich, 88–9, 90, 94;
and setting up of Suffield testing range, 94–
5; and CW weapons in WW2, 114; supplies
clandestine CW weapons to SOE, 201;
Microbiological Research Establishment
founded, 151; post-war BW work, 152,
157, 158, 164, 168, 222, 266; use of service
volunteers in experiments, 174, 183–4; and
accidental gassing of William Cockayne,
176–7; and death of Ronald Maddison,
178; suicide of Director, 178–9; post-war
CW work, 177; and Nancekuke 'out station', 179–81; develops VX, 184–5; develops CS, 194; and Markov case, 198; expertise in defence, 227, opens new 'Battle Run',
228; present-day size, 37; 40, 49, 64, 117,
121, 173, 183, 190, 244, 248, 255.
Posen Military Medical Academy, 85
Possev, 220
Powers, Gary, 221
Pravda, 140
Project Bluebird, 205
Project Often, 210
Project Tomka, 47
prussic acid, 199
psittacosis, 97, 161, 202
Public Health Laboratory, 82, 84

Q Fever, 161, 170, 172, 218

radioactive gas, 124–5
Ramsay, Captain, 25, 27
Randle poison gas factory, 113
Raubkammer training area, 58, 59, 60, 62
Reagan, Ronald, 231, 233
Red Cross, 49, 234, 259
Reutershan, Paul, 193
Rhydmwyn gas factory, 114
Ribbentrop, Joachim von, 135, 253
ricin, 198
ricketts, 97
Rift Valley Fever, 161
rinderpest, 95, 97
Robertson, General, 7
Rocksavage poison gas factory, 113
Rocky Mountain Arsenal, 117, 182, 196, 217
Rocky Mountain spotted fever, 161
Roosevelt, Franklin D., 95, 96, 117, 118, 122,
123, 129, 135, 136, 163, 164, 201
Roskill, Stephen, 82

Index

Rothschild, General J. H., 165, 170
Royal Air Force, 44, 88, 90, 111–12, 119, 158, 176, 179, 180, 250
Royal Army Medical Corps, 17, 25, 40
Royal Engineers, 7, 25. *See also* Special Brigade.
Royal Navy, 155
Royal Society, 69
Rüdriger, Colonel, 54
Ruwet, Colonel Vincent, 207
Sahara, 52, 259
Saigon Children's Hospital, 193
St. Thomas's Hospital, London, 168
Salisbury, 157
Salisbury Plain, 21, 37, 41
salmonella, 76, 80
Salt, Major, 44
Sandoz Drug Company, 187
San Francisco, 156–7, 209, 255
San Francisco Examiner, 144, 208
sarin (GB) 54, 58, 59, 61, 64, 138, 176–80, 182, 217, 232
Saudi Arabia, 259
Savannah, Georgia, 166
Schnitzler, Baron Georg von, 61–2
Schrader, Dr Gerhard, 53, 54, 56, 57, 65, 99
Schwirkmann, Horst, 199–200
sclerotium rolfsii, 99
Scotland Yard, 197, 198
SD, 89
Second World War: Hitler considers using CW, 57, 59–60, 62–4; Allies consider anti-crop warfare, 98–100; British contingency plan to use anthrax, 104; belligerents pledge to abide by Geneva Protocol, 107; belief that CW would be used in, 51, 107–8; Churchill warns Germans against using CW during, 252; Ribbentrop threatens Italians with CW, 253; British plans to initiate CW to repel German invasion, 109–12, 115, 250; movement of CW stocks during, 108, 119, 125; fears surrounding Normandy landings, 123–5, 247; British consider initiating CBW in response to V-weapons attacks, 125–35; likely effects of CBW on course of, 130–5; CW very nearly used in, 106, 135–6, 137; total CW stocks during 58, 108, 118; clandestine use of CBW during, 88–94, 198, 200–4, 208; most records relating to still closed xii, 86, 248; 52, 54, 106, 143, 149, 151, 160, 161, 168, 173, 177, 183, 185, 191, 193, 230, 252, 253.
Selassie, Haile, 49
Sergeant missile, 166, 171
serratia marcescens, 156
Servizio Chemico Militare, 43
Seventh Day Adventists, 167
Seveso, 193
sex hormones, 204
shellfish toxin, 211, 212, 213, 214, 262
Siberian Regiment, 11
Singapore, 119
SK, 9
smallpox, 76, 79, 153
Snajdr, Vladimir, 91–3
soman (GD), 138, 148, 176
Somer Lost, 58
Somme, Battle of, 19–20
Southampton, 157

Soviet Union: casualties in WWI, 8, 10–11, 242, 32; post-WWI work on CW, 43, 50; and Geneva Protocol, 45, 46; collaboration with Germany, 47; British fear of, 51, 84, 136; alleged use of BW against Japan, 75; use of BW by NKVD, 89; fears of German attack, 135, 145, 252; captures German nerve agents, 138–9; post-war Allied fears of, 139–40, 143–4, 145, 150, 225–6, 229; stages Khabarovsk war crimes trial, 140–1; work on BW, 141–4; states position on CBW, 144–5; Red Army training, 145; and Penkovsky allegations, 146–8; extent of Soviet arsenal, 148; seeks to interrogate Japanese BW experts, 152–3; clandestine use of CBW agents, 198–200, 205; and BW Convention, 218–9, 228; claims not to possess biological weapons, 218–9; alleged continued BW development, 218–22; develops VR 55, 235; and proposed CW convention, 228–9; post-war CW stocks, 229–30; NATO presumes will use CW, 230–1; alleged use of CW in Afghanistan, 232–3, 236; alleged to have supplied CW to Egypt, 226, to Yemen, 234, 235, to Vietnamese, 234–5; and T-2, 236–8; 30, 48, 59, 63, 85, 108, 126, 211
Spain, 44
Spandau CW laboratories, 54, 58, 66
Special Air Service, 214
Special Brigade, 11–13, 19, 20, 21, 29
Special Operations Executive (SOE), 89, 90, 200–1
Speer, Albert, 62–3, 247
'Squirt', the, 114
SS, 58, 60, 61, 62
Stalin, Joseph, 62, 129, 135, 142, 252
Stamp, Lord, ix, 84, 96–7, 202
Stashinstzy, Bodgan, 199
State Department, 221, 235-6
Stimson, Henry L., 95–6
Stoff 146, 65
Stokes mortar, 22, 23
Stoney Mountain, Manitoba, 157
Strasburg University, 60
Stuttgart, 194
Substance 83, 65
Suffield testing range, 94–5, 173, 174
Supply, Ministry of, 112–13, 114
Sutton, Graham, 69, 70
Sutton Oak, 50, 179
Sverdlovsk, 220–2
Sweden, 162

T2, 236–7
tabun (GA), 53–4, 56, 59, 61, 62, 64, 65, 66, 67, 138, 148, 176
Tandanoumi Arsenal, 47
Tanganyika, 213
Taranto, 121
Tass, 221, 237
Tay Minh Hospital, 193
tear gas, 9, 44, 194–5, 201, 233
Tempsford aerodrome, 90
tetanus, 76, 79, 80, 142
Thailand, 165, 234, 235
Thatcher, Margaret, 237
ticks, 167, 168
tick encephalitis, 76

273

Index